A CURIOUS MIX OF PEOPLE

A CURIOUS MIX OF PEOPLE

THE UNDERGROUND SCENE OF '90S AUSTIN

Greg Beets and Richard Whymark

University of Texas Press ❧ Austin

Requests for permission to reproduce material from this work should be sent to:
Permissions
University of Texas Press
P.O. Box 7819
Austin, TX 78713-7819
utpress.utexas.edu/rp-form

♾ The paper used in this book meets the minimum requirements of ANSI/NISO Z39.48-1992 (R1997) (Permanence of Paper).

Library of Congress Cataloging-in-Publication Data

Names: Beets, Greg, author. | Whymark, Richard, author.
Title: A curious mix of people : the underground scene of '90s Austin / Greg Beets and Richard Whymark.
Description: First edition. | Austin : University of Texas Press, 2023. | Includes index.
Identifiers: LCCN 2022062249 (print) LCCN 2022062250 (ebook)
    ISBN 978-1-4773-2813-2 (paperback)
    ISBN 978-1-4773-2814-9 (pdf)
    ISBN 978-1-4773-2815-6 (epub)
Subjects: LCSH: Underground music—Texas—Austin—History and criticism. | Punk rock music—Texas—Austin—History and criticism. | Rock music—Texas—Austin—1991-2000—History and criticism. | Nightclubs—Texas—Austin—History. | Punk rock musicians—Texas—Austin—Interviews. | Rock music fans—Texas—Austin—Interviews. | Alternative radio broadcasting—Texas—Austin—History. | Underground press publications—Texas—Austin—History. | LCGFT: Oral histories. | Chronologies.
Classification: LCC ML3477.8.A97 B44 2023 (print) | LCC ML3477.8.A97 (ebook) | DDC 781.6409764/31—dc23/eng/20230130
LC record available at https://lccn.loc.gov/2022062249
LC ebook record available at https://lccn.loc.gov/2022062250

doi:10.7560/328132

Book design by LMRonan

The publication of this book was supported by the Lowell H. Lebermann Jr. Endowment for UT Press.

CONTENTS

A CURIOUS MIX OF PEOPLE

NOBODY HERE BUT US WOUNDED CHICKENS

AS SOON AS ANYBODY STARTS INTERVIEWING ME, AND THEY START SAYING "PUNK ROCK," I STOP THEM BECAUSE IT WASN'T PUNK. IT WAS DIY. WE WEREN'T PLAYING PUNK. PUNK IS LIKE A COSTUME, AND THAT'S NOT WHAT WE WERE DOING. THAT HAS NOTHING TO DO WITH WHAT WE WERE.

TIM KERR

JANUARY 1, 1990, WAS A CLOUDY, COOL day in Austin, Texas—an appropriate forecast for a city nursing a wicked economic hangover.

If revelers from the night before regretted one too many Shiner Bocks while watching Glass Eye at Liberty Lunch or the Reivers at the Cannibal Club, the more circumspect genus of banker or real estate speculator might well have regretted falling prey to the false promise of endless growth. It was a lifetime away from 1984, when Austin-based Lamar Savings was giddy enough to file an application with the state to open a branch on the moon.

"Today's pioneers are the businesses who are willing to expand their horizons and explore the immense possibilities available in outer space," said chairman Stanley Adams when announcing the lunar satellite office.[1] But by 1990 Lamar Savings was defunct, and Adams was under federal indictment for misapplication of $121.1 million in funds.

1

From 1989 to 1990, the population of the fifth-largest city in Texas actually *declined* by 0.2 percent (from 466,499 to 465,622)—a slight but significant change for a city that had gained population every year since 1960 and every half-decade before that going back to 1840.

According to the business section of that morning's *Austin American-Statesman*, at least 65 percent of the city's apartments and at least half of the downtown office buildings were owned either by the federal government or the financial entities that had lent real estate speculators billions during the '80s real estate boom. The Resolution Trust Corporation became one of the city's largest landlords. Office occupancy rates hovered around 65 percent. In the previous four years, 322 Texas banks failed, and more were to follow. Local celebrities like John Connally and Willie Nelson declared bankruptcy. Although Austin wasn't an oil town, the statewide impact of the worldwide collapse in oil prices compounded the local misery.

But it wasn't all *that* bad.

Unlike other Texas cities, Austin had a bulwark against the economic ruins of irrational exuberance in its education and government sectors. As the '90s dawned, the University of Texas at Austin's enrollment hovered around 50,000. Even in a recession, college kids must eat. And despite Texas raising its legal drinking age from nineteen to twenty-one in 1986, the ever-replenished abundance of single young people ensured a vibrant bar and club scene, though under-twenty-ones now got marked with stigmatic "Xs" on either hand upon entry.

With the modest-yet-stable wages of public employment shaping the local market, Austinites stung by economic woes at least enjoyed one of the lowest costs of living in the US. Being a human guinea pig in a Pharmaco study on jock itch treatment could net you $100—enough to make the month's rent if you had a roommate or three. Even a minimum-wage gig, slapping meat on bread at a sandwich shop, could cover a makeshift Saturday brunch of sixty-five-cent breakfast tacos eaten on the curb in front of the Airport Boulevard location of Tamale House as 727s screamed overhead on their final approach to Robert Mueller Municipal Airport.

Apart from being cheap, Austin was livable. For outcast intrastate arrivals from the flat, sprawling suburbs of Dallas and Houston, it was an easy place to fall in love with. Austin's hills and trails and parks and springs were exotic and enchanting. If the city lacked its larger Texas cousins' world-class art museums and four-star dining, it made up for that with easily accessible and highly participatory cultural offerings that usually centered around live music performed by local musicians. The barrier to entry was low and the potential for transcendence was high, particularly when the inebriants were flowing.

The perennial question for local politics was how to keep Austin from being ruined. The flashpoint for this conflict in 1990 was environmentally suspect suburban development up creek from Barton Springs. The Capraesque saga pitted a former UT football player turned mining/real estate company CEO named Jim Bob Moffett against a ragtag army of over eight hundred earth-friendly citizens who lined up to testify against Moffett's proposed four-thousand-acre planned unit development overlooking Barton Creek in an all-night city council session on June 7.

Backed by an influential but badly outnumbered coterie of supporters in business garb, Moffett attempted to shore up his good-guy developer credentials with the council. But when he bragged that his grades were the highest of any UT football player in his class, the gallery erupted in guffaws. Late into the night, an earthy woman recovering from dental surgery approached the podium and tearfully beseeched Moffett and his ilk to turn away from the death culture. Early the next morning at session's end, the council unanimously rejected the development.[2]

Whether it was the Armadillo World Headquarters being replaced by a bank building or the centuries-old tree known as Treaty Oak being deliberately poisoned, the root-taking phase of a citizen's love with Austin often materialized as anxiety about losing a quintessential piece of the city's culture, followed by grousing about how much better things used to be before that quintessential thing went away. If you were a young person arriving in Austin for the first time, listening to older people bray about how great the Armadillo or the One Knite or Soap Creek Saloon or Raul's or the Beach had been could get a little tedious.

Paradoxically, despite this preeminent fixation on falling from paradise, Austinites generally loved to talk their city up and clamored for Austin to get more attention on the national stage. What form that attention took varied wildly. When *National Geographic* ran a cover story on Austin in June 1990, they dutifully reinforced the dominant cultural paradigm by adorning that cover with an Austin High School couple dressed up for prom in formal western wear. At the other end of the spectrum, street buskers turned major label recording artists Poi Dog Pondering showcased the sun-bleached T-shirt and baggy shorts crowd by filming their music video for "Living with the Dreaming Body" in front of the emblematic "Austintacious" mural by Kerry Awn, Tommy Bee, and Rick Turner at the corner of 23rd and Guadalupe.

Roger Kintzel, publisher of the *Austin American-Statesman* at the dawn of the '90s, doubled as chairman of the Austin Chamber of Commerce. This seeming conflict of interest—along with a prodevelopment editorial bent—prompted the city's contrarian class to dub the daily newspaper the *Real-Estatesman*.

The *Statesman*'s chief competition and philosophical adversary was the *Austin Chronicle*. Formed in 1981, the alternative freebie entered the '90s as a two-color biweekly tabloid running about forty pages per issue. The *Chronicle*'s position on development in the Barton Creek watershed was best reflected by its 1990 Halloween issue, which featured a sinister depiction of Moffett on the cover, suitable for cutting out and wearing as a mask.

Despite the barbs and slings, this us-versus-them characterization wasn't absolute. Case in point was the 1985 episode of MTV's *The Cutting Edge* that was shot on location in Austin. Produced by IRS Records, an indie label helmed by Miles Copeland and distributed by A&M Records, *The Cutting Edge* aired late Sunday night. If you lived outside the broadcast contours of college radio with no independent record stores nearby, *The Cutting Edge* was probably the only place you were going to learn about bands to the left of R.E.M.

IRS publicity director Cary Baker screened episodes of the show on the A&M lot in Los Angeles that had once been Charlie Chaplin's movie studio. When the episode featuring the North Carolina music scene screened in 1984, *Statesman* music critic and *Rolling Stone/Creem* veteran Ed Ward[3] told Baker *The Cutting Edge* needed to do an Austin episode.[4] So they did.

Hosted by Fleshtones vocalist Peter Zaremba, the resulting show spotlighted the shambolic sounds of bands like True Believers, Doctors' Mob, Timbuk 3, and Zeitgeist (who became the Reivers in 1987) along with a young McDonald's employee turned local cult songwriter named Daniel Johnston. Many young pilgrims who became principal figures in Austin music during the '90s were watching at home, making travel plans. From the show's point of view, Austin was Valhalla for skewed youth, replete with backyard barbecues, crowded clubs, and an eccentric cast of artists with day jobs.

Though the production was appropriately slapdash, it's worth noting that the local chamber of commerce arranged comped crew accommodations at the Driskill Hotel and airfare on American Airlines.[5] Even at a nascent level, the money folks knew there was something salable afoot.

In 1986 *Chronicle* publisher Nick Barbaro and editor Louis Black partnered with local music industry veterans Roland Swenson and Louis Jay Meyers to launch the South By Southwest Music and Media Conference (SXSW). Initially conceived as a regional variation of New York's then-ascendant New

Music Seminar, the four founders struck out on their own when NMS got cold feet. Strategically scheduled during spring break when UT students were out of town—and East Coast music execs needed a break from winter weather—SXSW was set up to draw media and record label interest to geographically challenged musical acts from Austin and surrounding environs. Alternative papers from the southern and southwestern United States cosponsored the festival and brought bands from their respective cities to Austin.

In 1990 badged SXSW attendees went to music business–related sessions at the Hyatt Regency Hotel on Town Lake during the day before joining wristband holders to see bands at night. Some 424 showcasing artists played across twenty-three stages. An army of unpaid volunteers served as swag-bag stuffers, registration desk jockeys, and stage managers in exchange for admission. Between low living expenses, no one making much money, and SXSW itself still a chancy business proposition, it seemed a fair enough trade. Beyond their occupational utility, the volunteers served as cultural ambassadors for the city and its laid-back vibe. It was entirely appropriate that SXSW ended with a barbecue and softball game.

The four-day conference kicked off with the Austin Music Awards at Palmer Auditorium on March 16. Despite SXSW starting to attract artists of note from further afield, such as X vocalist Exene Cervenka and Mitch Easter–helmed jangle pop combo Let's Active (Nirvana had a showcase scheduled, but it was canceled), the awards show maintained its primacy. On the same night Stevie Ray Vaughan accepted his award for Musician of the Decade, Johnston appeared before his largest crowd to date, battling the auditorium's atrocious sound with just an acoustic guitar. While flying home to West Virginia aboard his father's private plane the next day, Johnston suffered a manic episode and threw the plane's keys out the window, forcing his onetime war pilot dad to make a crash landing. Just over four months later, Vaughan was killed in a helicopter crash after a show in Wisconsin.

As the long, hot Texas summer set in, mysterious white stickers with the word "SLACKER" written in black began appearing all over town. Someone slapped one on the jungle-themed front window mural at the Cannibal Club, the key local venue for nascent underground rock since opening as Club Cairo at 306 East Sixth Street in 1988. Manager Brad First was thoroughly annoyed as he tried to scrape sticker remnant off the mural without damaging the paint. It would be several more weeks until director Richard Linklater's era-defining film emerged on July 27, 1990.

Garnering mixed reviews at film festivals, *Slacker* was far from a sure thing. Aside from a West German TV deal, the film had no distribution.

So Linklater deftly parlayed his experience as founder of the Austin Film Society to independently book the film into the Dobie Theatre, a triscreen arthouse housed in a high-rise dormitory building next to UT.

The cryptic sticker campaign culminated with a glowing cover story in the *Chronicle*. Casting *Chronicle* editor Black as a mentally disturbed curmudgeon probably didn't hurt Linklater's publicity campaign, but the director's vision and talent proved true. He successfully bottled the ethos of the town's creative malcontent class circa 1989 and held it up for the light. "No plot, no major characters, no suspense," summarized *Chronicle* film critic Chris Walters. "Just fleeting glimpses of bohemia in its twilight phase." The film's long, successful run at the Dobie convinced Orion of its commercial potential, ultimately leading to its national release.

Much of Linklater's crew and cast of nonactors was drawn from the local music community. It would've been difficult to circulate in Austin music during the early '90s and not know at least one person who appeared in or worked on *Slacker*. Members of Ed Hall, Glass Eye, Poi Dog Pondering, and the Texas Instruments all appear. Having nonactors act in a movie paralleled the DIY punk aesthetic of nonmusicians starting bands.

Not everyone was impressed or amused with *Slacker*. It was a good date movie in that it stopped doomed pairings dead in their tracks. If your date didn't laugh out loud when the old anarchist portrayed by UT philosophy professor Louis Mackey fantasized about blowing up the Texas State Capitol, best to part amicably and search for someone better aligned with your life goals.

So this was Austin at the top of the 1990s. A central business district full of empty office spaces and boarded-up warehouses. A true college town that noticeably slowed down when the students were gone. A regional jewel not quite ready for prime time that had taken its economic licks and was looking for a way forward.

The start of a new decade often prompts searching out sources of hope and renewal. In Austin some might've looked to twenty-five-year-old personal computer builder Michael Dell, who would soon become the youngest-ever

Austin skyline, 1994, by Richard Whymark.

CEO of a Fortune 500 company. Others might've put stock in brassy Texas state treasurer Ann Richards, who would win the Democratic gubernatorial nomination and parlay Republican oilman Clayton Williams's rape joke into an unlikely victory in the November general election.

For the rest of us, it was the Butthole Surfers. Heirs to the throne of wonderfully strange Texas music once held by the 13th Floor Elevators, the Red Krayola, and the Legendary Stardust Cowboy, the Buttholes prompted scores of bad acid trips with psyops-grade aural assaults, coupled with visual stimuli like medical education films of genital reconstruction surgery. While shock value may have been the hook, the band's defiant spirit and unwillingness to be boxed in by convention kept the music interesting.

After years of building a substantial cult following through endless touring, the Butthole Surfers took a break from the road and returned to Texas toward the end of 1989. Longtime drummer King Coffey, a Fort Worth native who cut his teeth in a teen punk combo called the Hugh Beaumont Experience, suddenly had some down time.

On January 1, 1990, while others slept off their hangovers, Coffey made a New Year's resolution to start a record label showcasing Texas bands. He couldn't have known it at the time, but with the luxury of hindsight, we can now time-stamp Coffey's resolution as the opening shot in an underground rock renaissance that scorched and evolved previously conceived notions of what Austin music was all about.

Brian McBride: If you got off an airplane at the Austin airport—before it moved to its new location—you would hear, "Austin is the Live Music Capital of the World." What that meant is that Austin was the boogie rock capital of the world, where all of these Stevie Ray Vaughan wannabes could hang out and have a continuous crowd. That was the frustration about Austin.

But at the same time, it was also a source of hope. I fundamentally believe that for whatever is the dominant culture at the time, there is an equally opposite counterreaction that happens to that as well. It produced bands like the Butthole Surfers, and Ed Hall, and Crust, and Moist Fist. That reactionary tendency is something that I appreciated more than the stereotype of what Austin should be.

Michael Letton: Texas has always prided itself on *This Is Where the Individuals Are*. This is where some of the crazy people go and settle. Austin seemed to be the oasis for the more artistic, more leftist side of the equation. The university helps that.

Robert Zimmer: There's just something in the DNA of the people that live there. In some ways it's self-perpetuating because places develop a reputation and people want to move there. Austin has been that way for forever.

King Coffey: I love the bands that came out of Austin in the '90s, but they didn't grow out of a vacuum. I think Austin has always been able to look to our history of what came before us. As punk rockers in Austin, we always looked to the Big Boys and the Dicks. They are our gods. Those two bands really threw down the template of what Austin punk rock would become for decades. They both played punk rock, but they played it to what made sense to them.

Susannah Simone: Austin was more friendly and tolerant and inclusive than other punk scenes in the US. Even though there were two kinds of electronic bands, six hardcore bands, and a couple of new wave bands, everybody went to each other's show and knew each other. If you wanted to be in a band, you were in a band. That's what the Big Boys kept telling you at the end of every show, "You like this? Go start your own band!" And everybody kind of took it to heart.

Mark Fagan: Bands like the Big Boys and the Dead Kennedys were saying "Start your own band. Do your own thing." Before that, being a rock star was kind of this unreachable goal like Rush, or Black Sabbath, or Van Halen. I love those guys, but I'm not Eddie Van Halen. We were encouraged by the bands we looked up to do our own thing.

King Coffey: For the Big Boys, they took the punk attitude and energy, but fused on their love of soul and funk music to do their thing. The Dicks took that same root of punk but fused on the blues and turned punk a different direction. Both bands are also really theatrical and had a big visual presentation to them.

Bands that came after them—like the Butthole Surfers and Scratch Acid—borrowed a lot from what our big brothers were doing in the Big Boys and the Dicks. I'm sure if you asked the Big Boys and the Dicks what inspired them, they might reach back all the way to the freaks of the '70s, or even the 13th Floor Elevators.

Janet Hammer: Austin bands in the '80s were some of the major contributors to the punk rock scene throughout the United States, because a lot of the biggest punk rock bands from Texas were from Austin.

Marc Fort: You've got to remember, Austin was a small college town up until the '90s. There was only a handful of clubs that the majority of people were going to.

Roger Morgan: Not every city had a hub of clubs—little smoky dives and whatnot. And SXSW was only just sort of starting up. Just having the ability to go out and see bands and meet artistic people—that had a big influence.

Rick Carney: When we moved here in 1986, we thought that this was *the* place to be because of the Big Boys, MDC,[6] the Offenders. And we get here and all those bands are broken up. So we were in the middle of rebuilding an entirely different scene.

In '86, you could walk around downtown and buildings were boarded up. It was not a good situation. It was the end of the real estate bust of the '80s. More than half of downtown was vacant. More than half of Sixth Street was vacant and there was nothing alive on Red River at all.

Gary Chester: Back then, all the buildings were empty. If you could go back in a time machine with Doctor Who, you could be richer than Dell.

Rick Carney: Was that a good situation? No. But it allowed us to come in and create a culture where we didn't have to have a lot of money or infrastructure, because we could do it ourselves.

Jennings Crawford: There wasn't this purity test you had to go through. Everybody was like, "Oh you play music? Cool. And you're from Austin, so you probably have a sense of humor about it." It seemed very casual, very tolerant, and kind of emblematic of what Austin was back then.

Jonathan Toubin: Dong Huong is this little scene where Crust, Ed Hall, Pocket FishRmen, ST 37, Coz the Shroom—probably about seven or eight bands—all came from.

Gary Chester: Playing at Dong Huong[7] was a step *up*. That's when we used to play at people's houses. We played some gigs at a nudist apartment complex.

Cris Burns: A little Vietnamese lady ran it. I never saw them make any food. Maybe one boiled egg and a piece of toast. And we started having punk rock shows there.

Brant Bingamon: We were at Dong Huong's, and we looked at a band poster and it said, "Trouser Trout." This was right when we were maybe going to play there the first time and we were like, "Those fuckers! They're stealing our whole thing right here. Who the fuck is this?" Then we found out and it was (guitarist) Buxf (Parrot) from the Dicks and all of his cool, cool friends. We started to realize if we just figure out one more band that's got a fish reference, we could package this as the fish fry and we could make some food. Back then we were always like, how can we get even like ten people to go to the show? Like what could we do? Free beer? Free food? Free stuff! So we had our first fish fry.[8]

Jonathan Toubin: The L.A. punk scene started out in Chinese restaurants because no one would book them. In Austin, it was a Vietnamese restaurant.

Brant Bingamon: Ed Hall had a totally unique sound. Did they influence anybody? Maybe. They were the coolest band, but people didn't wind up playing like them for whatever reason.

Cris Burns: They were very influential as far as the do-it-yourself philosophy of just making your own band and making your own records and making your own scene.

Larry Strub: The very first little insemination of Ed Hall was when I lived at 21st Street Co-op and there was a talent show, and that's when we formed. After practices we would climb to the top of a building that was being constructed across the street. That was before Liberty Lunch had put their roof on, and we could watch shows from the top of that building.

Jason Christian: Dongfest[9] was Agony Column, Hickoids, Squat Thrust. All those bands were incredible.

Ryan McDaniel: The first show I went to was when I was fourteen. My sister was dating Jason Christian. He sang for Squat Thrust. They were playing Noisefest 2 in Waterloo Park, and they were amazing. They all had mud caked all over them. They had Aztec masks and an Aztec backdrop. There were all these skinheads and punks. It was strange and cool.

Jonathan Toubin: Squat Thrust. This is by far the most interesting band to ever be in Austin, at least in terms of performance. They outdid even the Butthole Surfers on the level of just imagination and effort.

Ryan McDaniel: In the middle of their set, they had these chickens and papier-mâché eggs. They threw them over the backdrop and they all hatched. But the messed-up part was that all the skinheads started throwing the chickens around. And this chicken hit me in the head! I had the worst headache, but the best time of my life.

Jimmy Bradshaw: Uh, the chicken show. That was pretty infamous. That was just not very well thought out. We brought ten live chickens to a show. There really wasn't a whole lot of an idea other than having chickens running around on stage.

Once they became airborne, there were some deaths. Yeah, that really upset a lot of people which now, thinking about it, is not very cool. But at the time you don't think about repercussions when you're doing this shit. Once you pass a point, you're obligated to stick with your guns and be like, "Roll with it!" Your pride won't let you go, "Oh we've fucked up. Sorry."

An animal ambulance was brought out for wounded chickens, which is probably a little bit overkill in the other direction. The police talked to us. When you're talking to the police because your band killed a chicken or two on stage, it's kind of a surreal situation and it is pretty comical. Sorry that the chickens didn't get to live their full life and do the things they really wanted to do. But I guess they had to die for art, or lack thereof.

Jason Christian: Wade [Longenberger] always had a different idea for every show. He would be Santa Claus on roller skates with Christmas lights.

Jonathan Toubin: Squat Thrust had a friend that was, I believe, a dwarf that used to dance on one of the speakers. They often played on stilts to make it another weird difference. They figured out if you get a bunch of trash bags, put them together, and put a fan inside, it makes a bubble. At first, they started having their singer sing from within a bubble. *Then* they figured out if you weld a bunch of trash bags, you could fit the whole band in a bubble. And there's Wade, and he learned how to drink and run around and run upstairs on [stilts]. I remember seeing him walking down Sixth Street on his stilts in an orange jumpsuit breathing fire. And nobody noticed. The *Chronicle* was like, "Some bluesmen played on Sixth Street . . ." I was like, "You're missing it! You're missing it!"

Jimmy Bradshaw: At the time it just felt like that's what a band did. Put on a *show*. Obviously we weren't going to wow people with our awesome licks. We were fucking awful. But that was part of the fun too—some certain thrill in creating absolute chaos in front of a bunch of people. Maybe better than applause is just a bunch of confused faces.

Jason Christian: It was so hard for us to get shows because every time we would get a show, somebody would do something fucked up and we would get banned. When we showed up at Mexic-Arte, James Follis—the dwarf—got naked and got on stilts and everyone flipped out. So Mexic-Arte banned all nudity. And then the next time he was on stilts in a cape, making love to a severed pig's head. So they said, "No more nudity. No more animal parts. And no more Squat Thrust." Oh man!

Jimmy Bradshaw: When we were playing at the Ritz, there was a riser behind the drums. I realized I could make these giant papier-mâché spread legs, and I made this big vagina with all these wigs. And then I think it was Matt Pyle in there with all this liver and raw meat. Now, it just sounds so bad, and so dumb. But at the time it was like, "God, this is great! It's gonna be this giant spread legs and vagina and meat flying into the audience and . . ." Yeah, that pissed a lot of people off. We were opening up for some touring band and of course when you throw something in an audience it tends to come back during the headliner's act. Needless to say, we didn't get to open up for them ever again.

Hunter Darby: Playing the Ritz, you could smell the speed cooking upstairs. It was really sketchy.

Laura Creedle: Happy Family did a SXSW showcase with Sister Double Happiness at the Ritz. We had one of the best shows we'd had ever had, and Sub Pop was there and they were like, "We dig you guys!" They felt like they were sort of excluding women. And then we broke up three weeks later.

Jonathan Toubin: By 1990 the Ritz was in flux. It wasn't open often, so what happened is that most of the underground bands at the time did the bulk of their gigs at Austin house parties and at co-op parties. The co-ops did have a hippie-ish element here and there, but 21st Street, Pearl Street, Taos—they had a more progressive element, and they would hire a lot more of the punk bands to play at some of their parties. Little factions of punk kids were here and there in these co-ops, so a lot of the music scene existed primarily in this juncture of house parties, co-op parties, and a very rare gig at Cannibal Club, opening for a touring band.

The Cannibal Club was the most official venue. They booked a lot of the more popular bands that did punk and noise and all these grungy things. Mudhoney played there. The Mentors played there.

Tim Stegall: The Cannibal Club on Sixth Street was before Emo's and the Cavity came along. That was where you would see the Gibson Brothers and Rollins Band with the Dwarves opening. That caliber of acts.

Craig Koon: The Cannibal Club's bread and butter was road shows that Liberty Lunch wouldn't want to touch. Horrible, sludgy noise, or really freaky people. Like an early Melvins show. The nice people at Liberty Lunch would just be like, "Really? Okay. Well, maybe someday."

Jonathan Toubin: The Cannibal Club also did a lot of indie rock. Indie rock is what they called college rock back then because adults didn't listen to it. You have these jangly bands, you have the folky stuff. You also had a very big funk scene, some of them being more traditional James Brown style. Some going on a more post–Big Boys tip, and some of them being very in the [Red Hot] Chili Pepper variety. Other than funk, the other big thing seemed to be a lot of Soundgarden-esque grunge. You'd have a band that was kind of punk like the Cows play, but the openers would inevitably be this band Faucet—the more Soundgarden variety.

Russell Porter: In the early days, all the cool touring bands played at the Cannibal Club. The Dwarves and L7 and everybody. It was just a place to raise hell.

Britt Daniel: The Cannibal Club was great. When I moved down to Austin, it really blew my mind that on a Tuesday night you could go see a touring band there for two bucks. And you could go talk to the bands.

Lisa Rickenberg: When I first moved here in '89, a lot of AmRep[10] and Touch and Go touring bands were coming through.

Lauren Robertson: I'm from Bible Belt, insanely Christian, East Texas. It was pretty traumatic. I had been around all these fucking weird Christian freaks and football players at pasture parties, and then I'd show up at Cannibal Club and the Cows are playing and I was like, "Whoa! Now this is the shit!" That was a very transformative experience.

Dave Prewitt: I really ended up religiously going to the Cannibal Club to see the hoot nights.[11] Jesus Christ Superfly did a Manson hoot night and so they played the Beatles, Charles Manson–style. Buick MacKane played there all the time so I would go hang out with Alejandro (Escovedo) and those cats at that club for hours on end.

Britt Daniel: Skellington was my first Austin band. The very first time that I got on stage was at the Cannibal Club. The reason that we got the gig was because it was a punk rock hoot night that Carl Normal was throwing. We played a Ramones song. I asked him if the Wipers qualified, and he said that wasn't '77 enough. It was pretty phenomenal. I remember feeling this wall of volume hitting the back of my legs for the first time, and it was a really cool feeling. I think I might have read in "Dancing About Architecture"[12] that Carl was throwing this thing, and so I just called him up. He said he'd be in the *No Reply* T-shirt because he was doing the *No Reply* fanzine.

Carl Normal: We played the Cannibal Club a lot. The main reason is that our later-to-be guitarist, Dan Carney, owned the Cannibal Club. And the reason he booked us is because he thought we were kind of crappy, but he was a huge fan of English punk, and knew I was a Damned fan, which was his favorite band. So we hit it off. I think we were the only band doing a high-energy pop thing. That's really where we cut our teeth.

Brent Prager: The Cannibal Club definitely instigated and catapulted a lot of bands.

Tim Stegall: I would say the genesis of the Hormones started the night the Didjits played the Cannibal Club in September 1991. The Didjits were this manic trio. An American version of the Damned or something like that.

Their singer, guitar player, songwriter, Rick Sims, was this smarmy character in a game-show host's suit and little round glasses. Completely yanking the crowd's chain. He was one of the most sarcastic frontmen ever. We were watching this and there's this incredible energy going on. Bodies were flying, but everybody had a smile on their face.

I turned to Ron [Williams], and I said, "You want to start a band like that?" He just grinned at me and said, "Let's do it."

It was about a month later when the Cavity started up.

In 2023, comedian/podcaster Joe Rogan reopened the ninety-three-year-old Ritz Theater as the Comedy Mothership.

THE CAVITY

THE CAVITY CREEPS

ON THURSDAY, MARCH 21, 1991, CARL NORMAL, British-born front-man for Austin pop-punk concern Stretford, walked into the Ritz Theater at 320 East Sixth Street to see Happy Family perform. The oblique art-punk quartet's debut LP, *Lucky* (50 Skadillion Watts), had been one of 1990's most compelling local releases. A couple of weeks later, Normal published a review of the show in the April 1991 edition of his photocopied black-and-white zine *No Reply*.

"Unfortunately, Happy Family fell victim to the Ritz's legacy of shit sound tonight," he wrote. "There were no vocals, [and] when there were, there was feedback from hell everywhere and the band was justifiably agitated. They didn't put on one of their better shows, which is a shame because there was a healthy crowd in the house tonight and the Family deserve better than this."

Two days after the Ritz show, Normal caught Happy Family again when they played a party at Taos Co-op, a student housing cooperative across the street from UT at 2610 Guadalupe. He also reviewed this show in the same issue of *No Reply*.

"Happy Family came on and played a great set of their effervescent songs that gained momentum and climaxed in three or four pounding rockers, with singer Cindy Widner's screaming vocals sending the drunk college kids into a dancing frenzy," Normal wrote. "It was dark, dirty and beer-drenched and reminded me how badly Austin needs a small club venue for the punk/

17

underground stuff," Normal wrote. "I want a place where I can see the Rock-busters, the Friendly Truckers, Pocket FishRmen, and any other bands that are worth a damn play every weekend."

Happy Family broke up within the year, leaving would-be contrarian anthems like "We Love You We Don't Love You" and "Where's My Tribe" sadly underrecognized. But Normal's sense of injustice was remedied within months when the Cavity opened in September 1991.

"I remember reading that and going, 'Bing! There's my call to arms!'" recalls Cavity co-owner Staryn Wagner. "Carl and I discussed the article and the state of the scene. I told him what I was thinking about doing and he said, 'Yeah, I think that's exactly what this place needs.' It helped motivate me to hear someone else say the same things I was thinking."

Sandwiched between two gay bars,[1] the Cavity—also known to regulars as the Cavity Club—was located in a signless, windowless building at 615 Red River. The space had previously housed a cultish radical eco-arts collective called Zendik Farm. As a BYOB venue, consumption knew no official bounds. Ironically, this meant minors could be admitted so long as they didn't run afoul of Austin's downtown curfew. The all volume/no nuance sound system bore many of the same characteristics Normal had lambasted the Ritz for, but by serving as a steady homebase for the "punk/underground stuff" at a time when there was none, the Cavity unquestionably checked the most important box of all.

Starting with a grand opening night bill featuring Stumpwater, Meat Lovers Pizza, and Warthog 2001 on September 20, 1991, the Cavity incubated a cohesive sense of scenedom among a burgeoning contingent of younger, rawer bands that otherwise couldn't count on steady gigs at the Ritz or the Cannibal Club. Anyone who could pick up a phone could count on getting booked at the Cavity at least once.

Wagner served as the club's booking agent, while Squat Thrust guitarist/vocalist Jimmy Bradshaw mustered startup money. However, it was Dave Hermann, the club's Frank Zappa–resembling manager, who served as the "face" of the Cavity and embodied its most extreme proclivities. New York–based DJ/producer/club owner Jonathan Toubin—who frequently performed at the club as guitarist for Cheezus and Noodle—likens the Cavity triumvirate to a modern-day Yalta conference.

"Churchill, as played by Jimmy Bradshaw," Toubin posits. "FDR will be Staryn. And Stalin—of course—will be Mr. Dave Hermann, may he rest in peace."

The Cavity always existed on the fringe of legality and the verge of closure. It operated on a handshake deal with an absentee landlord and without superfluous bureaucratic formalities such as a certificate of occupancy. Hermann and Wagner actually lived in the club—illegally—to keep their costs of living low enough to make the venture viable. When Bradshaw and Wagner had had enough, Hermann bought out their interests in the business for the princely sum of one drink (each).

Fairly or not, the area around the Cavity had a rough reputation. The club lay halfway between the Salvation Army shelter on Eighth Street and the revelry of Sixth Street.[2] Despite being just a couple of blocks away from police headquarters, the drug trade at the corner of Seventh and Red River was brisk and violent crime wasn't unheard of. There was even a tenuous connection between the Cavity and the most infamous crime committed in Austin during the 1990s.

On November 17, 1991, a woman was abducted from the street outside the club, taken to San Antonio, and sexually assaulted at gunpoint by three men who were later briefly considered suspects in the Yogurt Shop Murders that took place in north-central Austin on December 6, 1991.[3] In their fruitless haste to find the killer or killers (the murders remain officially unsolved as of this writing), Austin police started bringing in band members and other so-called PIBs, or "People in Black," for questioning.[4] Even so, authorities mostly left the Cavity to its own strange devices because they didn't serve alcohol.

Against all odds, the Cavity lasted for a year and a half, hosting one last blowout in February 1993 helmed by primitive garage rock queens Pork and hesh-tinged potty mouths the Rockbusters. Ultimately, it was the 1992 opening of Emo's a few doors down at 603 Red River that ended the shoestring club's run. The Cavity couldn't survive against a neighboring venue that sold cheap drinks, didn't charge a cover, and brought in national touring acts like Killdozer and L7.

But what a run it was. The Cavity's fleeting success served as proof of concept for the alternative-minded music venues that followed. Many local bands nurtured by the Cavity, such as Normal's Stretford, teenage hardcore miscreants IV Violent People, unhinged math-rock maestros Gut, and San Antonio avant-punk émigrés Glorium graduated to bigger stages and musical ambitions as the '90s progressed. More esoteric musical strangeness abounded in the form of the Personalities, who played a medley of Beatles songs with the word "pus" (e.g., "All You Need Is Pus"), and Lucky Jewell, a onetime *Gong Show* contestant who sang tuneless-but-enthusiastic cowboy songs. Future big-name acts like Green Day, Chumbawamba, and Bikini Kill made pit stops at the Cavity on their way up. And no chronicle of the club would be complete without discussing the truncated gig scum-rocker GG

Allin perpetrated there in 1992 that ended in a hail of teargas and bodily waste.

So sit back, strap in, and don't forget your hand sanitizer. It's going to get dirty . . .

Craig Koon: The Cavity was the spark. That's the scene. The Cavity was really what got it going. That was one of the most exciting places I had been to in years of going to clubs in many cities. It actually felt like you were being a part of something that was going on. Not London '77, but you're thinking, "This is cool. Something's going to come out of this. This is actually going to build beyond this. Who knows what is going to be the next thing? If I'm not there, I'll miss it."

Jonathan Toubin: The minute that Cavity became even a glimmer in people's eyes, people got really excited. It was definitely the place where a whole new thing started, and it allowed Austin to do something that other towns had been doing for many years, which is have a functional DIY punk venue.

Staryn Wagner: The town had one punk club—the Cannibal Club. Brad First—good man—did a lot of good things for quite a while, but it wasn't my scene. He had his twelve bands that got to play. If you weren't one of those twelve, it was garage parties. The Ritz wasn't really happening in the latter days of the Cannibal Club. It had already sputtered out.

Jimmy Bradshaw: I went up to Alaska to work on a boat for three months and busted ass. And that's the financial cornerstone of the Cavity.

Dave Hermann: Jimmy came back from Alaska with a whole lot of money and a dream of buying an ultralight. I talked him out of his money.

Jimmy Bradshaw: I'd never had money and was really uncomfortable with it. I was showing up at parties with extra beer and big bags of weed and buying acid by the sheet just to share. I guess I had some moment of clarity. "I need to do something with this money cause otherwise I'm just going to be broke in six months and have a really bad hangover."

Dave can smell money. He said, "Hey, this guy Staryn and I want to open up something."

Staryn Wagner: We went to talk to the owner in San Marcos. He's some old bubba. Giant Texas-sized desk. Cigar in the ashtray with a cup of whiskey.

"It's 500 bucks a month. Anything goes wrong, you fix it or just deal with it. Do you want it?" We never signed anything. We moved in because neither Dave nor I were living anywhere else.

Jimmy Bradshaw: The place was Zendik Farm prior. It was a fucking disgusting mess. They were like a pseudo quasi-religious hippy, cultish, patchouli-drippy bunch of weirdos bonded by LSD and a leader, Wulf Zendik. He was like a Manson wannabe without the political ideas. I guess there was a resurgence of the '60s thing. It was really gross and weird.

Carl Normal: The Cavity opened in '91. That became my home away from home. Exactly what a true, underground club should be—run by people who cared about the music. Nothing flashy—a dance floor and a stage—but people came in droves. And there was an atmosphere. It was just the right size for the local scene at the time. Some of our best shows were there.

Cris Burns: It was definitely a do-it-yourself, underdog kind of scene. Sometimes the music was dangerous-sounding stuff, sometimes funny. Something like the Factory of Andy Warhol, but the Austin punk rock version. There were always a lot of creative weirdos there. It was some sort of surreal cabaret show.

Staryn Wagner: We did all the drywall with corrugated steel, which people went at. It didn't bust in, so the kicking ended. There was graffiti all over the place.

Bill Jeffery: I donated a painting there. It lasted two nights before it got vandalized.

Staryn Wagner: To build the skate ramp in the backyard, I ripped off a construction site over by Campbell's Hole. We had to rewire the entire place, man. But we never got an occupancy permit. We didn't sell alcohol, so we didn't need to worry about TABC. They'd come busting through sometimes. That was always more humorous than anything.

Russell Porter: We were the first band that played the Cavity. Our friends that lived behind us in Stumpwater—Eddie Housworth and all those guys— they kept hearing us practice and they liked our songs a lot. So they got us to open their show at the Cavity.

We were Warthog 2001 then. I was the drummer. I traded an ounce of pot for some drums. I bought a pitch-shifter toy at Toy Joy and started singing through that. It just sounded funny.

Jonathan Toubin: Dave Hermann of the Cavity was the manager of Warthog 2000,[5] who later became FuckEmos. Needless to say, they played at the Cavity very often, and he would accommodate Russell by plugging the pitch-shifter into the PA. It actually sounded like the best thing I ever heard. Or maybe the worst.

Dave Hermann: We had a preopening—Warthog and Vampire Bondage Club. Then we opened up the weekend of my birthday and it was pretty freaking insane.

Jonathan Toubin: Stumpwater were my favorite band back then. Their singer Eddie Housworth used to oil himself up and wear a flasher coat. But instead of seeing Stumpwater at a little house party getting shut down by cops, they were on a real stage at a real venue. Seeing these bands as headliners on a weekend would've never happened at Cannibal Club. It was a very exciting moment.

Sean McGowan: It was a catch-all for people with problems. But it gave a lot of people work, and it gave a lot of people community. You kind of came in there broken and it helped you to get fixed. For the people that lived there—because people actually lived there—they didn't charge. You could sleep on these couches.

Karla Steffen: Dave Hermann sometimes let me sleep in the weird little crawlspace under the sound booth at the Cavity Club when I was too tired to walk back to campus. I was seventeen, had just moved away from home, and I think I spent as much time at the Cavity as in my dorm room. Sometimes I even studied there before they opened for shows, sitting on top of the skateboard ramp out back, watching people sell drugs in front of the police station.

Craig Koon: There were people living under the stage. The fourteen-year-old English kid with the top hat. I don't think he was English, he just liked to adopt the accent. Ted Milton was in a fantastic band called Blurt. When Blurt petered out, he did spoken word and poetry. He's on stage reading from his little books of poetry and from under the floorboards comes retaliatory voices. He's looking around and the kid in the top hat crawls out. He's heckling the poor man who took it in good stride and was bantering back and forth at the Dickensian youth.

Jimmy Bradshaw: Unicorn Magic wanted to be the anti–punk rock punk rock band. We started playing all these really cheesy songs I was writing for shits and giggles. As awful as possible and really, really sweet. Painfully ugly. And then only play with the heaviest, hardest bands we fit the least in with. And that's where the Cavity came in, because I could book us. Now you have to endure this for the next half hour. I guess the bow on it all is that we were all majestically fucked up the whole time, trying to sing about rainbows and puppies.

Tim Stegall: There was Greg Beets's band that he had going with Jonathan Toubin, Cheezus. They were kind of freaky. They had all these bizarre songs like "Sally Has Maggots." That was about some news story that they read about a couple's sexual fetish where the guy would eat food out of the woman's vagina. One time they stuck tuna inside her, and it ended up rotting and she had maggots. I mean, this is the kind of subject matter these guys were coming up with!

Jonathan Toubin: Our influences were the bands in Texas. The Hickoids, the Dicks, Big Boys, Butthole Surfers, Crust, and Ed Hall, and Pocket Fish-Rmen in a big way. When Warthog started, it might have been more Agony Column and the Offenders. With Stumpwater, it was Birthday Party as filtered through Scratch Acid. And Meat Joy. Weird bands like that. All these different bands that were around the time the Cavity started were all very regionally informed. But we were not the first generation.

Brant Bingamon: Seeing the Big Boys, Biscuit [Randy Turner] always did something different. Every single show Biscuit did something interesting. It's a just-in-Austin thing. People like to dress up. Like the Uranium Savages.[6] We're just part of a tradition. We didn't invent it.

Craig Koon: The Pocket FishRmen were doing fun, energetic shows and they were kind of it. People kind of viewed them as being these freaks.

Jonathan Toubin: When John Peel[7] died, he had a box of his fifty most important records, and the Pocket FishRmen's single "The Leader Is Burning" was amongst those fifty records.[8]

Cris Burns: He would be like, "Here's a smashing new hit from the Pocket FishRmen from Austin, Texas." A good rock-'n'-roll voice.

Brant Bingamon: At that point we had been talking about doing a show naked for a while. It was one of the early Cavity shows. Because for some reason, it was an interest.

Cris Burns: We might have stolen some of that from Ed Hall because we had blacklight paint all over us. There were a few girls dancing naked as well. It was quite drafty indeed.

Brant Bingamon: For years afterwards, I was still pulling my dick out, which is so stupid. But of course Snoopy[9] has never really shied away from that type of thing.

Cris Burns: I remember his drumstick broke and it went straight down and pierced his member. But he didn't miss a beat . . .

Brant Bingamon: . . . any more than the ones he had already been missing before!

Cris Burns: We played the Cavity on Halloween night. We were inside this spaceship we'd made out of gold foil and stuff. Someone was supposed to pull the rope, the spaceship would open up, and we would come out. But of course the thing wouldn't open and so you had to kick your way out of the spaceship.

Brant Bingamon: You're forgetting what happened earlier with Smell of Blood.

Cris Burns: Oh yeah. We were playing on the Cavity roof and throwing gallons of fake blood, and we squirted on the audience below through a foam rubber penis thing. Our friend Colleen [Cude] was dressed as a giant dancing tampon for the Smell of Blood show. The TABC were trying to shut us down. They were all too fat and they couldn't climb on the roof, and it was a real Keystone Cops kind of deal going down.

Brant Bingamon: And Dave was probably happier than ever because he was getting in trouble for something.

Dave Hermann: I'm dressed up as a dominatrix. I got on a freaking vinyl teddy, my hair's up about six feet tall. I look like fucking Frankenstein's bride dead twice over. I got a whip and the cop comes up to me and goes, "Put the whip down on the bar." So I put the whip down on the bar. I walk up to him and he keeps walking backwards all the way up to the barrier. You could see his fellow officers just cracking up behind him.

The officer says, "You can't have a band on the roof." I'm like, "Well, they only got about ten minutes." "I'll give you twenty." What can you say? There's a different attitude now, man.

Rick Carney: Because we didn't sell alcohol, we were completely under the radar as far as what we could get away with. That all changed with the Yogurt Shop Murders, though. All of a sudden, we were under scrutiny. They had linked some suspects to the Cavity as patrons. A lot of folks were questioned and just called in to the police station to talk about it. That was a weird little episode.

Carl Normal: We did Sid's Birthday Bash at the Cavity, which was a huge success. The whole thing was trying to get all the bands I liked together in a one-night minifest. And that will help every band move forward. *This is a scene.* If all our fans come, then there's going to be some cross-pollination, right? And everybody will form bands. And before you know it, Austin will truly be *Punk Rock and Roll Central.* But it didn't really work out like that.

Paul Streckfus: The small local shows where it was a ton of bands playing— like those punk festivals—were really the coolest shows. Where everybody was there, like Gomez and Gut and Yuck, El Santo, Lather, Noodle, Bucketful, Stretford . . . so many bands.

Rebecca Cannon: I did like Cavity, but it was a dirtbag hole. All these Riot Grrrl bands I liked played there. And Stretford played there a lot. I got my start playing trumpet at the Cavity Club with Stretford.

Carl Normal: I think our sound was right for the Cavity. We started out as kind of a punk racket, and then we got a little bit more sophisticated. Adding horns was my need to bring more melody into the band.

Jennings Crawford: Seeing that original Stretford lineup of Carl playing bass, Tony [Nelson] on guitar, and Ken [Dannelley, drums] as this trio, I was

ABOVE Carl Normal (bass), Terrie Bomb (saxophone), and Rebecca Cannon (trumpet) of Stretford at the Cavity, 1992. Photo by Greggae Giles.
RIGHT Carl Normal of Stretford at the Cavity, 1992. Photo by Greggae Giles.

like, "Why is he singing with an English accent?" And then talking to him after the show he still has the accent and it's like, "Man, he's really keeping this going . . ." But they were such a cool different thing from what you would expect to come out of Austin. Unashamed pop punk with all the ba-ba-bas and melodies. They were loud, melodic, had hooks. I loved it. It coincided with my rediscovery of a lot of English postpunk stuff.

Bill Jeffery: Stretford was so much fun. I got fired from Stretford because Carl went on a soul-searching thing to Europe. He came back and he goes, "Bill, I want to be a serious band and I just can't do it with you dancing about all the time." I danced while I played trumpet and he wanted to be taken

seriously. But I got to say, Stretford was one of the best power-pop bands in the fucking world. I loved playing. It was an honor.

Ryan McDaniel: I think the '90s Austin scene really started going around '91 or '92. Stretford was starting to get really good at that time. Jesus Christ Superfly had come around in '91 and they were awesome.

Tim Stegall: You had that whole thing going with Tallboy and Jesus Christ Superfly, where they were prefiguring what Nashville Pussy and Zeke did. They were combining redneck aesthetics, Motörhead, and classic punk rock. Jerry Renshaw from Tallboy was a great guitar player. Rick Carney wrote really good songs. He had a certain drive and certain vision that took Jesus Christ Superfly beyond the city limits in a lot of ways. Tim Kerr had just gotten Jack O'Fire going. This was some of the first garage rock happening in Austin, alongside the Inhalants.

Lisa Rickenberg: I was working at Sound Exchange, so I put up some flyers and that's where I met Dave Haney. That was how the Inhalants got started. I was getting into a lot of the early Cleveland and New York punk kind of stuff. Dave Haney had been into '60s garage for a long time so we met in the middle. We had a similar aesthetic. Neither one of us were very proficient, and neither one of us wanted to be super noodley. We were also kind of on the overeducated side for punk rock. David is a professor. Richard[10]—our second drummer—was also a professor, and I was wasting my undergrad degree. We weren't raging party people.

Ryan McDaniel: The Cavity started doing parties that would start at two a.m. Bands like Gut and Glorium would play these keg parties, and no one could do anything because it wasn't a bar.

Paul Streckfus: The Cavity was where Glorium got introduced to all the bands in Austin, 'cause we were from San Antonio. We moved here in '92. One of the first shows that comes to my mind was American Psycho Band at the Cavity. I got my face split open. This guy in front was just freaking out and thrashing his head and split my jaw open. I had to go to the hospital and get stitches. But then we played at the Cavity with johnboy and Gomez and Gut and Yuck and Lather and Noodle and all the bands like that. Ryan Richardson was at our second show there. We played with the Mieces and he was like, "Hey, let's do a seven-inch!" So EV[11] Records put out our first seven-inch. And people were into it. Then Roger Morgan from Unclean Records offered to put out a seven-inch. Lisa Rickenberg engineered that and helped Roger produce that at Lone Star Studios.

Staryn Wagner: It was a start for a lot of kids, man. I used to get calls from moms: "My kid's only twelve years old. Can he come to your club?" I'm thinking, *Ma'am if you knew what this place was like some nights . . .* But my response is, "Oh, yes ma'am. We do not serve alcohol. There is no alcohol served here."

Graham Williams: I had to tell my mom I was staying at someone else's house, but one of the first times we went to the Cavity, we were sitting on that skate ramp and I remember Roger [Brown], the bass player for Intent, walking by. The guy I was with had an Intent shirt and he was like, "Nice shirt!" and started talking. He was telling us where to go for shows, where to buy records. So through that little network of seeing bands in all-ages venues, you were able to meet each other. A lot of people started bands with each other because of that.

Staryn Wagner: IV Violent People was the first real, full-on, underage show we had. And straight-edge, which was really great. Every kid shows up with the money to get in. We didn't have that luxury with the older folks. When the all-ages shows were over, the place was clean. It wasn't soaked in beer and cigarettes. No vomit. No broken bottles. I loved those. We got money and we didn't have to clean up. It was after the IV Violent People show that Dave was like, "Staryn, you need to book more of those."

Ryan McDaniel: I had my first high school punk rock band called IV Violent People and we needed a singer. Our guitar player Houston [Ritcheson] knew Chepo [Peña] and introduced us at Aqua Fest when the Ramones and Debbie Harry and Tom Tom Club played.[12] He was in a band called What? at the time. I told him I liked his demo and I thought it sounded like the Descendents. He became our singer. I turned him onto Kiss and we would dress up as Kiss at certain shows and do a silly amount of Kiss covers. We've had this crazy punk rock science-fiction silly brotherhood going on since 1990.

Around 1992, IV Violent People broke up. The core of that band was Chepo Peña, Brandon Burke, and myself. We decided to start our own band and be more poppy, so we started Gomez.

Jonathan Toubin: Gomez would be really more into that California punk rock sound.

Ryan McDaniel: For the longest time we were the only melodic, poppy band that was in the punk rock vein. I think that helped us because we were different. Everybody else did more heavy, kind of Dischord music, which was awesome. But we had our own thing.

Michael Letton: Chepo was the scary punk rock guy in the halls.[13] He would dress up like Glenn Danzig and walk down the hall. I wish I'd bought their music before they sold their name to the British band.

Cindy Widner: The Cavity is not the first thing that comes to my mind when I think of Austin in the '90s—though I enjoyed its nutso environment and shows as much as the next guy. Maybe it was too punk rock for me.

Dave Hermann: We were getting amazing shows. Antiseen. Crazy shows like Nimrod. That was awesome. It was *the* bondage show going on. There were a lot of things going on at that club that were completely underground, that could not happen anywhere else. Period. Eugene Chadbourne. Three Day Stubble. They're not going to play the Cannibal Club. They were playing the underground places back then. The only other place that had shows was Chances, an underground lesbian bar. They had good punk shows.

Kerthy Fix: I would say the Cavity Club was much more hardcore, more humorless in booking policy than Chances.

Cindy Widner: There was humor, but it was the humor that thinks GG Allin is brilliant.

Laura Creedle: The Cavity was a very *boy* space. The pictures on the wall. The attitude. At the same time, there was a certain "Everybody is free to do what they want" atmosphere. You have to dive deep for the inclusivity and the generosity of spirit while still acknowledging that, yeah, there were issues there. There were times that I felt very welcomed there and other times not, but I do remember it well in a lot of regards.

Dotty Farrell: For the people that went there, it had a meaning to them that was special. But when I walked in the Cavity, it felt like a bunch of sheetrock and junkies hanging out. It wasn't my scene. We were all going to Chances!

Rebecca Cannon: I think Cavity was close to some other's hearts, but I wasn't so much into a GG Allin type of thing, like those real gross bands. It was funny, but stinky.

Staryn Wagner: Very good friends of mine never, ever showed up to a show. They were afraid.

Dave Hermann: I don't know why they were afraid. Okay. So, you have a show like GG Allin. You're going to have some violence. Mainly from GG. You're paying for the violence. You're paying to run away from shit and to hopefully not get hit by him.

Staryn Wagner: Or any parts of him.

Dave Hermann: I swear, that's all Staryn wanted, though—a freaking GG Allin show at the Cavity. That was freaking huge. It was a lot bigger than Chumbawamba, I'll fucking tell you. That show took over the whole block. Vampire Bondage Club came on and freaking rocked. Everything was covered in plastic.

Ryan McDaniel: The Murder Junkies[14] came to the Cavity and it was a big deal. I think it was the first time GG Allin ever played in Austin.

Dave Hermann: The place is fucking packed. It's five hundred people in a three-hundred-person space.

Craig Koon: Kelly Petrash and I were wise enough to stand outside because I've seen GG Allin before. I knew better than to be close.

Dave Hermann: People pay and they go in. And then they go out because they're scared.

Staryn Wagner: Because we were BYOB, everybody brought their own. Dave said, "There will be no bottles." You know how much pain and blood there would be from bottles at a GG Allin show?

Ryan McDaniel: Bones was a really big GG Allin fan. He went up and shook his hand. I was like, "Dude, he probably still had fecal matter on it and stuff!" He was like, "No dude, he had gloves on his hands, so it's clean." And then the show started and GG started doing his thing and he was still wearing those gloves, which you knew he had been wearing the whole tour.

Bones DeLarge: People were throwing turkey basters, bananas, anything. He's putting everything up his butt. It was pretty insane. This guy starts screaming at him about four or five yards from the stage. This kid's like, "You gross motherfucker!" and [Allin] threw shit and it fucking hit this dude. This guy's like, "Fuck you, you motherfucker!" and then [makes splat noise]. It just hits this guy in the face and the guy starts going [makes retching noises]. I was standing right next to him, and I start laughing like, "Oh dude, you fucking idiot!"

Ryan McDaniel: This one skinhead is on crutches and starts swinging it at GG Allin. I don't know what he was thinking—skinheads aren't known for being the smartest guys in the world. GG just reaches down, snatches that crutch, jumps into the audience, and starts swinging the crutch like a baseball bat. I see everyone rushing toward the back. I'm like, "I better get the fuck out of here, too." I jumped down off the riser at the wrong time because I hit the ground and, "Bomp bomp bomp." He cut my face. The blood starts trickling down. I'm freaking out, thinking that he had gotten my eye or something. It was really close.

Dave Hermann: The next thing is the tear gas. That was awesome.

Jimmy Bradshaw: The crowd was making this mass exodus and there was a choke point. I'm up in the sound booth starting to see people pile and I instantly thought about the Who concert[15] and it was like, "Oh fuck! Is my name on any actual paperwork for this place? Am I going to go to jail for this death that's going on right below me?"

Staryn Wagner: All of a sudden, a parade of police cars and ambulances comes flying around the corner of Sixth Street, and I knew exactly where they were going. It was like thirteen police cars and three ambulances.

Officer Charles Smith (Austin Police Department): Upon arrival at the Cavity Club I notice numerous people running out the front door. Dispatch had prior advised me that a fight was in progress and that a white mail [*sic*] was onstage and was defecating.[16]

Jimmy Bradshaw: I locked myself in the office and was counting out the money while the cops were banging on the door.

Officer Charles Smith: I saw an arm holding a spray cannister [*sic*] above the crowd's head, and it appeared that a member of the crowd was spraying the Mace. I was pushed by several subjects and I immediatley [*sic*] pulled my night stick and readied it for use.

Dave Hermann: The tear gas has hit me, and I look out the front door and see all these cops. I get the key to the back gate.

Staryn Wagner: To get out the front you had to go through the tear gas . . .

Dave Hermann: . . . and the police. So, I go to the back and open the gate. People were running out of that bar into the gay bars *covered in shit*. I see GG sitting on the stage, and these cops will not go near him. He's covered in shit, bleeding, wearing a pair of gloves, a pair of boots and collar. And he's got an erection.

Staryn Wagner: Smallest penis I've ever seen. Holy shit, I'd be angry, too.

Officer Charles Smith: Upon the arrival of EMS they transported the white male to Brackenridge for his injury's [*sic*].

Staryn Wagner: The event was still far from over though, man. People piled up out front. Police going in and out trying to figure out what the hell had happened there.

Officer Charles Smith: Allen [*sic*] was found to have a warrant to revoke probation out of Flint Mich. After Allen [*sic*] received treatment for his injury's [*sic*] I transported Allin to Central Booking which [*sic*] which he was booked in on the warrant.

Staryn Wagner: The cop cars are all lined up across the street, and there's this kid walking along each car, pissing on the handle of every cop car.

Jimmy Bradshaw: You know, the things you don't hear about GG Allin shows is the next day I'm on a ladder, cleaning feces off the wall, walking around and going, "There's a doo-doo nugget . . ." Gloves and bleach.

Jonathan Toubin: People weren't always accustomed to the kind of behavior that was going on there. The way the three of them ran it, it was a rawer level than some of these bands were accustomed to. Chumbawamba quit after the first song because it was too violent.

Alice Nutter (Chumbawamba): We played the Cavity Club in '91. There was a scrap and we said, "Right, we're going to carry on and we're going to give you ten seconds, 'cos if you want a fight you may as well have a fight to any music—we're not supplying it. Unless you stop, we're going to stop playing." And they didn't, so we just stopped playing and put our stuff away.[17]

Bones DeLarge: Chumbawamba came out in dresses and umbrellas. They said, "No more fighting . . ." and some dude started a fight in the pit. Dave Hermann goes out and tries to stop the fight. Dave Hermann ends up *in* the fight. So the band stops playing.

Richard McIntosh: One of my favorite shows there—the Dogshit Rangers—was just a free-for-all. Ten people on stage. Everyone's on drugs. They poured flour all over themselves. They just looked crazy. There's a keg and somebody had broken off the tap, so it was just a stream of beer coming out of it. This punk rock chick at the keg looked like she was sixteen. She had a mohawk, but she was pregnant, and she was filling up her beer. I remember going, "What the fuck is going on?"

Michelle Rule: Pork was a band I liked right when I first moved here. They're bad asses. Riot Grrrl lo-fi minimalist chicks with tattoos who were just so rock 'n' roll.

Craig Koon: They were just having fun making music. This is the stuff I like about music. Just having fun, not caring about what anyone thinks of it. If you make some bucks and get some beer, that's great.

Chepo Peña: Their EP recorded at the Cavity was one of the first seven-inches that came out in the '90s on SubPar—Craig Koon's label.

Dana Smith: We didn't know what we were doing, clearly. And yet we made our way. What was important to us is that we did it ourselves. Always.

Edith Casimir: I felt like everybody was way tougher and scarier than us. When we started playing at the Cavity, everybody seemed to get so much cooler so fast. I got shy and put my head down. People got more into drugs, and everybody got a little creepier, but it didn't really affect me because I didn't really run around that. I was at the Hole in the Wall drinking with the old men.

Dave Hermann: There were months when it was just like, "Here's the money. We got to make this last . . ." Then SXSW came and were sucking our you-know-whats. They took us to dinner, wined us and dined us. They wanted us to be part of their little gig so bad.

Staryn Wagner: Dave never wanted to be in it, but I thought, "Okay, this will be an opportunity for us to have a couple of cash-in nights." I was so fucking broke, eating at the Sally [Salvation Army]. If I had fifty bucks in my pocket, I was really doing good.

Dave Hermann: They were offering us like two grand a night, you know?

Staryn Wagner: The funny thing is, the person I was dealing with was Steve Chaney[18]—a guy who I had worked for at the Texas Union on campus. I got dollar signs, thinking, "Yeah, man, I'm going to have money!" But I'm torn inside because SXSW was so *not* what we were about. Steve Chaney shows up at the Cavity, and he's like, "All right. Staryn, I got the paperwork. We're going to sign this."

I was like, "Steve, fuck it. We're not going to do it." He was like, "Staryn, thank god, man. I just haven't been able to figure out what the hell you've been thinking. This is not for you guys." I was like, "All right. Take it easy. Thanks, anyway."

So we set up some awesome shows and we were packed, and there were record label folks in the place. I'm so glad I ditched all that SXSW. They got their thing. We weren't it.

Dave Hermann: By this time we had a reputation. Some good, some bad, but whatever. If you got to Austin, the Cavity is a punk club, period. It's a fucking *punk* club.

Staryn Wagner: We were pretty much as raw as it got.

Dave Hermann: Some of the stuff should've been a lot worse, but a show like Crash Worship where there's thirty or forty naked women running around in the club. . . . You really can't tell what's going on and there's all this rhythm, and the whole club is breathing. The club was indestructible. There were fires being built in the middle of the floor.

Staryn Wagner: Crash Worship reminded me of a show Blort put on. Blort had two drummers, a bass player, and Chuk [Hell] singing and playing guitar. Real tribal sound. One time, they had this kid pinning live roaches to his cheek. Just a little freak show going.

Jimmy Bradshaw: Chuk Hell had brought a really flammable liquid rubber glue, lit it up, and kicked it everywhere. It was like napalm. Everywhere it hit, it left a little trail of fire and then of course it goes into the crowd.

Staryn Wagner: The crowd's kicking it back and forth and then—whoosh— it goes right through the hole in the front of the stage.

Jimmy Bradshaw: It flies way back under this wooden stage. Everywhere it's just a trail of fire. And I'm chasing it around and had to crawl under the stage and then, "Oh wow. How do you put out a fire without, you know, anything?" And if I tried to pad it out, it just gets on you. . . . I was pretty sure for a few minutes we were done.

Staryn Wagner: We were *it* for about four to six months.

Dave Hermann: And then Emo's opened. After a year, when Staryn and Jimmy left, it became a free-for-all. It was basically, "How long before I get kicked out?" At that point, Emo's had taken everything that we had worked on. Everybody was going there.

Ryan McDaniel: The Cavity started going downhill and part of the reason was because Emo's opened up.

Bones DeLarge: Emo's kind of came in right around the time the Cavity was ending, and they were trying to compete with Cavity.

Marty Volume: They outdid them.

Ryan McDaniel: Emo's was great and a home for me and my bands for many years, but you can't discount the impact of the Cavity on Emo's and the scene.

Kathleen Hanna of Bikini Kill at the Cavity, 1992. Photo by Lisa Davis. Courtesy of Austin History Center.

Staryn Wagner: Emo's came and had every bit of money they needed. And had free shows.

Jimmy Bradshaw: It wasn't gonna last much longer. I realized that. Dave and I were sitting in Emo's, and I was like, "I want out." He said, "What do you want for your part of this business?"

"A bourbon and Coke please." And that's how I cashed out. Trying to make money—that's not rock and roll or punk rock, you know? Be famous? Why would you want that? It's horrible.

Staryn Wagner: I sold my share to Dave for one beer over at the Crossing.

Dave Hermann: After Staryn and Jimmy left, I actually got Rick Carney to do the booking. He knows everybody. He started booking crazy shows like Green Day, and these MTV one-hit wonders.

Rick Carney: I booked one of Green Day's first shows in town. I booked Sublime's first show in town. We were doing all-ages shows with bands like Crash Worship, Impotent Sea Snakes, and Antiseen.

Jimmy Bradshaw: I don't remember Green Day. It's probably 'cause they suck.

Dave Hermann: Goddang, I hate those little asswipes. I was like, "You're coming to my fucking club, and you're going to bitch at me in Texas about your rider? I don't think so." This is the end of the Cavity—the last six months. We're still getting these great shows in. Bikini Kill . . . those poor girls. This is my best friend's freaking birthday, and we had her chained up to the ceiling. We were spanking her. They're totally offended.

Tim Stegall: Kathleen Hanna, Miss Queen Riot Grrrl, was supremely pissed off by that huge painting of the clown offering a lollipop to the little girl. Then Gomez got up there and closed their set with "Lick It Up" by Kiss.

Chepo Peña: We played with them at the Cavity and we played "Lick It Up," like we did every show at that time. We had no idea who they were or what Riot Grrrl was. We were like nineteen years old.

Tim Stegall: So, Kathleen Hanna gets up there and proceeds to deliver this ten-minute feminist lecture about how wrong this band was, what a bunch of male chauvinist pigs they were, and how wrong that pedophile painting was.

Chepo Peña: I might have been outside when she said that. I don't recall hearing her rant about us. She was probably right.

Dave Hermann: Those last six months were complete insanity. The club was out of control. They'd come turn the water off during the day and I'd turn it back on at night. I tried to talk the landlord into letting me do SXSW.

He's like, "You haven't paid the rent for six months. I got people over there telling me what's been going on over there."

There was a last weekend. Rockbusters played. Pork played. Swine King. Really good bands. The last weekend just totally rocked.

Dotty Farrell: The one time we were supposed to play at the Cavity, Lindsey Kuhn made this badass Day-Glo poster. And then the club closed down the night before. So the show never even happened.

Karla Steffen: I've never loved a shitty punk rock club the way I did the Cavity. It's a place that could never exist in whatever Austin is now.

EMO'S

JOHNNY CASH SAT HERE

IN AUSTIN MUSIC, MOST ROADS ULTIMATELY LEAD back to Willie Nelson. So it is with Emo's, the Austin outpost of a club first established in Houston in 1989.

The Houston Emo's was located at 2700 Albany—where Montrose meets the Fourth Ward—in the former DePelchin Faith Home orphanage building (c. 1913). When owner Eric "Emo" Hartman went scouting for an Austin location, he landed at 603 Red River. The stark brick building with concrete floors had been a garage in the 1920s. In the late '80s and early '90s, the building housed country-themed Raven's and its roots-oriented successor Poodie's Red River Saloon, both owned by Poodie Locke, Willie Nelson's longtime road manager. In 1987 blues-rock quartet Omar and the Howlers filmed the music video for "Hard Times in the Land of Plenty" on the indoor stage.

After a hastily arranged soft opening during SXSW, Emo's officially opened on April 24, 1992, with a local double bill of Jesus Christ Superfly and Trouser Trout. Then came the May 29 blowout with Killdozer, Poor Dumb Bastards, and Cherubs to solidify the business template. Although Killdozer was a well-known act on the national underground touring circuit, the show was free for patrons over twenty-one. The eighteen-to-twenties paid just $5. A robust bar business subsidized the live entertainment.

Up through 1994, spoiled Austin music fans of legal drinking age paid nothing to see essential underground rock acts like the Jesus Lizard, Unsane,

© LYMAN 1994

the Didjits, Superchunk, and Jon Spencer Blues Explosion that fans in other cities were paying $20 to see. A noisy cadre of local bands—including Cavity graduates like Gut, Blort, Crown Roast, and the American Psycho Band—also played regularly and grew their audiences. Even the FuckEmos—who changed their name from Warthog 2001 after vocalist Russell Porter was refused entry to Emo's—ultimately became club favorites.

When Emo's opened, the critical mass of downtown Austin venues that regularly featured original live music clustered up and down East Sixth Street in the four blocks between Red River and Brazos. But the Red River strip had its own live music history prior to the '90s.

The 13th Floor Elevators established their mid-'60s psychedelic primacy at the New Orleans Club on the corner of Red River and 11th. The One Knite at 801 Red River presaged Emo's no-cover policy during the early to mid-'70s, incubating young up-and-comers like Stevie Ray Vaughan, Marcia Ball, and the Flatlanders. Future Cannibal Club owner Brad First ran the Cave Club during the '80s at 705 Red River, hosting the Butthole Surfers, Scratch Acid, Sonic Youth, and Ministry in the former Snooper's Paradise Pawn Shop that had previously inspired Doug Sahm to write a mash note to Austin called "Groover's Paradise."

If clubs like the Cavity provided advance reconnaissance, Emo's served as the beachhead for a live-music invasion of Red River that would spread north from East Sixth Street during the '90s and ultimately culminate years later in the establishment of an official cultural district. Of course, Emo's was long gone from Red River by then.

Emo's was not just a live music venue in its early days. Though its submoniker "Alternative Lounging" was already dated by 1992, it accurately pegged the club as a place to meet up and hang out. Because it was free to get in, patrons didn't necessarily wind up there to see the band playing that night. Friendships, romances, and bands started and ended on the patio that linked the smaller indoor and larger outdoor showrooms.

Emo's was a loud club. Grunge and punk alternated with gangsta rap on the jukebox between sets. The bands were usually loud and audience members gabbed loudly regardless. Often someone would yell in your ear while pressing a finger down on your tragus to dull the ambient squall and increase the odds of you understanding what was said. Whether you did or not, it was usually easier to just nod and act like you did.

LEFT Poster for Thinking Fellers Union Local 282, Moist Fist at Emo's, November 4, 1994, and poster for Ed Hall, Sixteen Deluxe, Stars of the Lid at Emo's, December 16, 1994, both by Lyman Hardy.

Garish, highly irreverent artwork adorned the Emo's walls. To the right of the outdoor stage was a giant mural depicting infamous Texas criminals Lee Harvey Oswald, Charles Whitman, Henry Lee Lucas, George Hennard, and David Koresh, each brandishing a rifle with a flaming Lone Star flag in the background. To the right of the indoor showroom entry, a Frank Kozik mural clearly not authorized by Hanna-Barbera depicted a grown-up Pebbles Flintstone garbed in bondage gear while engaging in prehistoric dom play with Dino the Dinosaur. Such artwork embodied the timbre of a time that reflexively held sentimentality at an ironic arm's length and celebrated the roasting of sacred cows, preferably with bottle rockets up the backside.

As the '90s progressed, Emo's branched out from its initial slam-bang pedigree. The abrasive road acts like Seaweed and Cows that made up the nonlocal side of 1994's *Live at Emo's* compilation were joined by emergent post-rock purveyors like Tortoise and Low. More avant-leaning metal bands like Napalm Death and Neurosis would play, and Hartman's unintentional namesake subgenre was well-represented with shows from totemic emo acts like Sunny Day Real Estate, the Promise Ring, and Austin's own Mineral.

Emo's was always an in-demand venue for SXSW. When the indoor and outdoor stages could no longer contain all the action, the club began setting up a third stage in a tent in a lot near the southwest corner of Red River and Sixth. A 1999 showcase from L.A.'s Streetwalkin' Cheetahs made the decade highlight reel when MC5 guitarist Wayne Kramer joined them to rip through an elongated reading of the MC5's "Looking at You."

The first era of Emo's ended in 2000 when Hartman sold his interest in the club to Jason Sabala, who had worked his way up from security to become manager and co-owner. Sabala brought in Frank Hendrix as partner. Then Hendrix bought Sabala out, becoming sole owner.

Hendrix wisely retained Graham Williams as talent buyer for the club. Williams started working security at Emo's in 1998. Although he was only twenty, Williams had been a Cavity kid who fronted a straight-edge punk band called Direction and learned to book shows in classic DIY fashion. Bolstered by Hendrix's investment, Williams's astute booking kept Emo's relevant into its second decade.

The Red River location of Emo's closed in 2011. Unlike most club owners, Hendrix owned the increasingly valuable land Emo's sat on. Faced with a growing tax burden and the difficulty of retrofitting the venue with modern-day amenities, he cashed out and hired architect Michael Hsu to design a new Emo's at 2015 East Riverside Drive. On December 30, 2011, Killdozer returned to play one last show on the main stage.

In 2013 Hendrix sold Emo's to C3 Presents, the Austin-based multinational concert promotion company started in 2007 by Charles Attal, Charlie Walker, and Charlie Jones. The following year, C3 became a subsidiary of Live Nation—the largest concert promotion company on the planet. While the Emo's name and logo live on at the corner of Riverside and Burton, its current incarnation bears only the faintest resemblance to the club Hartman started.

Despite all the piss-takes and revelry, Emo's wouldn't have survived the '90s—or beyond—without running like a business. The staff were irreverent enough to embrace a band called the FuckEmos by putting their debut CD on the club's jukebox, but shows ran on time and jobs were performed professionally. That couldn't always be said for the Cavity. Working at Emo's was a cool job to have, but it *was* a job.

Beyond its musical legacy, several Emo's alumni parlayed the experience into running their own successful businesses. After leaving Emo's, Williams launched a series of independent promotion companies, including Transmission, Margin Walker Presents, and Resound. Sabala opened a namesake club in Portland, Oregon, before returning to Austin and opening Buzz Mill Coffee. Noah Polk cofounded the local pizza chain East Side Pies, while Jason Ward opened a vinyl mastering house in Chicago with Shellac/Volcano Suns bassist Bob Weston.

If there was one moment at which Emo's became one of the key transformative venues in Austin music history, it occurred on March 17, 1994, when Johnny Cash performed a short set in the main showroom for SXSW. Cash was promoting his Rick Rubin–produced *American Recordings* and finding more favor among alt-rock audiences who revered him than on country radio. Joining Cash on that night's bill was Beck, who at that point was primarily known for scoring an oddball radio hit in "Loser."

Traditional country had already established an unlikely toehold at Emo's when Don Walser and his Pure Texas Band brought their weekly residency there from demolished Burnet Road honky-tonk Henry's Bar & Grill in 1993, but Cash's appearance drew international coverage for both the club and SXSW as a whole. The barstool on which he performed was immediately taken out of circulation and ceremoniously suspended above the inside bar until the club closed.

If anyone questioned the Man in Black's feeling about playing in a club with a men's room once deemed "too disgusting to shit in" by satirical news outlet *The Onion*, the answer came when he got to the final line of "A Boy Named Sue" that night.

"If I ever have another boy," Cash ad-libbed, "I'm gonna name him Emo."

Pocket FishRmen playing the original Austin Emo's outdoor stage, 1992. Photo by Greggae Giles.

Eric "Emo" Hartman: Emo: a self-inflicted nickname. In Chicago I used to work at some of the punk bars. A girl was coming by all the time, and she kept bugging me. "Come on, tell me your name."

I was trying to think, who's the weirdest person I know? Emo Phillips. So I go, "My name's Emo. If you laugh, I'll kill you." These guys heard that, and they started calling me Emo.

When I first wanted to do Emo's, my partner's like, "Isn't your nickname Emo? It's your idea. Let's call it Emo's."

I wanted to have a place where I had really cool music on the jukebox, really cheap drinks, and a place to hang out and play pool. That's where we started out in Houston with Emo's.

Graham Williams: Austin is this music capital, but it wasn't the best stop for a touring band. Not until later. I remember having to go to Houston a lot to see bands that wouldn't come to Austin.

Eric "Emo" Hartman: A lot of bands that played in Houston were always telling me about how Austin's great, and how it'd be so cool if there was an Emo's in Austin. The location on Red River had been sitting empty for a long time. The first time I walked in, there were wagon wheels and a bunch of dead animal heads on the walls.

The landlord and his buddies would come in after hours, drink their Crown Royal, play ping-pong, and listen to music. I told them about what I wanted to do. He's like, "That sounds like a gay club." I'm like, "No, it's going to be a music venue."

I didn't really want to use the term "punk rock," because it made him nervous.

We had planned on being open by South By Southwest. With TABC licensing it took a little longer, so we used a catering permit and put butcher paper behind the bar saying, "Coming Soon! Emo's." We were just going to use the outside stage. Then all of a sudden, South By Southwest called us and goes, "We just lost a venue, Can we use that inside stage?"

So Thom [Bone] from Butt Trumpet built a stage. We were painting the stage right before the bands were loading in. We opened up for South By Southwest and closed down right after that was done.

Rick Carney: We [Jesus Christ Superfly] were the first band to headline Emo's, on the soft opening on Friday night.

Eric "Emo" Hartman: Saturday night we had Agony Column. We had a line around the block. It was crazy. That was a good kickstart to everything. After that, I flew in the first touring band—Killdozer. That's the big grand opening tradition.

Rick Carney: There was a certain sense of that was *the* place to be. Part of it was their policy of the shows being free if you were twenty-one [or over]. So you could see Jesus Lizard for nothing.

Dave Prewitt: In the more metal days of *CapZeyeZ*, there was a fuck-those-guys mentality because those were the cool kids, you know? They looked down on the douchey hair-metal guys and they had to play grungy, no leads and things. That meant something so deep you don't understand it, and that was Emo's, man. And I guess you believe something until you go in yourself. So I think the thing about Emo's that kept me going was the fact that they touched on all of that metal shit I thought everyone hated on top of all the new stuff.

Susan Shepard: Crust were one of the first bands I saw at Emo's when it opened in '92. The singer was wearing a diaper and pulled it down and started setting his pubic hair on fire with a Zippo lighter. I was like, "This is awesome!" I must've been sixteen.

Jennifer LaSuprema Hecker: When Emo's opened it changed our teenaged lives.

Susan Shepard: They didn't really keep out teenagers. Later they started kind of enforcing you had to be eighteen to go in, but I don't remember having a problem with that. Thanks, Dave Fisher and Dave Thomson!

Brant Bingamon: It was a revolutionary place when it opened because it was so legit. It was committed to alternative music exclusively. More so than almost any other club in town.

Eric "Emo" Hartman: Next door, the Cavity Club was the true punk rock place. There were guys living there—squatters. Those were great guys. There were a lot of bands playing there too, so it was like I just happened to walk in at the right time back in '92.

Graham Williams: Emo's was free and everyone who was into anything weird was like, "This is where I'm going!" Their only competition was the Cavity—a place that charged.

Staryn Wagner: We never had a bad relationship with Emo's. I walked over, and was like, "Hey, guys, I own a place called the Cavity."
    They're like, "Oh, yeah. Hi. We know of you guys. We're hoping that we have no impact on you. We think that it'll be a good combination." Had the potential to work out . . . Didn't. They came in, they had [Frank] Kozik do artwork there.

Eric "Emo" Hartman: I went around to different artists and said, "I'll buy the material if you want to paint it and we'll hang it up here." Lindsey Kuhn did a really great piece on these famous Texas mass-murderers that was on the wall forever.

Jason Sabala: It was something that most people looked at like "This is cool!" because the guys were all holding rifles. But it's pretty dark. It's all Texas killers so it's got the Texas flag in the background. Mr. X had some photos up in the small room. Bobby Love had an elephant in there for a while.

Staryn Wagner: Emo's had all these artists do some really cool, demented stuff. There's some old clown standing up there in his whitey-tighties with a raging hard-on, and a rainbow wig, holding a lollipop, giving it to this little kid who's just like, "Oh, lollipop!" But they paid all these artists. Stuff we couldn't have done.

Eric "Emo" Hartman: We had one painting in here that the police didn't like. After that first weekend, they said, "If you keep that on the wall, we'll be here every day." We took it down, and actually gave it to Cavity because they didn't have a license or anything.

Bones DeLarge: You have people fucking donkeys, you have women with syringes on their arms and stuff like that.

Ryan McDaniel: Jason Ward—who was Jason Saucier back then—started booking bands. We gave him what little recording we'd done, and he gave us our first show. Dave Thomson—probably one of the coolest guys on the planet—was the heart of Emo's in their first few years. Every band that he liked, he would let them know they had a place there. And that's what bands need. They need that core place that makes a scene. And Emo's was that in the '90s.

Jason Sabala: The beauty I always loved about Emo's was the inside room. You could look down the stage and there was a skateboarder, there was a hippie, there was a cowboy. There was a crazy mix of people that were all there enjoying the music.

Bones DeLarge: I remember taking Dicky Barrett from the Mighty Mighty Bosstones down to Emo's, and he couldn't believe that he's going to see Gas Huffer for free. I'm like, "Dude, they just make the money off the bar."

Eric "Emo" Hartman: I like to think that people saw those bands here because they didn't have to pay. There's Sixteen Deluxe and Spoon—those big bands—but there was also Noodle, Butt Trumpet, Squat Thrust, Jesus Christ Superfly, johnboy. There's so much great talent. The '90s were just magical times here. You'd have as many people here to see an Ed Hall show as you would to see Ween. Sixteen Deluxe would sell out. Spoon would sell out.

Michelle Rule: Emo's was luxurious. We played at Emo's back when they would give you towels and a cooler of drinks in the green room. It was great. That was the first club we played where we really got paid.

Graham Williams: It was the spot for weirdos. The youngsters who were probably into punk and hardcore in the '80s had got a little bit older and wanted to hang out at a bar and this place had both things they liked. Bar life and rock.

Jason Reece: One of the first shows that I saw at Emo's was Don Walser. That was an immediate impression of just how crazy and diverse this town is going to be.

Conrad Keely: There was all these punks doing this two-step slam dance, and I'm like, "This place is fucking weird!"

Janet Hammer: Brainiac, Rocket from the Crypt—a lot of those bands played Emo's and then got really big. Radio big. It was kind of the Eldorado of rock 'n' roll.

Jason Sabala: I'm not tooting our own horn, but I think that we would have to be one of the most instrumental aspects of South By, by having the inside/outside room. We could flip a room and do day parties. It allowed for Man's Ruin and all the different labels to come through and we just ignited it. The labels didn't go to the highest bidder. They came to us because they *wanted* to be there. And once we had the Annex across the street, that's three huge fucking stages. In the '90s, Red River and Sixth Street was ground zero of South By.

Eric "Emo" Hartman: Two days before South By Southwest '94, we're all in here cleaning. All of a sudden there's a knock at the door. I look through the peephole.

I'm like, "That's Johnny Cash!"

He shakes my hand. "Hi, I'm Johnny Cash."

"Yes, sir. I know who you are."

He was the most gracious gentleman. It just happened to be one of his songs playing on the jukebox. He was like, "Oh, my manager called and told you I was coming."

"No, we're great fans."

When he first walked in, he looked over at the small stage and goes, "Is that the stage I'm playing?"

"No, we have a big stage outside."

He asked what kind of place it was.

"It's a punk rock place."

He's like, "This is really cool looking."

He went up and shook everybody's hand. To be the legend and how nice he was to all of us. He had just flown in from Australia because he just got off the Highwaymen tour down there.

Lindsey Kuhn had made posters for us. He signed one for all my employees. It was a little disappointing that the show was private, but I probably let two hundred people through the back gate. He closed his set with "A Boy Named Sue," and the last line of it was, "If I have me another boy, I'm going to name him Emo." You can't get any better than that. I still get tingles about it.

Paul Streckfus: All the nationally touring bands would hit Emo's. Jesus Lizard would play there, but they had Austin roots from Scratch Acid. We saw Boss Hog there. Jon Spencer played there. Everyone played Emo's. We played with the Ruins, Shudder to Think, and Lungfish. The Dischord bands were coming down.

Eric Hartman: L7 were on tour with Beastie Boys. They played at the old Coliseum, over there by Lake Austin, and said they wanted to come over and play at Emo's. They used a fake name, but everyone got the word out.

Paul Streckfus: In '94, things really started to feel like they were moving in Austin. Lots more bands were popping up. Kids from Copperas Cove were moving here. The Carbomb guys moved here. They started playing out and we started doing shows with them. Then they started doing 100 Watt Clock and the Satans. Trail of Dead moved here in '95.

Conrad Keely: Things were getting dark in Olympia, Washington. Lots of friends were dying from overdoses or from weird accidents. There was even white supremacist violence that was affecting the town. Then Mia Zapata was murdered. And then Kurt Cobain killed himself. From 1991 until '93, things went steadily downhill. The core group of scenesters that had created the Olympia scene became very rigid and really cliquish. We got sick of it, and Jason was just like, "I'm getting out of here, I'm moving."

And I said, "Well, you're not leaving without me, man."

Jason Reece: It seemed so dark.

Conrad Keely: Seeing bands like Beat Happening and Bikini Kill was part of our Olympia education. They didn't have assigned roles. They were very flexible in who played what. We brought that to what we did here.

It was a really magical time because we were happy not to know anybody. The only people we knew were Jason Morales and Chepo Peña. Chepo invited us to a couple of Sincola shows, but we couldn't get a show, so we organized one for ourselves. It just so happened that the night that we played, Paul Streckfus and Lauren Robertson were riding by on their bicycles.

Lauren Robertson: I saw Trail of Dead play their first show. It actually was through Chepo because he was in Sound Exchange and told me about it. I had been at the Muffs show at Liberty Lunch and was on my bike with Paul Streckfus and was like, "It's a cool name: . . . And You'll Know Us by the Trail of Dead. It has this western feel to it."

We rode our bikes over and saw them at this coffee shop on Congress. They looked really strange and did not fit with what was happening in Austin. So I invited them to play at my house for their second show, and we introduced them to lots of other bands.

Conrad Keely: At that one house show we went from knowing a handful of people to suddenly knowing pretty much everybody in the hip Austin music scene overnight.

Jason Reece: Glorium took us under their wing and were giving us opportunities to play shows and expose us to people.

Paul Streckfus: I remember feeling sort of like a big brother band to these other bands that were getting established and really enjoying that and helping to foster this sense of community.

Lauren Robertson: One memorable Glorium show that stands out was because Princess Di had just died. The Prima Donnas did a show with them at Emo's, and they projected the psychedelic oil light show thing with Princess Di's face and it was all swirly and fucked up. I think it said, "Lady Died," and they kept making Princess Di jokes. She had literally died that week, so it was really fucked up.

Paul Streckfus: There was a ton of different crossover stuff going on. Gut, Lather, Noodle—that stuff was more proggy. Gomez and Star 69 and Stretford, Inhalants—bands like that were kind of more straightforward and more rooted in pop-punk. Windsor for the Derby played at Emo's with us for the first time. Andromeda Strain broke off and formed the Paul Newman group. Neil [Busch] joined Trail of Dead. I wish somebody would map it all out. It would look like a beautiful mess.

Conrad Keely: We played a *lot* of house parties. Us and the Crack Pipes and Gut and Zulu As Kono. We basically just said yes to everything. There was a time where we were playing once a week in Austin.

Jason Reece: And then getting banned.

Conrad Keely: The clubs didn't like us because of our reputation. We would break things.

Lauren Robertson: I remember Trail of Dead playing their first shows at Emo's. They used to destroy all their equipment and then Kevin [Allen] could reconstruct everything.

Conrad Keely: We were banned from Hole in the Wall for years. We got banned off and on from Electric Lounge. We got banned from Emo's, but then the girl that banned us from Emo's—Margaret [Dickenson]—she wanted to manage us. So then we found our niche. Emo's became our fortress.

Graham Williams: In the early Emo's days, the bar numbers were insane. One-dollar Lone Stars, and a Monday night with Jesus Christ Superfly would bring $10,000. How is this possible? I can't get it to rain $10,000 at a sold-out Circle Jerks show! But this happened on a Monday with a local band with one opener because it was free to get in. And people would go there at happy hour.

It was just packed from five p.m. to two a.m. Both rooms. Small bands are playing to eight hundred people outside. Everything was built around that for a long time when there weren't many alternatives.

Eric "Emo" Hartman: We lived and died by the bar. If people didn't drink, then I'm losing money. I wasn't making any money at the door. We'd take the door money from minors, and it'd all go to the band.

A lot of bands worked that way, but then Nirvana hit and all of a sudden, the explosion of what they called "the alternative." Then the guarantees went up, and some other competition came into town. That's when I had to start charging a little bit of money from the adults, just to keep up with the Joneses, and keep up with music that we wanted to do.

Tim Kerr: Eric started charging because you started getting a whole bunch of asshole frats coming in there and not being respectful but causing fights. Prices went up to hopefully weed some of them out.

Jason Sabala: We had a bunch of Round Rock Nazi skins come through, and I remember it was time to throw them out because the pit was going, and they do their little thing where they lock arms in the middle. The culture of punk rock wasn't going to stand for racism. I had a bigger guy in a half nelson. I was trying to drag him to the door, and then everyone else was trying to kick people out. But I lost my grip and it had gotten really hairy. Finally, the cops got those guys out. That was a night I would say got out of hand.

Tim Kerr: And prices went up because bands all started having these ridiculous guarantees. They all started wanting deli platters. That's not DIY. That's not punk rock. You're hook, line, and sinker, just another Led Zeppelin now. You're now part of this whole conglomerate.

Jason Sabala: Bands had to start getting paid. Reverend Horton Heat could only come through so many times and play for 25 percent of the bar. They stayed as loyal as they could as long as they could, but at the end of the day, the jet needs fuel, man. You still got to get the van down the road to the next spot.

Tim Kerr: Nine times out of ten, we gave all the money to the touring band because it's like, "You have to pay for gas." That mentality is how it should be. And then you got "professional musician" mentality. That's why Fugazi would only charge five bucks at the door. Period. Because they're not going to play that game. And it's kind of sad that when Pearl Jam took on Ticketmaster they didn't cite Fugazi as the example, because that's where that came from. That's literally why they decided to take them on—Fugazi had already proven that you could do this.

Eric "Emo" Hartman: When we first opened up, everyone was drinking here. Then Lovejoy's [604 Neches Street] opened up and Casino El Camino [517 East Sixth] opened up, so it became this little triangle. The pie got a little smaller. Then I had to make a tough decision. I go, "Well, let's charge $2, that way we can cover the cost."

Jennifer LaSuprema Hecker: When it went up to $2 for under twenty-one, we went home directly and wrote the angriest rant ever. "This is bullshit! I don't know what they think they're doing, but they're certainly not support-ing art!" We were outraged! We had been stabbed in the back! I may have said I wasn't going to go there anymore. But I'm sure I was there the next night.

Eric "Emo" Hartman: We got a lot of flak from people, like, "$2?" I'd be like, "Well, if you go to Houston or Dallas, it's $20."

Jason Sabala: It had a ripple effect everywhere. Behind the bar you didn't get tipped because they'd paid at the door. And then the bands were like, "They're not buying as much merch!" It's ridiculous, but it is what it is.

Eric "Emo" Hartman: Plus, Electric Lounge opened up. Stubb's opened up. When the agents are looking to book shows, they're supposed to get the most they can for a band, so they'd come to me, and I'd have a ceiling. Stubb's would say, "Well, I'll pay double that."
I understood that. I was never going to hold the bands back. Luckily for me, a lot of bands would come back. When Offspring blew up, that first song hit when they were on tour. They were bumping all their shows from playing three-hundred-seat places to three-thousand-seat halls, but they told their management, "We still want to play Emo's."

Jason Sabala: I remember when the Dwarves played and there was a guy—Bung—right in the front row just egging them on. And HeWhoCannot-BeNamed reached out with his guitar and smacked him on the top of the head and busted him wide open. Later that night, I was in the front room talking to HeWhoCannotBeNamed. Bung's out of the hospital and he comes flying out of the cab, his head all wrapped up like a mummy. He's like, "Where the fuck is that guy?" And HeWhoCannotBeNamed was actually an older guy

Poster for the Impotent Sea Snakes, ST 37, and Squat Thrust at Emo's, November 6, 1992, by JasonAustin.

with glasses like a schoolteacher, but Bung had no idea because on stage he was the naked one with the mask on.

Eric "Emo" Hartman: With a liquor license, unless you pay for adult entertainment, you can't have nudity. Whenever a band would get on stage and expose themselves, I'd always be like, "Please, don't let the cops walk in." Impotent Sea Snakes always did a few things where—if the police walked in—I would be going to jail. There was nudity.

Jonathan Toubin: We created the Noodle All-Male Leather Revue. We made these flyers at Kinko's, where I cut-and-paste our heads onto Leathermen bodies. We had a dancer—Lee Roy Chapman, rest in peace—who was the go-go dancer for FuckEmos. He had a giant "LOSER" tattoo, dancing in sunglasses and a cowboy hat.

We had this great, mixed crowd—the Leathermen and the punks. I went around the neighborhood all day in my buttless chaps and g-string just to get comfortable. We were putting it all on at the show and, in a big hurry, I zipped my skin into the chaps and there was blood everywhere. But it was great and we sold out the outside of Emo's with that.

Jason Sabala: The Man Scouts of America played a South By day party. They dressed in little scout outfits and their guitars had flamethrowers on the end. So when they hit the big part of the music, the guitars were shooting these flames. And then any of those Japanese bands really just fucking got you. Electric Eel Shock was one of those bands that I really loved.

Dotty Farrell: One time, Courtney Love is at Emo's and she's being so obnoxious and she's so drunk. She's going around screeching and making Courtney Love sounds. She went into the men's bathroom and she lost her purse. And so she's stumbling around going, "Where's my purse?"

The next day I'm working at Planet K[1] and my friend rolls up. He pulls out Courtney Love's credit card. He's like, "We went to Fiesta and bought $275 worth of groceries and cigarettes and signed it 'Kurt Cobain.'" And he went shopping with that card over and over and over again. Finally, he was at Tower Records and the guy was like, "Dude, I got to keep this."

Susie Martinez: Emo's was mostly a lot of dudes. I played there because of the Hormones and Tallboy. We opened for Fear and DOA. And then John Yarbrough, the [Tallboy] bass player, would always be like, "Yeah, but Susie, you have the biggest dick!" We made stickers that were like "Tallboy—potty mouth motherfuckers." I mean, it was just the vibe of the club, you know? That's kinda how I got into Emo's and got Handful in there because if any girls could handle that, it was us!

Eric "Emo" Hartman: We got typecast as the punk rock bar. People looked *not normal*. They were always thinking they're all on drugs, so we had to make sure that we were real stringent. Plus, we had all ages in here, so we had to be really sure that we didn't get caught with fake IDs.

Graham Williams: I've never understood when venues have sort of an in-between age policy. If you're worried about people underage drinking, eighteen to twenty-one is prime underage drinking age! You don't have to worry about a nine-year-old sneaking a shot of whiskey. I remember Green Day played Emo's, and they lowered it to sixteen but they wouldn't go down to fourteen, so me and none of my friends could get in. Imagine football games being like, "Sorry—we have beer at the stadium. You can't come in, kids."

Eric "Emo" Hartman: Whenever we busted someone with a fake ID, we'd confiscate their license and staple it to the wall. It became quite a collection. Some people we caught— when they became adults—would go, "Look, there's my fake ID up there!" TABC thought it was funny when they came in.

Russell Porter: I got kicked out one night when Jennifer [Walker, Porter's spouse] was at the bar talking to the bartenders after two a.m. I went outside and she wouldn't come out, so I bum-rushed the door to get back in and they threw me out on the street. I was the drummer then, so I put "Fuck Emos" on my bass drum. Eventually we looked at that and decided that would be a really good band name so we became FuckEmos. It wasn't even *The* Fuck Emos. It was just FuckEmos.

Eric "Emo" Hartman: They were Warthog 2000 at one point. One of their biggest fans was drinking somewhere and decided to paint "Warthog 2000" on the police station. The next day, the head of this area for the police department walked in [saying], "Listen, I know this band plays here. If they play here and you don't call me, I'm going to shut you down."

FuckEmos (*left to right*): Sean Powell (drums), Russell Porter (vocals), Ed Rancourt (guitar). Photo by Sean McGowan.

At that time Cheney Moore was booking the club. I said, "We can't play them here right now because the police want them bad. We don't need that hassle."

The next day, Russell called trying to get a show. Instead of explaining to him why he can't play here, Cheney basically said, "Emo said you can't play here anymore." That's the first thing that set it off. That night his wife was in here and he came strolling up. I'm like, "You can't come in Russell."

Eric "Emo" Hartman: Jack Black was here one night, and he's like, "I want to know the story about the FuckEmos. I saw them in San Francisco—they're hilarious."

Russell Porter: Dave Thomson—the manager of Emo's—used to come see us at the Cavity and he liked us a lot. He was like, "You guys have to come play at Emo's!" Those guys all got the joke.

Brent Prager: Playing at Emo's really elevated the band to a new level, a following and status. And then Frank Kozik sent the band into yet another level with distribution that went all over the world. So it went from dumpster–diving cassettes to real fans in Norway above the Arctic Circle.

Russell Porter: [Frank] Kozik and Craig [Koon] put it out on Rise Records. It was so weird actually even having anybody wanting us to play with them because we didn't want to be a band.

Brent Prager: I will say one thing for Russell—which he won't say—is that his lyrical genius is definitely the main ingredient that was the magnetism. That's what caused this tape to circulate and have people hand it to other people. It was a special thing. They didn't give it to just anybody. I don't think ever before had there ever been such an onslaught of badass songs within three or four months.

Russell Porter: Getting into the Emo's jukebox was the best thing that ever happened. You couldn't walk through that place without hearing that shit.

Cris Burns: FuckEmos were great. I recorded a few albums after *FuckEmos Can Kill You*. I had that Stupendous Sounds studio from '93 to '98 and worked on *Lifestyles of the Drunk and Homeless*, and *Celebration*.

John Spath: We—The Administration—decided that we were going to do a real quick low-budget video for the FuckEmos ["Barf Baby"], which we knew was never going to play anywhere except for on Austin Public Access. We shot that on one roll of film and the whole idea was just to throw a bunch of soup into this batch and that would be our barf. We shot it in the men's restroom of the original Emo's, which was the most disgusting place in the universe. I lit it with a fluorescent shop light, and we shot it on 16mm.

For music playback, they had the song on the Emo's jukebox so we fed a quarter into the jukebox and hit the numbers. The jukebox was in the other room, so they had to crank it up really loud. There was a lot of people in it, barfing and making out and doing all these gross things in the restroom. But Sean the drummer never showed up. Russell from the FuckEmos had the idea that Miss Laura should fill in. So she gallantly came down and sat on the men's toilet at Emo's and filled in for Sean's parts.

Johnny Motard: We played more shows with FuckEmos than any other band. We always thought of it as this good combination because we're both just as crazy and just as fun. But we sounded nothing like each other. And fans fuckin' loved it. Punk rock to me wasn't this particular sound or fashion that you had to be into. It was a life you fuckin' led that you turned into music.

Mark Fagan: I have a FuckEmos shirt that says "Rohypnol" and it's got a big pill on it. They were very open. For a while, everyone was on shitloads of Rohypnol. It was this drug—roofies, the date rape drug—and we took it recreationally for fun. You would turn on the news at night and they'd be talking about this crazy drug.

Johnny Motard: I first came in contact with Rohypnol in the early days of Emo's, a year before the Motards got together. That shit was just around, man. You didn't have to pay for it. You could take one of those and drink three beers and not even remember the evening.

Mark Fagan: People were doing meth. Coke. Heroin. Drinking to excess. Smoking weed. I wish I could remember things better than I do, but we were fucked up a lot of the time.

Chuck Trend: It wasn't in the context of you're a *rock star* and you have all the pressures of touring or living out of a van. People for the most part went home and slept in their own beds, so it really was recreational.

Mark Fagan: And then also addictive.

Johnny Motard: We all got bad habits, bro. Mine was booze. It almost killed me. First show we ever played I got shitface drunk. It turned out well, so I kept doing that over and over.

Chuck Trend: I'm just surprised there weren't more drug casualties than there were.

Bassist Angele Moyesos of the Cryin' Out Louds at Emo's. Photo by Sean McGowan.

Mark Fagan: There were a couple, but it's surprising that everybody made it out as well as they did. Everybody in the FuckEmos is still alive. We're all very happy about that. Everybody in the Motards is still alive.

Graham Williams: In the mid-90s we were driving the ship into the ground. And that happens with lots of businesses where the old guard does it one way, and it's kind of hard to change because you're used to it. But there's new people who are like, "Well shouldn't we do it this way? This makes more sense." The club was going through that at that time. We just had to tear the Band-Aid off and say, "This is not a hangout lounge anymore. It's a live music venue."

Rick Carney: By '97, things were turning a corner a little bit. I know it did for us as a band. It was harder to tour. You could feel a change in town at that point. It seemed like that's when we had a really big influx of the dot-com folks and the California folks. The character of the city changed a little bit, for better or worse.

Graham Williams: By the end of the '90s and into the 2000s, Austin was *the* spot to stop. No one skips Austin. You *cannot* miss this city that's going to make you the most money, have the most people to play to, have the most fun in. And that was not only thanks to Emo's, obviously. It was SXSW more than anything.

There's good and bad with South By of course, but South By put Austin on the map as a music-culture place. Booking agents would stare at a map of the state when they were routing their tours and Austin used to be irrelevant. Then they were coming here every year for SXSW and seeing a packed crowd in all these venues. Even if it was just a bunch of laminates that weren't even people from Austin, it still felt like, "I got to get my bands here!"

Jason Sabala: But by the time we got into the aughts, there was a huge shift because our bathrooms still were shitty, and the green room sucked compared to these other places. Bands had completely flipped and wanted to play nicer venues.

Eric "Emo" Hartman: Right around 2000, the music was changing. The bands coming up weren't really a lot that I liked, and it was turning more and more into a business. Less fun in a sense. Guarantees kept getting higher.

Jason Sabala: It got very frustrating trying to get the bands when the competition got a little deeper and a little darker. The agents would be like, "Hey, I want to bring the Melvins in." And we would offer five grand. C3 offered seven. And all that was really happening was the ticket price was going from $15 to $25. So the people who were really getting punished during that time were the concert-goers. It was very sad to see.

Eric "Emo" Hartman: All of a sudden, bands that would play here forever, they're playing Stubb's. Even the local scene got a little bit stretched out. There weren't a lot of bands coming up.

Graham Williams: Stubb's opened down the street and they started grabbing Queens of the Stone Age and all these Emo's regular bands. And all these awesome AmRep bands don't draw like they used to. So if Unsane plays, there will be a couple hundred people, not a thousand people.

Eric "Emo" Hartman: I sold the club and, unfortunately, the guy that owned it ended up selling the Kozik Flintstones painting.

Jason Sabala: Once that piece got sold by Frank Hendrix, it really rubbed a lot of people the wrong way. Frank invested in the club, but that wasn't his piece to sell. Frank says he gave it to a beer distributor guy. That guy sold it to some guy in Germany to pay off his school debt, but I cannot confirm. Who knows?

Eric "Emo" Hartman: The rumor was it got sold to some Japanese art collector who paid an unbelievable amount of money for it. I was upset when I found out because I was never going to try to make money off it. Every other painting in here stayed to almost the end. I know they transferred some of them over to the new location where they reopened Emo's.

Conrad Keely: You can't help but see how things have changed. I live a block away from the new Emo's and it's not the same at all. You don't go there to meet up with a bunch of friends and hang out and drink. Not at all.

Jason Sabala: When we moved Emo's over to Riverside, it just changed the dynamic. We've really lost that connection. That small midlevel club had that energy.

Graham Williams: The Emo's we know is for sure closed. It's almost like they licensed the name. They don't care about the name. Now anything can play there, right? It's just a big venue. Why not call it Riverside Theater? I remember right when I walked in, there's a Chippendales poster and a Rick Astley poster.

Jason Sabala: After we sold Emo's to C3, I never wore my Emo's jacket or flew the flag ever again. But when I really wrote it off is when I saw that the damn Chippendales were there. Dude. There's no coming back from that.

RADIO

NONE OF THE HITS, ALL OF THE TIME

QUALITY MUSIC ALWAYS HAS THIS AMAZING WAY OF FINDING A PATH TO EXPOSURE. I HAVE A LOT OF FAITH IN PEOPLE'S ABILITY TO RESPOND TO QUALITY IN MUSIC AND ART. THAT'S ONE OF THE SAVING GRACES OF OUR CULTURE AND I HOPE IT WILL CONTINUE TO BE.

ROBERT ZIMMER

AT THE DAWN OF THE '90S, AUSTIN'S radio landscape revealed surprisingly little about the town's status as a live-music mecca. A naive listener could be forgiven for not being able to tell the Austin radio market apart from that of any other second-tier market dominated by mainstream country and contemporary hit stations. To the extent local and nonmajor label music got any airplay at all, it was typically consigned to pigeonholes on the far fringes of late night or overnight slots.

Although KUT-FM was licensed to the University of Texas, it was a professionally run National Public Radio (NPR) affiliate, not a true "college radio" station run by students. Nonprofit KAZI-FM was the only station in town programmed for the Black community, somehow working in everything from nascent hip-hop to public affairs. On the commercial band, album-oriented rock stalwart KLBJ-FM hosted local acts on its weekly *Local Licks Live* showcase, but otherwise hewed closely to many of the same rigid AOR axioms developed by radio consultants like Lee Abrams. If you were in an Austin band that was loud, young, and/or snotty, you were more likely to garner airplay on adventurous college stations in other cities—most notably Rice University's KTRU-FM in Houston—than on stations in your own town.

But major changes were on the horizon for Austin radio. As the '90s unfolded, new stations signed on and new formats emerged. Music that had previously been relegated to the left end of the dial became commercially viable under the catchall "alternative" designation. More stations integrated local music into their programming, giving local bands more opportunities to be heard outside of nightclubs. Despite a national trend toward corporate consolidation and homogenization of commercial radio, Austin became a much more adventurous and interesting radio market during the '90s.

On the commercial end of the dial, so-called rimshot stations licensed to nearby smaller towns began targeting the Austin market in earnest. In January 1990 Bastrop-based KGSR was unsuccessfully broadcasting a New Age/Jazz format at 107.1 FM. In a bid for prestige and profit, they hired respected longtime KLBJ-FM DJ/music director Jody Denberg to reprogram the station in the emerging "Adult Album Alternative" or "Triple A" format pioneered at KBCO-FM in Boulder, Colorado. KGSR provided an outlet for the less raucous, more mature alternative rock entrants. Suddenly local stalwarts like Alejandro Escovedo could be heard on commercial radio in the middle of the day so long as it wasn't his more decibel-pushing material. Even the Replacements got spins with "Sadly Beautiful" from their 1990 swan song, *All Shook Down*.

"'Gary's Got a Boner,' needless to say, is out," Denberg told the *Austin Chronicle*.[1]

Further up the dial at 107.7 FM, Georgetown-licensed KNNC took to the airwaves on Halloween 1991 as Austin's first true commercial alternative rock station. Despite its weak signal, K-NACK quickly found a youthful audience with a playlist dominated by first-generation Lollapalooza acts like Jane's Addiction and the Red Hot Chili Peppers. The station's emblematic "Babyhead" logo began appearing on bumpers and guitar cases all over town.

Though there was no small amount of sneering from underground cognoscenti at the commercialization of alternative music, there was promise for local bands at the margins. DJ Ray Seggern's Sunday night *Home Groan* show offered a confined-but-reliable new channel to reach potential fans. Seggern also produced station-branded CD compilations of local music. A few local tracks—including Sincola's "Bitch" and Meg Hentges's "This Kind of Love"—even made it into regular rotation on K-NACK.

Ultimately, K-NACK's weak signal would be its undoing. In 1995 another rimshot station licensed to Giddings signed on at 101.5 FM. KROX, or 101X, called itself "Austin's New Rock Alternative." With a more powerful transmitter and a larger wallet, several K-NACK veterans defected to 101X. By 1997 KNNC abandoned alternative rock for the ossified-but-safer classic rock format.

Musically speaking, 101X's bill of fare was a more constrained take on K-NACK's alt-rock format, but the new station was adventurous enough to give its morning drive-time slot to Butthole Surfers vocalist Gibby Haynes and local actor/raconteur Robbie Jacks, who played Leatherface in 1994's Austin-filmed *Return of the Texas Chainsaw Massacre*. Haynes and Jacks made for some of the most entertainingly obtuse morning radio in Austin history, but their unorthodox approach (e.g., calling the latest hit record from Live a "puke chunk") guaranteed a brief tenure. As for the station itself, 101X continues to broadcast alt-rock as of this writing even though the cornerstone artists of its genre are now further in the past than those of classic rock were when the alt-rock format first emerged.

If you were making or otherwise in the market for music with scant commercial potential, the real action in '90s Austin radio was down at the left end of the dial, where 91.7 FM loomed as Austin's last available noncommercial frequency. The battle to bring 91.7 FM to life began in the early '80s at Whitehall Cooperative, a housing co-op near UT that is the oldest of its kind in Texas. While living at Whitehall, community radio enthusiast Jim Ellinger started researching what it would take to put a noncommercial radio station on local airwaves that reflected the cooperative ideal.

Initially, the radio spectrum itself conspired against Ellinger and his fellow advocates. Because Austin's FM broadcast contour extends to within less than 199 miles from the US/Mexico border, new frequency allocations were subject to a binational treaty negotiated in 1972 to end the powerful "border blaster" stations in Mexico that made American household names out of characters like goat gland "doctor" John Brinkley in the 1930s and nighttime DJ Wolfman Jack in the 1960s. Such an undertaking typically involved money and/or political clout.

With the former largely nonexistent, Ellinger called the office of US senator Lloyd Bentsen, a conservative Democrat who represented Texas in the Senate from 1971 to 1993 and was Democratic presidential nominee Michael Dukakis's running mate in 1988. After hearing Ellinger's case, Bentsen's office called the FCC to express interest in having 91.7 FM allocated to Austin. The subsequent allocation was the first-ever modification to the 1972 treaty.

Texas Educational Broadcasting Cooperative, the nonprofit corporation founded by Ellinger, filed an application for the frequency on July 4, 1986. The proposed station would be called KOOP-FM and would feature music, voices, and viewpoints not otherwise heard on local airwaves. KOOP's application was accepted on June 25, 1988. A thirty-day period during which other entities could apply for the frequency followed.

Meanwhile, over at UT, the Students Association had formed an ad hoc committee called the Student Radio Task Force in the spring of 1986 to bring a student-run radio station to the university. The SRTF, led by chairman Kevin Tuerff and vice chair Sara Beechner, held benefit shows, sold T-shirts on UT's West Mall, raised money from alumni, and won the support of university administrators. In September 1987 KTSB was officially established under the auspices of Texas Student Publications. The call letters stood for Texas Student Broadcasting, though some joked it actually stood for Tuerff and Beechner's initials.

KTSB's mission was twofold: to provide UT students with broadcasting experience that could potentially be parlayed into careers and to play "alternative" music that couldn't be heard elsewhere on Austin radio. In 1987 the term "alternative" still connoted any music outside the mainstream as much as it referred to the defined subgenre of rock music future stations like K-NACK and 101X would program.

In lieu of an actual broadcast frequency, KTSB started as a cable FM station airing over Austin Cablevision. In order to hear the station in stereo, intrepid listeners had to patch a cable TV signal into their stereo receivers using a signal splitter from Radio Shack. Lazier listeners could simply hear it as background music when the public access channels scrolled school lunch menus and the like.

Despite having a large, well-endowed university behind it, KTSB was a spartan operation when it began cablecasting on April 11, 1988, by playing Jonathan Richman's "This Kind of Music." It was initially housed in the shuttered Varsity Cafeteria. The station's ancient mixing board came from KLBJ's storage closet, and the carpet on the studio walls came from the recently demolished Villa Capri Motel.[2] Initially the station didn't even have a bathroom, which meant DJs heeding nature's call would have to put on a long record and hoof it over to the restrooms in Jester Center dormitory.

From the beginning, KTSB's goal was to become a proper FM station. An early incarnation of Spoon had a song alluding to this ("When We Go FM"), and KTSB's dial position at 91.7 Cable FM left no doubt about where the station intended to land. On July 22, 1988, just three days before KOOP's application would've become final, UT filed a competing application on behalf of KTSB for the 91.7 FM frequency. The application was accepted on September 20, 1990.

The FCC didn't want to have a competitive hearing to decide which station would get 91.7 FM, so they gave KOOP and KTSB ninety days to work out an agreement over what to do with the frequency. Representatives of the two competitors met privately but were unable to come to a resolution by the end of 1990.

With two competing applications for the last local frequency of its kind, the KOOP/KTSB conflict attracted press attention and strong opinions. Because KOOP wasn't a station yet, there was no way to compare the two competitors from a listening perspective, but its vision for opening the airwaves to the underserved certainly aligned with the notion of broadcasting in the public interest. Furthermore, there was the question of why UT should be granted a second radio frequency for the exclusive use of its students when they already held the license for KUT.[3]

Within KTSB itself, not all student staffers supported UT's position. A significant number of them favored negotiating a frequency sharing arrangement with KOOP. Some even met unofficially with KOOP representatives to help bring this arrangement about.

UT initially tried to argue that KTSB's live sports broadcasts and time-sensitive university news coverage were incompatible with a shared-time station arrangement. KOOP, for its part, was amenable to a shared-time solution. Upon further review, an FCC administrative judge ruled the two stations would have to share the frequency on alternate days of the week.

Neither KTSB nor KOOP felt alternating broadcast days would be viable, so the administrative judge's decision was appealed to the FCC review board. On October 23, 1992, the review board ordered both stations to negotiate in good faith toward a fair and equitable schedule for sharing the frequency.

In June 1993, KOOP and KTSB submitted a timeshare agreement to the FCC that split the broadcast day between the stations. KOOP would broadcast from nine a.m. to seven p.m. weekdays and nine a.m. to ten p.m. on weekends. KTSB would broadcast during the other dayparts. The FCC granted construction permits to the two stations in September 1993. Because another station was already using the KTSB call letters, the UT station became KVRX in January 1994.

At the time KOOP/KVRX agreement was inked, it was only the fourth shared frequency arrangement in the United States. Many were skeptical that sharing a frequency could work, but the adversarial nature of the frequency fight ultimately yielded to cooperation. By the end of 1994, Austin had two new noncommercial stations delivering divergent views and sounds.

On November 15, 1994, KVRX began its FM broadcast with DJ April Fresh playing "FM" by the Slits as station volunteers past and present celebrated at historic downtown watering hole Scholz Garten. KOOP went on the air December 17, 1994, with Ellinger reading a quote from Margaret Mead: "Never doubt that a small group of thoughtful, committed citizens can change the world; indeed, it's the only thing that ever has."

As of this writing, the two stations have shared 91.7 FM for over twenty-five years. While the past quarter century hasn't come without conflict, controversy, and uncertainty, each broadcast day is a living victory for the lofty yet seldom realized standard from the Radio Act of 1927 requiring broadcasters to operate in the "public interest, convenience, and necessity."

Bob Simmons: We used to call them underground stations. Countercultural or avant-garde. Anything that we could do to be unique and distinguish ourselves from commercial radio.

Paul Streckfus: College radio was how you learned about stuff. Not until '94 did the internet come around.

Carl Normal: Back then, the student-run station was really the only radio station that represented the Austin underground. Commercial radio stations don't play independent records. Having said that, we played on KLBJ once, which was bizarre.

Jett Garrison: Before KVRX actually went on the FM dial, it was only broadcast on cable.

Susan Shepard: I had my mom take me down to Radio Shack, and they told me how to hook up a cable adapter so you could listen to KTSB. I would hear stuff on there like the Flaming Lips, and Sonic Youth, and wanted to go see these bands down at the Cannibal Club that I couldn't get in to.

Ty Pearson: KVRX is what got me into going to all the shows. Just meeting people and getting my first taste of punk rock. It took hold of me immediately.

Kerthy Fix: If you were a DJ, you were at the hub of the world. It was this springtime of indie rock. The college radio circuit was super active. There were loads of small labels putting out little indie records, and they were all flowing into college radio stations. Jad Fair records and the first Nirvana record and Flaming Lips. And Sonic Youth—so influential.

Britt Daniel: I DJ'd there for my senior year, and then I ended up actually taking classes for the next two years just so that I could keep DJ'ing. The guy that DJ'd after me was this guy, Brad Shenfeld. I didn't know anything about him other than he did a blues show. I was very impressed that he got Ian Moore to come up to his radio show to be interviewed. I wanted to keep going because we were on cable and we were always going to get an FM channel, but it just kept getting delayed.

Craig Koon: It didn't help that it was cable only. There was a small group of people working to get it on the air. They were very dedicated.

Robert Zimmer: I was there right before the radio station went FM. I was part of the big conflict between the University and KOOP. They fought for years over the frequency 91.7.

Kerthy Fix: It was really hard to put KOOP on the air. There was a lot of in-fighting over who was going to control this community radio station. It was kind of difficult to mesh KTSB and KOOP, but we knew we needed it. It seemed really important for the community.

Jim Ellinger: The very last night of the Armadillo[4] was live on NPR. I made $500 producing that and said, "Let's move to Austin!" But Austin didn't have community radio. I was fairly well connected and spoke to some lawyers and engineers and radio consultants. I said, "Can we put another station on the air in Austin?" They were always very polite.

They said, "Not really. You got this Wolfman Jack Treaty." What the fuck is that? If you weren't on the table of allocations for frequencies in your country—Mexico or the United States—you had to get the other country's permission so as not to interfere. And even if you *broadcast* into the 199-mile buffer zone, you had to get the other country's permission.

Well, lacking a suitcase full of $100 bills I didn't have a way to do that. We applied to the FCC for the license. They said, "No. You'll broadcast into the broadcast zone." And I persevered. I persisted. Back during the Ann Richards era, we were a fairly prominent family within the Democratic Party. Senator Lloyd Bentsen was a friend of the family. They're not supposed to get influence from politicians at the FCC, so a very carefully worded strategic phone call said, "Senator Bentsen's office understands this case is very difficult.

Should the Senator's office be able to help, we would be pleased to do so." And that worked.

For the first time ever, they modified the so-called Wolfman Jack Treaty so that if you broadcast into the buffer zone but did *not* reach Mexico, you could apply.

Kerthy Fix: Jim Ellinger made an application for community radio, and they fought and fought. When I was at KTSB, he was lobbying us because time was on his side. We would all graduate and we would want to go to KOOP, so his argument was persuasive.

Jim Ellinger: Up until then, the students had been on cable. They were anxious to get on the air. They felt KOOP radio and myself personally was an impediment for them getting on the air. I was clearly the bad guy. And we duked it out. There were a hundred newspaper stories about the so-called radio war that lingered on and on and on.

Jett Garrison: It came to a standstill. We soon realized that nobody's going to get it until we figure out a solution.

Jim Ellinger: The students did a very smart thing. They hired Bob Simmons. He was much smarter and much more experienced than me, to be sure.

Bob Simmons: All I was trying to do was preserve the peace. Don't lose the license. Don't embarrass the Tower.[5] That was my gig.

Jim Ellinger: On public access TV, Max Nofziger—Austin's legendary hippie city councilmember—said, "You need to give it up, Jim. You're not going to beat the University of Texas."

Bob Simmons: We had the best legal talent in the world working for Texas Student Publications in Cohn and Marks and a guy named Richard Helmick. Cohn and Marks was LBJ's old law firm at the FCC. Those are the guys that had the FCC clout.

Jim Ellinger: That's when it became quite serious. Now the Tower's involved: the president, the chancellor, the board of regents.

Come the day of the second hearing, and there's four lawyers at the table. The attorney, John Crigler, was waiting. He says, "They're going to ask The Question: 'Do you have the funds in hand to build and operate the radio station for six months? Yes or no?' If it's no, you're out. You're going to have to answer honestly. Do you have the money in hand?"

"No."

But they *didn't* ask The Question. Did they make a mistake? No. This is UT. They don't make mistakes. It wasn't clear at first why, but we had our own Deep Throat—a source in the Tower. He said that the powers that be at UT would prefer that students not get on the air, and that the community radio group didn't get on the air. They didn't want nobody on the air.

Bob Simmons: Bill Cunningham was the UT president at the time, and they were none-too-happy about having student radio.[6] They were sure it was going to embarrass them in some way. They weren't happy about the whole idea, but they couldn't be *seen* to be unhappy about it.

Robert Zimmer: We ended up negotiating. I was one of the people with Kevin Tuerff who negotiated a deal to split the station in half. That split station still survives to this day. KOOP is on the air during the day. KVRX is on the air at night.

Ty Pearson: KVRX definitely got the raw end of the deal. KVRX was on from like nine p.m. to nine a.m. or some ridiculous time. Those three a.m. to seven a.m. shifts—no one was listening. KOOP had the times when everyone was actually awake and listening. But in the end you're just doing it because you love music and you're having fun.

Robert Zimmer: We ended up being voted the Best College Radio Station in America by the National Association of College Broadcasters before we even went on FM. I was really, really proud of that. It came because we made a conscious decision to turn the corporate model upside down and gave all the control to the people who knew the most about the music—the DJs. They were members of the community and went out every night and saw these bands. And the result was extraordinary.

Jett Garrison: I remember the day when we flipped the switch to FM. That party was at Scholz Beer Garten. You felt like, "Wow, we were a part of making this happen!" And people were there who had been a part of KVRX back when it was KTSB. That was the beautiful thing about KVRX—you just didn't want to leave.

Jim Ellinger: It was December 17, 1994—the Big Day for KOOP. Very modest studios. And Jenny [Wong][7] showed up for the sign-on and said a few words. There's a picture of her pointing at the clock showing she was eleven minutes late. It was Bob Nagy the brilliant engineer, myself, and a few others. We've been waiting all these years. We hooked up a microphone, did a transmitter check, did some mic checks, and people started playing music and just kind of slipped into their roles. And there we are. It was set in stone. That took a mere eleven years.

Scott Gardner: The very first KOOP studio was on San Jacinto Street. The studio was downstairs, and our office was upstairs. There were band rehearsal spaces in the building, too. I can remember having KOOP meetings upstairs and hearing the Inhalants rehearsing. I'm going, "Oh my God—that's the Inhalants!" Sweatbox is on the second floor, and then the KOOP studios were up on the third floor—the Penthouse! And that was pretty crazy. KOOP went on the air on December 17th, 1994, and then Bob Coleman and I get our first *Garage Show* on December 24th, '94. That was pretty cool.

Tim Storm: Scott and Bob had a radio show on KOOP and they would play local bands. I can remember the Reclusives having made our first record. We'd just got the test pressings. At rehearsal, we opened the box and ran down to the radio show to deliver the vinyl to them to play, which they did. This is like something out of Memphis in the '50s!

Scott Gardner: And with Sweatbox right down there, you had people like Tim Kerr and Mike Mariconda producing and recording bands, and they'd just bring them up. "Yeah, I just recorded this! Let's play it!" So I got to interview all these really cool garage bands.

Robert Zimmer: At KVRX, we made a really, really aggressive push to support local artists. Spoon is a fantastic example when they were running around with demo tapes. You had all these clubs who were supporting local music and alternative and independent music, but they were getting no support on the radio at all. We thought that needed to be remedied.

Brian McBride: KVRX is a radio station that didn't just try to play records, but also tried to be a part of the community and throw live shows or parties. It was a conduit for the music scene in the most literal of senses.

Local Live was originally broadcast from the KVRX office. Photo by Richard Whymark.

Jett Garrison: *Local Live* is the self-produced, self-distributed CD that KVRX puts out from live performances in the studio. There have been some wild times in that studio. My favorite was Foreskin 500 playing nude.

Travis Higdon: Every year they did a CD of local talent. They had at least a couple of Battle of the Bands–type shows. It was the first time I ever saw Spoon—at a KVRX Battle of the Bands.

Britt Daniel: KVRX/KTSB helped us. The first thing that comes to my mind is reading in the *Daily Texan* that Skellington was in their Top 10. That blew my mind.

Ty Pearson: We broadcast the last four bands of a New Guild party—Guild Shock—on tape delay on KVRX. And by "tape delay," I mean we had Mike

Gomez (the Austin version) playing *Local Live* on KVRX. Photo by Richard Whymark.

Heidenreich and the *Local Live* production crew taping them on a cassette tape. It was somebody's job after the last four bands—Spoon, Starfish, FuckEmos, and Pocket FishRmen—to physically run the tape across campus and hand it to someone at the radio station who would then play the tape on the air.

Rebecca Cannon: Being a DJ also made me have to do these KVRX nights at Cannibal Club or Cavity or Blue Flamingo or at the Green Room or at Texas Union. That's what got me into the scene in Austin and realizing there's this whole local scene going on with girls that are in bands. It didn't seem like a dream anymore. If I was going to aspire to be something, it would be like what Kathleen Hanna from Bikini Kill was. That's all I wanted.

Once I realized it was something I could be part of, I started finding artists locally that really inspired me. Gretchen Phillips—I really looked up to her. She was so fiery and confident. And then Glass Eye. It was so magical the way Kathy McCarty sang. Just being able to see somebody that I looked up to in the club and be part of it was something. I'm like, "I can do this! I can be a part of it!"

Kerthy Fix: There was a lot happening with women in music in indie rock at the time. It was very exciting. I started a show on KTSB called *The Ho Show*, focused on women and queer musicians. Basically, I wanted to focus on all the interesting women and queers that I was seeing in music. I just wanted to give a fun party sensibility. At that time feminism felt really *heavy*. Really serious. But to me it was like, "Ladies know how to party! We *are* the life of the party! So let's create that energy around a more subtle feminist agenda. Oh, by the way, it just so happens that all the musicians you're going to hear on this show are women and queers."

Rebecca Cannon: When I found out about the do-it-yourself movement, something shifted in my brain. From the big arena rock concert to suddenly a tiny little room or a house party. You don't have to be special. You don't have to have tons of money and a manager and be on TV. You could just do this all yourself. It was a sense of empowerment that you didn't have to be part of this corporate infrastructure that seemed so out of reach. You could just do it at your own local level. What inspired me too in Austin was getting to know the female musicians that weren't just front people. They played drums, they played guitar, they ran their own label or ran the band.

Jett Garrison: My senior year in college, I was on KVRX, KGSR, 101X, and the Austin Music Network. I met so many female artists. Folks like Terri Hendrix. Rebecca from Sincola. Terri Lord, Gretchen Phillips, Sara Hickman, Trish Murphy. There was this really great community of strong female artists, and I don't know that they always got as much recognition. The women's music community started realizing that if they wanted to gig more, they needed to set up the gigs and gig with each other.

Rock 'n' roll is still a boys' club. It is really tough for female artists. I remember working with female musicians who were being told by record companies, "Well, we can't sign you. We already have a female artist." Lilith Fair was just a nail in the coffin to female artists because it was seen as, "You got your year! Sarah McLachlan gave you a voice." What the fuck?

Kerthy Fix: *The Ho Show* was a fun place to express something that felt fresh and new and to pull in all these influences, because there were so many women musicians here. Pork, The Damnations, Power Snatch, Eleanor Plunge, Two Nice Girls, Girls in the Nose, Gretchen Phillips. All the bands. Terri Lord and Darcee Douglas and Gretchen Phillips were super respected beloved members of that music scene and the community.

Power Snatch came and played live on KVRX. Each member of Power Snatch was an intellectual artistic powerhouse. Their influence, their intelligence, and a sense of humor and playfulness was so fantastic. Cindy [Widner] is a hilarious performer. Kate [Messer's] kind of over-the-top guitar playing. Laura [Creedle] would just write these crazy lines. With both of them as guitarists, it was like the guitar was an animal that they might not be able to tame. And Terri Lord—incredible drummer. Darcee Douglas—this steady tree of bass playing. The two of them really were the grounding that kind of held the whole thing together.

Rebecca Cannon: That's what I liked about the DIY movement in the '90s—a girl would say, "You know what, I want to be in a band." There was nothing that said, "No you can't do that, you're not good enough, you suck." It didn't matter because the type of music we wanted to do could suck but still be fun.

Brian McBride: Being a part of KVRX was great. I created *The Dick Fudge Show*. It was this weird, cartoon-based, surreal, pastiche, collage of random samples embracing the chaos. I was walking around with a handheld recorder. I would record anything. The sound of an ice cream machine. The sound of the bus when you got on it. I would take all of those sounds and cut them up on my four-track. Then I would go to the radio station, play some of the more quieter songs that I was into—maybe some Zoviet France—and layer them in. Eventually, a song would come out of that. It influenced me in a big way as the training for Stars of the Lid. It taught me about layering and timing.

There was one night when two of my friends were present. One is on acid. He's laying on the ground of the radio station while whatever chaos is ensuing. A UT police officer shows up and he just stands in the doorway. We have a nitrous tank. We're smoking pot. We're probably breaking every rule that the radio station established to prevent them from having to deal with something like this. We're all so fucked up that none of us know how to respond to this cop. He just stands there and he looks at us. Thirty long seconds pass.

He says, "I didn't really come here to do my job. I just like to visit the radio station when I get bored."

He points to the nitrous canister and he says, "What's that?"

We say, "It's nitrous oxide."

He says, "Is it legal?"

We're like, "Oh, yeah. It's legal, for sure."

He's like, "Okay. Just checking."

And then he leaves. It was definitely a heart-pounding moment in a lot of ways.

The type of music that Stars of the Lid were making was really like an underwater symphony. It wasn't really something that meshed with what the Austin music scene was about. Whenever we played, we put a premium on making sure that people could be comfortable, whether that was bean bag chairs, or a huge tank of nitrous. It's a strange thing to go out to a show and—instead of getting *up*—to go down. Something in our culture that is a little bizarre—you don't go to a bar to really relax. There's got to be pumping music to keep you going. Austin is a very rock-centric place—a lot of drums.

Robert Zimmer: There was this entire, burgeoning music scene—not just nationally, but locally—that was reflecting the changes in culture. The big record labels weren't aware of it. We would get all of these promos for the equivalent of Tiffany or Debbie Gibson. Seriously. We were just astonished that these labels kept pushing this crap. We were like, "Well, if they won't do it, we'll do it ourselves." It was really no more complicated than that. We had the arrogance to believe that we could get away with it. And we did. Most people identify the early '90s with grunge music, but it wasn't just that. It was all sorts of amazing genres like hip-hop and rap that saw themselves get a lot of wonderful, well-deserved exposure in the early '90s.

Nick Nack: I think the punk scene and the hip-hop scene are parallel in a lot of ways. But community and college radio is that vehicle that the music is delivered on. So everyone—all the DIY underground cats—would come to our show. I cannot underscore this enough: KVRX was the lifeblood of Austin hip-hop. And I ran in some pretty big circles. All these different southern traditional UGK-sounding [Port Arthur's Underground Kingz] cats would come up to the station. We had West Coast guys. And pretty famous people came through and free-styled. I met T Double, Mirage, Bavu [Blakes] . . . all these people. My show was *The B-Side Mix Show* on Saturday night, and Les Jacobs and Kari had a show on Thursdays called *The House of Phat Beats*. They had an amazing show, dude. I went to their show and got plugged into the community at large. It was a big community. But music in the '90s was not just KVRX, right?

Trina Quinn: K-NACK was one of the first alternative stations in the nation. Before that, there was rock and heavy metal, but no one was really tapping into the Smashing Pumpkins or Sonic Youth.

Robert Zimmer: When K-NACK came on the air, my very first reaction was panic. Then, after talking about it with everybody for a little while, I was like, "We don't have anything to fear from those guys." And here's why: Although they were branded as "alternative," it was still a corporate thing, and it was basically white male alternative rock. It's not to say there aren't some great white, male, alternative rock bands, because there are. Spoon. What we had over them, and what KVRX still does, is interest in diversity of culture and genres. You never would hear alternative hip-hop on K-NACK. Never in a thousand years.

Trina Quinn: We [K-NACK] would promote the *Home Groan* series of CDs and play everything from Sincola to El Flaco. Through us, I think a lot of local bands were able to open up for bigger bands that were coming through town.

Kris Patterson: K-NACK put out a compilation and we were the first song on there. K-NACK did feature Austin musicians, so it wasn't just Sincola. But we were on heavy rotation. The only other song I remember off of that was Meg Hentges's "This Kind of Love," which is an awesome song.

Robert Zimmer: K-NACK were somewhat supportive of local artists but, to me, a corporation can come in and do alternative as a brand but, really, it's just a brand. KVRX's focus always has been—and hopefully always will be—strictly about the quality of the music. Not about how much it makes and not about appealing to the lowest common denominator.

Trina Quinn: When the alternative format picked up across the nation, 101X showed up in Austin to play their alternative music, which wasn't exactly the same. They were more playing Hootie and the Blowfish, but they incorporated Stone Temple Pilots and the type of bands we played at K-NACK. We kind of knew that our ship was going to sink. We didn't have the money to compete. A lot of us stuck around and went down with that ship, proudly.

Some of us did not. It caused a big rift. I eventually moved on to 101X and stayed for many, many years.

Jett Garrison: It's no secret that 101X shut down K-NACK. I was there when that happened. That's the market strategy. 101X was the Starbucks that came in and put down the local coffee shop. No doubt about it. This was also in '96, when media was deregulated. No longer could you only own a certain percentage of stations in the market. You could have a monopoly. And that's when the Clear Channels started popping up.

Bob Simmons: The Communication Act of 1996, Bill Clinton. It was that consolidation that has probably had more to do with the destruction of creative radio than almost anything in the sense that you have all of these one thousand stations owned by one entity. They have four production sites throughout the country where you're programming for seventeen or eighteen stations at a time. Local ownership and local control is a thing of the past and diversity of opinion and all the rest of that.

Jett Garrison: Having been a noncommercial college radio DJ, it was great actually being able to support a band who was not getting recognition or exposure. Really pushing and promoting bands. And as I transitioned to commercial radio and watched commercial radio become more commodified, that aspect of being a DJ and actually feeling like you were contributing to something . . . for me, that went away.

Bob Simmons: Luckily, nothing ever lasts in radio for more than five minutes, except that radio waves are our most permanent creation. Remember, your program is still headed out there past Alpha Centauri somewhere. It'll be listened to someday again by some sentient being.

HOLE IN THE WALL

CHEAP MUSIC, FAST DRINKS, LIVE WOMEN

SITUATED JUST ACROSS GUADALUPE FROM UT'S COLLEGE of Communication since 1974, the Hole in the Wall was already an old-guard watering hole by the early '90s. Framed sketches of regulars, weathered sports pennants, and Elvis memorabilia adorned the bar's wood-paneled walls. During the day and early evening the place resembled a low-rent variation of the *Cheers* set or maybe one of the weathered beer joints the band X name-checks in "The Have Nots."

Marian "Billie" Cugini and her son, Doug Cugini, opened the Hole in the Wall on June 15, 1974, in a building previously occupied by a dry cleaner. They named the place after the Hole in the Wall Gang, a storied band of late-1800s outlaws back in vogue following the popular 1969 film *Butch Cassidy and the Sundance Kid*. The Cuginis ran truck-stop diners on the outskirts of Austin and opened the new establishment as a place where frugal working stiffs and academics could grab affordable sustenance and libations. Live music was an afterthought.

Singer/songwriters were the first to play Hole in the Wall. A young Nanci Griffith stopped by to ask for a gig that summer and wound up with a residency. Over the years, everyone from Doug Sahm to Townes Van Zandt to Lucinda Williams held court on the postage-stamp-sized stage backing up to a picture window overlooking the Drag. Former Velvet Underground guitarist Sterling Morrison even put in an appearance, moonlighting from his UT

English instructor gig in the mid-seventies with a band called the Bizarros. In the mid-eighties, a newly relocated folk-boombox duo from Wisconsin called Timbuk 3 parlayed a Hole gig into a record deal with IRS and a Top 40 single with "The Future's So Bright, I Gotta Wear Shades."

By the early '90s, the Hole's musical fare leaned heavily on Austin's bumper crop of what was then called roots rock. Teddy and the Tall Tops, Two Hoots and a Holler, and the LeRoi Brothers were all frequent flyers. Ex–True Believer Alejandro Escovedo's Buick MacKane channeled the squall of protopunks like the Stooges and the New York Dolls, but he was already one of the city's best-loved musicians. Younger, less-known bands pumping that kind of action were more likely to be found at the Cannibal Club, the Ritz, or even the Texas Tavern—a venue housed in the UT student union and forever ruined by a wall between the bar and the showroom erected in 1987 to preserve its all-ages status after the state drinking age went from nineteen to twenty-one.

Hole in the Wall may have been a dive, but it was not an underground club. By 1990 it was already a local institution. Graduate journalism seminars sometimes abandoned classrooms across the street to continue discussion over beer pitchers there. Its barstools were usually populated by longtime customers whose primary business there was drinking, not live music. So it spoke to the burgeoning nature of the local underground music scene when bands hatched from the Cannibal Club and the Cavity started showing up on the Hole's stage in the early '90s.

The shift was the work of Debbie Rombach, a longtime bartender/server who took over booking in 1989. In reviewing Rombach's monthly planners from the era, the shift toward louder, more punk-influenced bands first manifested in the summer of 1991. A June 28 gig headlined by Cannibal Club regulars Hand of Glory—featuring LeRoi Brothers vocalist Joe Doerr alongside ex–Poison 13 guitarist Bill Anderson—offers a subtle hint of what's to come. By the end of 1991 the Pocket FishRmen, the Wannabes, the Texas Instruments, Toby Dammit, and Pork had all been booked at the Hole.

In some respects, this shift was organic. Once a foothold was established, groundbreakers like Hand of Glory's Anderson pitched additional bands to Rombach. At the same time, it was not uncommon for local underground musicians to play in three or four different bands. Not long after Hand of Glory played the Hole, Anderson also began playing there with Joan of Arkansas and the Horsies.

A new band called Sincola played the Hole for the first time on a Monday night in 1993, opening for recent Iowa transplants Miss Universe. Spoon shows up on the Hole calendar for the first time in January 1994. Both

Sincola and Spoon became weekend headliners in relatively short order and played prominent roles in defining the venue's identity in the mid-90s.

Superego frontman Paul Minor launched the Rock and Roll Free-for-All at the Hole in 1994. Minor's consistent presence in Austin clubs since his early '80s teenhood meant he knew an astounding number of local musicians, which made the weekly Sunday night show a grab bag salon of sorts. Superego was the show's one constant, with a *Peyton Place*–sized roster of "guest" acts fleshing out the bill from week to week. The Free-for-All continued every week until 2002.

For years, faux-superstitious locals spoke of an "Austin curse" that kept the city's Next Big Things from making the jump to national success. The curse was invoked when critically celebrated mid-eighties acts like True Believers and the Reivers failed to make commercial hay of major label deals and continued into the '90s when Sincola and Sixteen Deluxe met similar fates. Even Spoon, whose most successful period would come in the next decade, were said to fall victim to the curse when Elektra dumped them after one album in 1998.

The Austin curse, such as it was, would be broken in part due to a tragedy unrelated to music. In 1997 Raymond and Lela Howard, an elderly Central Texas couple, went missing after setting out from their home in Salado to attend a summer festival in Temple. Eighty-eight-year-old Raymond was recovering from brain surgery, and eighty-three-year-old Lela was showing signs of dementia. Their disappearance made front-page news in Austin.

Something about the Howards' unfolding story triggered the imagination of Tony Scalzo, bassist/vocalist for Fastball. "I just started getting these ideas, well maybe they don't want to be found, maybe they're just like— they're sick of being responsible and they just want to go out and have fun," Scalzo recalled years later.[1]

Scalzo, guitarist/vocalist Miles Zuniga, and drummer Joey Shuffield started playing in 1995 as Magneto U.S.A. Zuniga and Shuffield were already veterans of a one-and-done major label stint with Big Car in the early '90s. Magneto's unabashed pop bent put songwriting over squall, and they honed their craft through steady gigs at the Hole. Within a year they signed a deal with Disney subsidiary Hollywood Records and changed their name to Fastball after a mercifully brief flirtation with calling themselves Starchy. Their 1996 debut, *Make Your Mama Proud*, failed to scale the charts.

Scalzo's songwriting instinct proved sound. With a guitar and Casio beat, he crafted "The Way," a borderlands-tinged pocket epic around his fictional resolution of the Howards' disappearance. Sadly, the story didn't end well for the Howards. On July 12, 1997, they were found dead in their maroon

Oldsmobile at the bottom of a ravine near Hot Springs, Arkansas. Even after learning of the couple's fate, Scalzo was smart enough not to let reality short-shrift the eternal.

"The Way" became a larger-than-life hit. It made the *Billboard* Top 10 in 1998 and helped Fastball's second album, *All the Pain Money Can Buy*, sell over a million copies. When the band performed on the *Tonight Show*, they regaled Jay Leno with a story about a Wednesday night Hole in the Wall gig in 1995 when a would-be thief wahooed Zuniga's second guitar and ran out the door. Audience members chased the perpetrator down Guadalupe and retrieved the guitar, leaving the still-performing band wondering where everyone went.

That same year, Cugini sold the Hole to Rombach, Mike White, and Hickoids/Gay Sportscasters vocalist Jeff Smith for $25,000. A proper stage with a proper sound system was built in the back game-room area. The low clearance made it easy for particularly acrobatic musicians to poke the necks of their instruments right through the drop ceiling. Bands also continued to play the front room.

Although the Hole remained just that through the end of the '90s, its profile continued to grow along with the city at large. As more movies were filmed in Austin, actors like Ethan Hawke and Natalie Portman would drop in to have a drink or shoot pool. The celebrity appearance to end them all occurred after the turn of the millennium when Hole frontwoman Courtney Love made the *National Enquirer* by locking herself in the Hole's squalid men's room for twenty minutes while in town to deliver a speech at the 2002 edition of South By Southwest.

Despite such renown, the Hole's reputation wasn't appreciating at the same rate as the dirt on which it sat. A giant "For Sale" sign appeared on top of the Hole in the Wall in November 2001. In January 2002 Rombach received word the club's lease would expire at the end of June. The Rombach era of the Hole in the Wall ended on June 30, 2002, when the Pocket FishRmen took the stage and delivered their ever-apropos salvo, "Go Out Smokin'."

The Hole remained shuttered for the better part of a year before the owners of the Austin's Pizza chain stepped in and reopened the club in May 2003. El Paso transplant Will Tanner purchased it in 2008. Longtime regulars can point out all the subtle changes, but the venue's role in the local music eco-system remains intact. The building itself and its famed yellow marquee still look much as they did in 1974.

Just as when it first closed in 2002, the Hole in the Wall continues to exist in a state of perennial precarity. The Jack in the Box that used to be next door is now a 162-room boutique hotel. Ever-higher rent, encroaching West

Campus gentrification, and the complete shutdown of live music as a result of the COVID-19 pandemic make the Hole's previous challenges seem breezy by comparison. Nevertheless, unlike the other fleeting haunts of the Curious Mix, the Hole endures at least for now.

Debbie Rombach: I started working at the Hole in the Wall December 23, 1978. It was a lot of folk singers. And experimental jazz, which I hate. Very early on when the Psychedelic Furs first played at Raul's, I had wanted to go down there and see them, but I couldn't get anybody to work for me, and I had to wait tables for one of those jazz bands.

There was some '50s and early sixties-style rock and a bit of blues. The Bizarros. Speedy Sparks. And Sterling Morrison from Velvet Underground when he was teaching school here. The Bizarros have this song called "Coma Victim" that could hold its own with any punk band on earth. It makes you think of the Sonics a lot.

Tim Stegall: When I first arrived there, it was mostly bar bands and country stuff, but not a lot of punky bands. Alejandro Escovedo's more rock 'n' roll band Buick MacKane was playing there quite a bit. The Reverend Horton Heat would come through about every three months before he was well known.

Debbie Rombach: I started booking in 1989 and I preferred the louder indie and punk bands. Everybody was so afraid that I was going to turn it into this punk rock heavy metal club. The Hickoids were one of my early bands that I booked. Jeff and I have had some notorious birthday parties, and we've actually been kicked out from behind our own bar on our birthday.

Unfortunately, I couldn't get Poison 13 because they broke up right when I first had a chance to do it, but Bill Anderson just funneled me bands. I first saw Bill in Poison 13. Any time he would come to me and say, "I think you should book this band," I would book them, and it would be right on. Hand of Glory, Joan of Arkansas, the Meat Purveyors, Drive-By Truckers. The Gourds were brand new and playing on a Monday night.

Tim Stegall: The Hole in the Wall was definitely starting to host more of those bands. It seemed like our little scene had suddenly become accepted in clubs other than just Emo's or the Cavity. I would say about '93 they started featuring more of the Inhalants. Pork, certainly. Gomez would be playing there, usually with Jesus Christ Superfly.

The Hormones at the Hole in the Wall. Photo by Sean McGowan.

Rick Carney: We were one of the first of that wave of punk bands to get into the Hole in the Wall. I think they were afraid to book punk at the time. After we got in there, they realized it wouldn't be so bad. Then the Cryin' Out Louds, the Motards, the other bands got in.

Andy Maguire: The stage isn't very high, so you're practically in the crowd with people, getting the energy back from the crowd. I can't say it was a lot of college students, but it kind of had that vibe. It was indie rock at the time. I don't think "alternative" had been coined as a phrase.

Britt Daniel: The vibe there was more like a saloon. Really dark. Everything was wood. In the back there was an area with pool tables and pinball machines. This was where people that wanted to drink that were a little bit

older than college age would go. It felt a little sophisticated. It was also right down the street from the Texas Showdown, which used to be Raul's.

Gretchen Phillips: Two Nice Girls started touring a lot around '89. It meant I was gone and lost touch with Austin in a certain way. So when Two Nice Girls broke up, new venues came into my life like Hole in the Wall. It was always a cherished venue, but I didn't see me playing there because it was more of a honky-tonk. And then it turned into such a great place to play.

Jennifer LaSuprema Hecker: I want to give a little shout-out to the Hole in the Wall ladies' bathroom. Two toilets not separated in any way. At the end of the night, everybody has to pee really bad, and you're drunk anyway. So there was always the bathroom line conversation of, "Hey, what's your name? You want to pee with me?"

Debbie Rombach: I'm one of the people who absolutely loved SXSW. I had a badge so I would always have one night during SXSW when I could go everywhere and see everybody. I'm downtown watching a band, and this guy who was supposed to be watching over Courtney Love was there and yells at me across the room, "Hey Debbie! Your sound system blew up and Courtney Love and Lawrence [Heads] are in the bathroom doing coke and wouldn't let anybody in!" I was like, "I think one or two people in this whole club did not hear you, do you want to shout it a little louder?"

Dotty Farrell: Doing coke off that nasty-ass toilet in the fucking Hole in the Wall? No. So gross.

Marc Fort: The shows in that front room had such an intimacy. You had little flickering candles on the tables and the heartbeat of the university right outside the window. You could see the drummer's ass as you were walking by.

Debbie Rombach: There's just something about that—having the cars going behind you. People walk through the front door and they can't miss you. It was a small space, but it really held the energy well and it kind of made it a little more exciting.

Jason Morales: Playing in front of that window, it's a rite of passage.

Debbie Rombach: Mike Hall put together our very first hoot night in the early '90s.[2] It was a cross-dressing hoot night. The guys all sang girl songs, the girls all sang guy songs. Mike Shea did a dress like Carmen Miranda that just blew everybody away. Then every December I would have a hoot night. Tim from the Hormones helped me set up the first one—the Ramones. Tim got Joey Ramone to record a little blurb for us that we could play over the stereo.

Every year I would come up with a different theme and any money collected went to HAAM[3] or SIMS[4] or Blue Santa or the Food Bank.

But on Sunday nights, we had singer-songwriter night, and nobody was ever coming in. It was dead. Paul Minor approached us about, "What if I put together these nights?"

Bryan Nelson: Those Free-for-All nights were really cool. That built a little scene. It was free to get in.

Jason Morales: It was down to earth. You could just drop in and play. And it was important for what we're talking about here for sure. If your whole band showed up and you were willing to get up there on their equipment, you could fucking go.

Bryan Nelson: That was a cool setup because a lot of bands would end up sharing gear and everyone would play a shorter set. There would be Sister-unaked, Peglegasus, Big Horny Hustler, and tons of other bands, always headlined by Paul Minor and Superego.

Debbie Rombach: Paul would have a band that was popular around town and then he would have two brand new bands. We would find bands and help them grow and give them a place to play. Paul really did a fantastic job setting those nights up.

Dave Prewitt: That was a party to be had. It didn't matter who was there. The normals were Allyson [Lipkin] on sax, Paul and the Superego guys, the Fastball guys, and anybody who was around. It was a great vibe. And it was pretty much the family. That was a big part of that whole '90s thing—the camaraderie.

Debbie Rombach: Dennis Quaid and Ivan Neville came in. Ivan came up to the bar and he goes, "Do you think they would let me sit in for a song?" And I went, "Hell, yeah! See that guy?" I pointed to Paul Minor. "He's in charge. Just tell him you want to play."

Paul just looked at me with big ole eyes and puts him up on stage. He's

Poster for Hole in the Wall twenty-three-year anniversary Free-for-All show with Sixteen Deluxe, Wookie, Superego, the Goin' Along Feelin' Just Fines, June 16, 1996, by JasonAustin.

playing Andrew's keyboards and Andrew [Duplantis] moves back to bass, standing behind them just going, "He's playing my keyboards!" It was pretty cool.

The guys from R.E.M. came in. Michael Stipe sat in the back and played Galaga all night. Mike Mills got up and played. The coolest was when Harry Dean Stanton came in to watch the band. We tried to make it a place where you could just come hang out and nobody would fuck with you, you know?

Dotty Farrell: It was so much fun when Exene [Cervenka] would come to visit. She would spend a week in town, and we'd go out to the flea market thrift shopping. She and Biscuit and Robbie Jacks had been friends forever. She just really loved Austin.

Debbie Rombach: Word got out that Exene was there, and I have a line down the street on a Sunday night for a free show because people wanted to see Exene sit in with Swine King. That was a pretty cool show.

Dotty Farrell: We didn't really think about that turning into a complete zoo, but it was a complete, insane mob of people just trying to cram into that room to see her. She had so much fun. We did "Monday, Monday" with her, and then she sang "Blue Spark" with Biscuit. It was just such a thrill to get to be on stage with her. It was so packed. I was wearing a Day-Glo psychedelic kaleidoscope wet suit, which was really hot. I had a cat suit on underneath it and about halfway through the set, my best friend came up and she was like, "You need to take that off, you're turning purple."

Hunter Darby: The Hole in the Wall talent show is still one of my top favorite concerts I've ever been to in my life. It was insane. People who weren't musicians get up on stage. This guy Pascal did a beatnik poetry thing, smoking a cigarette with a guy drumming behind him. He talked about meeting his lover, eating a bunch of dimes, and taking a poop.

Jennings Crawford: That place was one of the few places where they would give you a percentage of the bar, and you'd also get the door. It probably paid for most of our records, paid for our van, and allowed us to go out on tour.

Hunter Darby: People always talked about, "Oh yeah you guys played at the Hole in the Wall and there was a curse that you guys had. Something crazy was always going to happen. Princess Di died the night you were playing. The apartments behind it caught on fire and burned to the ground the night you were playing." I was like, "That's because we're there *all the time!*"

Jennings Crawford: We invented this mod persona for some dumb reason. I had gotten involved with a bunch of people that had Vespas, and we were trying to figure out reasons to have everybody ride their Vespas downtown. So we would show up wearing suits and ties, which was hilarious because all of a sudden some writers in town started talking about all of our Jam influences. We literally just put jackets and ties on. But it let us fit in more with some other bands. Like Stretford.

Michael Toland: I saw Stretford a lot with the Wannabes because they played together all the time. They had their kind of fake mod revival. That was a great time. I remember very well a show with the Wannabes and Stretford and the Pocket FishRmen. This must've been '92, '93. Jennings was telling me, "This is going to be our Death of Mod show." And so they were all wearing their suits, including the Pocket FishRmen.

Jennings Crawford: Brant [Bingamon] and Cris [Burns] and everybody show up, dutifully wearing their mod suits and ties. Then at one point Brant's got blood coming out of his mouth. It's fake blood, but it's all over him, like a scene from *Carrie*. And then their suits were covered in blood and their suits are off, and it's just Brant in his underwear and Cris in his underwear and it's the normal Pocket FishRmen.

Bill Jeffery: The Hole in the Wall was that whole Graham Parker thing of pub rock. It was ours and everyone knew each other. A lot of hugging. Inhalants. Motards. Wannabes. Sincola I loved. Pork was the all-time favorite.

Edith Casimir: Mary [Hattman] and Dana [Smith] had already worked with Spot [Glen Lockett],[5] but he didn't want to play drums anymore. They wanted a drummer who could keep it real basic. They just browbeat me into doing it. I said, "I don't know how to play drums," and they said, "Don't worry about it. It's punk rock. It's three-chord punk rock. We don't want any cymbals. And can you play standing up!"

Spot gave me my drums. He gave me the snare with great ceremony and said that it had been used by Black Flag. I thought that the whole snare drum was the Black Flag's snare drum but then I changed the snare at some point, and he yelled at me. He was like, "That was the Black Flag snare!" And I said,

"I thought you meant it was the whole drum." And he said, "No, it was just the springy thing on the bottom."

Ed Hamell: She played drums kind of like Mo Tucker. It was less grungy and more like the Fall. Dana loves Mark E. Smith. They were pretty influential—an all-girl band making it and pissing guys off because they were getting a lot of press because there was something pretty *real* about what they were doing.

Tim Stegall: I think at least two or three times a set, Edith would screw up her face and throw her sticks down because she's lost the beat. Nobody cared. They had just such charm and such great songs.

Jimmy Bradshaw: Pork had some magic going. Their songs are great and as individuals, all three of those women were awesome. And as a group it's fucking amazing.

Dana Smith: We felt that we had something to say. We were like, "Just see if we can play eight songs in a row and get it done." And we did.

Edith Casimir: Dana was such a tough nut to crack that me and Mary would be falling all over ourselves to do anything she wanted to do. And whatever she did was with this heart and soul like she was a hundred years old already. A couple of times she started bawling in the middle of "Only Love Can Break Your Heart" and stomped off stage because she was overcome with emotion.

Jimmy Bradshaw: Those Unicorn Magic/Pork shows at Hole in the Wall were blasts. At the end of the night, the majority of tables and chairs were upturned. Broken beer bottles. The floor was a quarter inch deep in beer. Somehow we got paid. Debbie would say, "You guys can't get this drunk and play here ever again." And then three weeks later it happened again.

Debbie Rombach: Pork and Unicorn Magic. That night they got married was so funny.

Jimmy Bradshaw: That was another one of those things that just felt right. "Let's get married!" People got involved and decorated the club. Who married us? Spot, I think. It was just an organic fucking adventure with Unicorn Magic and Pork.

Pork (*left to right*): bassist Mary Hattman, guitarist Dana Smith, drummer Edith Casimir. Photo by Sean McGowan.

Edith Casimir: That was a highlight of my life. That's my best marriage! I was aligned with Mike Belyea and Mary was aligned with Nathan [Calhoun], of course. Dana was aligned with Jimmy Bradshaw. But Dana knew I had a secret crush on Jimmy Bradshaw and that we might have to kiss. Because she's so good, she shoved me over to the Jimmy Bradshaw side at the last minute.

Lisa Rickenberg: I was super judgy about women in bands who I felt were— and this sounds really horrible—milking their sexuality as a selling point for the band. I was super resentful of bands like Pork who were successful. I felt that that was because they were cute girls in short skirts that bounced around a lot.

In retrospect, I love Pork. I love their records, and they were never anything but nice to me, so it was definitely jealousy. The whole thing is extra ironic because punk rock is all about "Anybody can do it!," and yet at the time I was like, "These women are not even bothering to learn how to play. They're just cute so people like them." I was so judgy about that. I'm sure a lot of it was just my own insecurity and feeling like I was in competition with other women in bands, which is really sad.

Edith Casimir: Back then there just weren't girl groups that much. I remember hearing about L7 and Shonen Knife and girl bands that were way better than us. It didn't seem like any big deal to be three girls, but I guess that made us stand out. Our songs weren't bad—literally three-chord punk. You can't really criticize a whole lot if there's not much there to criticize, right?

Dana should've totally been a rock star, and Mary always should've been a rock star. Me, not as much. But yeah, we didn't really stay friends. At the Hole in the Wall they wanted us to keep playing and Dana was like, "I got up at six o'clock this morning. I have three kids at home. I got to go home." And I said, "You big baby!" And she says, "You drunk!"

As far as I know, that was our last show. It was awkward.

Lauren Robertson: As a woman in Austin in the '90s, I have to mention how important Pork was. I loved them so much. They just meant so much to me, and to all the women in music at that time. Seeing an all-girl band was like the clouds parting. At the time, there just weren't that many women in music at all. And then after '95 there were a lot more.

Melissa Bryan: When all the women started playing, it really inspired me. I started putting the Shindigs together around 1994 or so. The Shindigs were always kind of weird. We weren't punk enough to play with the Motards or the Chumps, but then the pop bands were like, "Why is that girl screaming?" We had a lot of hooks, and it was real poppy.

We recorded three songs with John Croslin. We actually started our record with these two guys who were in Pariah—Kyle Ellison and Jared Tuten. Kyle said, "Yeah, come over to our practice space." It turns out this is the Meat Puppets' studio space at the ARC.[6] Kyle was playing guitar in the Meat Puppets at the time. We recorded eight or nine songs then needed someone to finish it. I knew Spot forever just from being around. It seemed really natural. Not, "I'll ask Spot, this legendary producer who worked on all these records that I just worship." It was a strange, full-circle thing, 'cause we started in the Meat Puppets' studio and then Spot finished the record.

Andy Maguire: I felt like punk rock was an opening for women to start playing instruments. We had nothing before then. It's the DIY scene. The women just went out and did it, but they never really get talked about. And that's true in almost any field. I think women have a really hard time going up to the top and getting recognized. And then when you do, it's like, "Oh look, it's a woman that can play guitar!" Why *can't* a woman play guitar? Why is that unusual? When I started in '83, there weren't many women playing bass. Tina Weymouth was like the only person that was known.

Some of my male friends at Berklee College of Music said that women couldn't play bass. Their hands are too small or whatever. So I went out and I bought a bass and I learned to play. So punk rock was there for me to step in and learn my instrument on stage.

Marc Fort: Spoon was another band playing great shows in the '90s, particularly when they had Andy Maguire in the band. Writers, including myself, would inevitably acknowledge their Pixies influence, but what better influence to have than the Pixies?

Britt Daniel: I really wanted to find somebody that would play guitar in a way that I was into. I had seen Sincola play and the lead guitar player, Greg Wilson—also known as Wendel Stivers—seemed to really have it together in terms of his guitar playing. It was these lead lines that contributed to making the song have more hooks. But then Sincola got big, so he ended up quitting Spoon. I met the bass player through an ad in the paper.

Andy Maguire: I'd done tours with Pigface and Chris Connelly and had come through Austin. I arrived in Austin in the summer of 1993 and started looking in the *Chronicle*. There was an ad for a bass player who was into PJ Harvey. I love PJ Harvey. Jim and Britt and I played and we just clicked. We played our first gig at a Battle of the Bands in that big warehouse thing over near the train tracks. Austin Music Hall. Britt took a lot of cues from really great songwriters.

Travis Higdon: I remember going to Hole in the Wall and seeing tiny shows when Britt was playing his acoustic/electric, which was totally like an anti–rock star thing to do. And he would wear those sunglasses onstage. But they sounded so good.

Spoon at Hole in the Wall (*left to right*): guitarist Britt Daniel, bassist Andy Maguire, drummer Jim Eno. Photo by Stephanie Black.

Debbie Rombach: We constantly had Spoon at the Hole, and the crowds just grew and grew and grew. Britt says that was their big break.

Britt Daniel: Hole in the Wall was a big one for me for probably ten years. It was a hard place to get a gig for a long time because the lady that booked it was not easy to get in with. But once you got in there then you were *in*. It was a great place to play because you could pack it, and it sounded good in there. That was the first place where I felt like something was happening with Spoon. I mean, to sell out anything was a big deal. It was the one room you could sell out because only eighty people would fit in there.

Travis Higdon: It always felt like we were witnessing something that was going to be big. Even back then, they would pack the Hole in the Wall. It would be wall-to-wall people and we'd be up there in the front row, screaming and having fun. They just sounded so fantastic. Britt had a vision that was fully realized from the beginning. You can listen back to the records and hear how he's stopped and kind of reevaluated the sound and changed it. It always sounded like they were going to be big.

Nanette Labastida: Hole in the Wall is where the guy from the record label came to see Fastball. Rob Seidenberg[7] came there with the invitation of Andy Langer[8] and that was *the night.*

Debbie Rombach: One night there was some frat guy in there. Miles had a guitar close to the door and as this kid walks out, he took the guitar. All of a sudden, the whole room empties out and goes running down the street. Everybody gave chase, got the guitar back, got the guy cornered, flagged down a cop. Every now and again we would get the people come in that quickly learned that their crap wasn't going to be tolerated. If they pulled a frat party thing, they were gone.

Nanette Labastida: When they were Magneto U.S.A., they were pop, because that's the kind of music Miles and Tony write. Most pop bands aren't usually underground, but they played all the same gigs with all the same bands in all the same clubs.

Chepo Peña: I always considered them part of the scene because they played the Electric Lounge and Hole in the Wall and Sincola played with them.

Debbie Rombach: Fastball and Spoon have had the best success as far as worldwide. But Sincola—watching them grow was really cool.

Kris Patterson: I started listening to the Pixies and the Breeders and was like, "I can do that!" So I called Greg [Wilson]—because it had been four years since Hundredth Monkey. "Greg—we got to start a band!"

Rebecca Cannon: My friend, Carl [Normal], from Stretford, needed a horn player, so I learned how to play a couple notes on the trumpet, and played three songs with Stretford. Really, Stretford was the big one that started it for me.

Kris Patterson: At that time I was living at the Farmhouse with Patrice Sullivan. That was the Poi Dog Pondering house. That's where Frank Orrall lived with Patrice. And Thor [Harris] lived there. And Sheri [Lane] from the Horsies lived there. It was a magical little place because Sincola was born there, the Horsies was born there, and Thor went and did all his amazing stuff.[9]

Rebecca Cannon: Carl started letting me sing one or two songs, but he said I was upstaging him. One day Carl called me and said, "I saw this ad in the *Austin Chronicle* and it said they're looking for a girl singer and they're into the Go-Go's and the Breeders." It was the first ad I'd ever answered, and it ended up being Sincola.

Kris Patterson: My ex, Kasey Joe [Smith], who was in Virgin Machine, was the first singer. She wrote the lyrics to "Hey Artemis." We did a demo with John Croslin and it was "Artemis," "Hint of the Titty," and a B-side, "Soap Boy." It was just amazing. Hearing that was like "Holy shit! We sound really good!" But then Casey Joe didn't last. Her heart really wasn't in it.

Rebecca Cannon: Carl was very supportive. He wanted me out of his band because he knew I needed to be singing and performing. And I was a terrible trumpet player.

Kris Patterson: Then we somehow got Chepo by putting something in the back of the *Chronicle*. He was just like a big goofy golden retriever and could fucking *play*. He was amazing. We told him right then, "You're in!" And he was like, "Oh my God! You're not scared? I'm in this band—IV Violent People . . ." I just remember standing in the backyard and him being super excited, "I can't believe I'm going to be in this band!"

Tim Stegall: I remember Sincola at the Hole in the Wall very vividly because Rebecca was on the floor, frightening the fuck out of me. She was certainly one of the most singular, interesting frontwomen I have ever seen. A very charismatic, very intense presence. She had these eyes. There's some sort of drama going on inside this girl. You only had a hint of what was to come.

Susie Martinez: Then Terri [Lord] became the new drummer. And that was Sincola right there.

Kris Patterson: I was dating Terri at the time and she's a badass. She had been with the Jitters in the '80s. That was a really popular band with Billy Pringle. And then she was in Bad Mutha Goose. Then right when Sincola started, she was in Power Snatch.

Rebecca Cannon: I was really young and had no idea how the music business worked. I never realized how lucky we were. Things happened for us really fast.

Kris Patterson: As a band we felt this chemistry and this buzz. We were immediately getting attention, so it was pretty magical.

Michael Letton: Sincola was very college-poppy with a darker edge. This was in the middle of the Riot Grrl movement. Bikini Kill was very popular. There were two male members in the band, but there was an obvious female vocal element to it. The lead singer was fascinating. She looked like one of those girls who was always sad or always pissed off or has some kind of dark past.

Chepo Peña: To me, it was pop-punk. That's why when we did those shows with Miss Universe and Stretford it was such a good deal because everybody was different, but they were all melodic.

Bill Jeffery: One time we [Stretford] played in San Marcos with Sincola. San Marcos still had a curfew, so we had to be done by twelve. The venue was weird, and it didn't seem like they usually had our kind of bands. Stretford did their thing. Sincola plays. There's some people in the audience heckling and they would not stop.

Michelle Rule: This rowdy, insane, soon-to-be-ex-boyfriend of mine was there and was really wasted. They were big Miss Universe fans.

Bill Jeffery: They kept heckling at Sincola, and they were saying louder and louder stuff. And it finally got to Chepo.

Chepo Peña: They threw a pitcher at Kris! I looked over at Kelly [Petrash], pointed to those guys and went, "Was it them?" And she went, "Yes." So I picked up the pitcher, smashed it over the guy's head, and ran out and hid in the dumpster.

Sincola's first show at the Texas Tavern, 1993 (*left to right*): Greg Wilson (guitar), Rebecca Cannon (vocals), Kris Patterson (guitar). Photo by Greggae Giles.

Bill Jeffery: And everyone's like "... and the show is done."

Chepo Peña: I got home and "knock, knock, knock." I pulled the curtain and it's the guy!

I opened the door and he's like, "Is Chepo here?"

"No, he's not here. I think he has a gig in San Marcos."

"Well I know that, I saw you there!"

I was like, "Okay well let me go check." I went outside and I fucking took

off. Did I mention he had an aluminum baseball bat? Then the next day he left a message on my machine saying, "Is this the bassist from Sincola? You're fucking dead motherfucker!"—which we put on the album!

And so I called that guy. I was like, "Hey man look, I'm sorry about that."

"It's okay, we were all fucked up."

And we made up.

Rebecca Cannon: We just had a chemistry together. Chepo was amazing on bass, and I was kind of crazy. I would writhe around on the ground and scream, and dress like a little kid. I looked like a twelve-year-old, crazy, insane asylum inmate. I wore nightgowns and pajamas. I put on a spectacle because I *was* kind of crazy.

Michael Crawford: Rebecca just has this captivating stage presence. She was really cute, but she had these crazy eyes. She would be so determined when she would be singing. The eyes would just open really wide and sometimes it was like these different weird personalities would come out on stage.

Kris Patterson: "Bitch" was brought in by Greg. That was his seed of the song.

Rebecca Cannon: Suddenly we're playing to seven hundred people at Emo's. I just thought that's how it worked. I thought if you were good, then good things happened. Now I know that's not the case.

Kris Patterson: The video [for "Bitch"] was by Kerthy Fix and Heyd Fontenot. The first layout for the video was each of us being a dog groomer and someone has a poodle. We didn't want to do that, so then it became these little vignettes of surreal things going on at the house on West Street.

Dotty Farrell: There's all these people in the line to get into that house. Darcee [Douglas] was the bouncer. She had to go throw the people down the stairs that were trying to come up the stairs. Heyd saw me and was like,

"You come too." We both had on black catsuits, and I had a leather bondage top over it.

Kris Patterson: What's beautiful about the video is it's such a Who's Who of Austin at the time. It's sort of like a living early '90s music yearbook.

Debbie Rombach: I really liked the '90s the best. There was a real coherent scene. It was so eclectic because I booked bands I wanted to see. I could see bands grow from when they first started learning their instruments to where they are now. Watching the bands grow musically, I'm happy to think that I had a part in that, having a venue that they could play at to hone these skills. It felt kind of magical to me and I miss it a lot.

BLUE FLAMINGO

THOSE HORSES *DO* BITE!

I THINK FOR ANYONE WHO REALLY UNDERSTANDS THE ENERGY OF PUNK
ROCK MUSIC, A SMALL VENUE IS IDEAL. IF EVERYONE'S PACKED IN
THERE, EVERYONE JUST VIBRATES IN UNISON. OR, IN THE CASE OF THE
BLUE FLAMINGO, THROWS PLASTIC BEER CUPS IN UNISON.

CARL NORMAL, STRETFORD

GIVEN ITS SPURIOUS BUSINESS AND LEGAL STANDING, no one was
particularly surprised when the Cavity sputtered out in February 1993. If
anything, the surprise was that a motley bunch led by a captain like Dave
Hermann kept the boat afloat for nearly a year and a half.

Not long before the club closed, Hermann outlined his plans for the Cavity
during a 1992 interview for an unpublished Austin Chronicle feature. "We're
going to have S&M, bondage and piercing displays," he said. "We're also going
to have a drag queen pageant. I'm building a runway for them to walk on and
everything."

While these plans never came to pass, they did anticipate the shape of
things to come at the Blue Flamingo. Located next door to the Cavity on the
drug-infested corner of Seventh and Red River, the Blue Flamingo opened
in 1992 as a low-rent gay/trans bar in the space previously occupied by

Buzz Moran (guitar) and August Alston (vocals), Big Horny
Hustler at Blue Flamingo, 1994. Photo by Greggae Giles.

Marilyn's. There was nothing trendy, glamorous, or cool about the club. Its
quotidian CD jukebox alternated Hank Williams Jr. with En Vogue, but the
drinks were cheap, and the vibe was welcoming.

Neither the size nor the design of the Blue Flamingo made it an ideal venue
for live music. There was no room for a stage, let alone a decent PA system.
But once the Cavity closed, there was still a need for a smaller if not gentler
alternative to Emo's. While simple proximity facilitated interplay between
the Cavity and the Blue Flamingo, it was the adventurous spirit of owner
Miss Laura that turned the Blue Flamingo into a launchpad for Austin's
emerging garage rock conflagration.

Miss Laura was a large Black trans woman who spent years running
adult book and video stores before opening the Blue Flamingo. Though her

decision to book bands was partially born of necessity since the bar-only format wasn't a consistent draw, her enthusiasm and support of bands was genuine. Whether it was drunken punk singers, down-market drag queens, or homeless families from the Salvation Army around the corner, Miss Laura became a mother hen figure to fringe dwellers of all walks. Her motto for the club—"A Curious Mix of People"—was spot-on in this regard.

The band that best embodied the reckless, anarchic spirit of the scene that developed around the Blue Flamingo was the Motards. Bred in the not-yet-gentrified rent houses of Hyde Park, the quintet's puke-spattered staccato sneer bombs took full advantage of the club's parameters. Since there was no stage, the entire club became a stage, with jostled, beer-sprayed audience members becoming almost as much a part of the show as the band.

The Blue Flamingo also played a role in Spoon's rise to national prominence. With faint echoes of the apocryphal Schwab's/Lana Turner legend, Matador Records honcho Gerard Cosloy dropped in on a Spoon set during an anti-SXSW showcase at the club on March 17, 1994, while most everyone else was clamoring to get into the Johnny Cash showcase at Emo's down the street. Cosloy ultimately signed Spoon to their first proper record deal.

Other frequent Flamingo flyers included the Chumps, the Reclusives, and the Phantom Creeps, all of whom tapped a sense of chaotic possibility similar to that of the Motards. The Dead End Cruisers and Lower Class Brats mined a Spirit of '77 British punk vibe, while the Nipple 5 cross-bred the Melvins with Black Oak Arkansas.

Craig Koon of Rise Records had a habit of bootlegging shows on a Sony Walkman, which he ultimately used to compile *A Curious Mix of People: Live at the Blue Flamingo*. Released in 1996 on Koon's one-off King's Mob imprint, the album presented bands like the Motards and the Chumps along with Cavity vets Stretford and the Inhalants in the rawest possible light. The recording quality is atrocious, but listeners can rest assured that it didn't sound much better in real time.[1]

By 1997 the Blue Flamingo was on borrowed time, beset by money problems as well as issues with the health department and alcoholic beverage commission. Citing poor health, Miss Laura pulled out of the business by year's end. The club continued hosting punk rock shows as the Blue Flame and then Purgatory before closing for good in 1999.

"The Blue Flamingo will live on no matter what," Miss Laura wrote in a letter published in the November 28, 1997, *Austin Chronicle*, "because it's in the hearts of the people, and the bands that they have produced."

Even after the Blue Flamingo closed, Miss Laura kept supporting the scene as her health allowed. For many years, she held a birthday party to benefit the

Miss Laura. Photo by Sean McGowan.

local chapter of the ACLU, an allegiance borne of her days running sexually oriented businesses and incurring the wrath of antipornography activists. When the city was considering a zoning change in 1986 that would've effectively closed her down, famed folklorist John Henry Faulk showed up to testify against the change.

"I was born and raised in South Austin, not a quarter mile from where that pornography theater stands today," the onetime blacklist target of Sen. Joseph McCarthy told the Austin City Council. "I think y'all know that there was a lot of masturbation in South Austin before there was ever a pornography theater there."

In some sense, Miss Laura's support of deviant music furthered her greater support of civil liberties in a manner that echoed Faulk's willingness to defend a porn theater in his autumn years. If drag queens and punk rockers needed a place to play, there was no reason in Miss Laura's mind why they couldn't find safe harbor in the same bar. It was curious, and it was good.

Jonathan Toubin: One day I ran into Dave Hermann, and he was wearing a leatherman outfit. A little black cap, a vest, leather pants. Maybe some chains. He's like, "I'm on my way to this place Blue Flamingo to work. Come in—I'll get you a drink."

Dotty Farrell: There was a whole lot of queer bars in that little strip where Blue Flamingo was. There was the Crossing. There was the Naked Grape. The first band I was in—Technicolor Yawns—played at the Crossing. The two lead singers in that band were both gay men, but they were in terrible drag and were hilarious. They got kicked out because the lead singer, Ray, was eating out Barbie's crotch. It was a male gay bar, and you couldn't eat out a Barbie doll's vagina, I guess.

Jimmy Bradshaw: There couldn't have been a better neighbor for the Cavity than a rowdy transvestite bar. That was just fucking perfect.

Ty Pearson: Once you went north on Red River past Seventh Street, all of those places that have now been clubs for years were just empty warehouses filled with squatters and down-and-outs. Homeless addicts. You did not walk over there. One block over, you had Sixth Street, which was frat central. A block east, you have the police station. And in the middle, you had the Blue Flamingo. It was perfectly placed. And Miss Laura was just the loveliest and friendliest person that I had ever met.

Jonathan Toubin: She was a large, Black, beautiful drag queen. Laura had a history before that of running businesses around Sixth Street. Some of them a little more illicit. The mystique going around Miss Laura, despite her being so sweet, was that she was something to be a bit scared of.

Jimmy Bradshaw: Miss Laura—one of those magical aliens in human form. I think the thing that really bonded us is we had the Impotent Sea Snakes from Atlanta, and I went over and grabbed Miss Laura and said, "You gotta check this band out!" Transvestite band playing next to a transvestite bar. At that moment, that was *it*. We became super friendly and the two places almost kind of merged, you know?

Jonathan Toubin: It was this really sleazy drag bar and a really unsavory place in a way that I really liked. It wasn't just a regular drag bar. This was some end-of-the-road, down-on-your-luck, track marks as far as they go, sideways wigs, stubble, make-up all smeared. . . . There were some normal queens there too.

Miss Laura: I always told Leslie[2] she could not come in with a bikini, so she put on this little bitty miniskirt and came in and had a drink. Miss Giovanni and all of those Mexican queens would be drinking their little beers, playing the jukebox, pushing Selena, and pantomiming. The whole scene was so unusual, and they had the S&M crowd down at a club behind us [Ohms].

Jonathan Toubin: Dave Hermann brought the link between the Cavity and the Blue Flamingo. He's the one who first started bringing bands there. I think Anti-man was the first band. They had their shirts off and they're sweating and playing this loud music, and these drag queens loved it. As with so many of the great music scenes that mattered in the world, this mix of gay and straight really made the night so much livelier than just a strictly heterosexual, bro-y, Emo's show.

Rick Carney: Miss Laura was fantastic to the bands. It was like playing a house party, and that's what I liked about it.

Miss Laura: The Cavity were basically put out of business. After Dave Hermann closed up, I felt it was at least my right to have his bands come over. Even though we wasn't as large, we still made room. We had an occupancy of thirty-five people. Most people don't realize that because we were always over capacity.

Craig Koon: The Blue Flamingo was originally a really seedy bar. Then it became gays and transvestites with a big chickenhawk scene. And they were totally mystified because their nice, quiet bar was taken over by these kids throwing full beer cans at each other and jumping up and down and screaming. It was a curious mix of people.

One day a really well-dressed man walked into a Motards show wearing a business suit. He's in there drinking and says something to someone at the bar.

And I hear, "We don't have a valet!"

And he says, "What?? I gave my car keys to that kid!"

One of the chickenhawks stole his car! The whole bar just erupted and this guy runs out . . .

Carl Normal: Miss Laura was a huge fan of Stretford so we got a lot of gigs there. Barry [Anderson, Stretford bassist] picked up a chick there one night and left with her. It wasn't a girl. That's just the kind of club it was. I think they went to another bar, and maybe a little conversation was had. Barry elected not to take her home.

Jonathan Toubin: I remember later you see a lot of the drag queens put their fingers in their ears, make a face, and run out once the bands start. The honeymoon didn't last very long with the clientele, but Miss Laura was a very big fan of the bands.

Miss Laura: I've always considered FuckEmos close friends so I did a couple of videos with them. One time I played guitar, and the other time I played drums. Russell and them took some pictures for an advertisement with the drag queens. They ended up commissioning a couple of young men to dance in front of them with no clothes on.

Russell Porter: Miss Laura was opening a bathhouse on the East Side. She invited us to play the grand opening and it was a beautiful thing. We had the winner of the swinging dick contest dancing for us whose butt was in Sean's [Powell, FuckEmos drummer] face. There were several people that were whipping each other with leather. People were stroking each other while we played. It was really weird and fun and just awesome.

Bones DeLarge: Everyone was friendly. The punks knew their boundaries. If you're into that, you're into that. If it bothers you, just leave. If you want to have sex with dudes, have sex with dudes. Isn't that what punk started out as? Everyone accepting everyone for who they are and what they are? Everyone should just accept everyone. And the Blue Flamingo was that place.

Britt Daniel: There was a slight exotic feel to this place. Also, it was a shithole. When you'd see shows, there were a lot of people. You couldn't move. It was just sweaty and a great vibe. The fact that there was no stage was a benefit. It really made the audience and the band, one. I saw the Motards there a lot. Some of the most amazing shows I've ever seen in Austin were Glorium at the Blue Flamingo.

Lauren Robertson: I remember it being so crowded that everyone would be standing outside the window on the street to watch the bands. And Miss Laura would let us dance on the bar. She was the best.

Miss Laura: We started something else that was unusual. Everyone would get in for free if you only wore underwear. Then we had a drag race. All of the guys was in drag and their girlfriends would be with them as men. They ran to Emo's. Then they went to one of the bars on Sixth Street and had to have a drink. During the middle of the race, I had some police officers chase them because every drag queen had to know how to run from the police in high heels. The last bit was a sprint back to the Blue Flamingo for safety.

We had belly dancers. We had all kinds of bands. The drag queens were pretty popular. We had male strippers on certain nights. It was an unusual place and that's what I wanted to make it. A curious mix of people. That was the best way to describe it.

Charlie Void: The Down Syndrome Army played at Blue Flamingo a lot. That was the place where I went when I would get out of jail to get free beers because, you know, it was a gay bar. The punk rock scene came in the nighttime. We brought Miss Laura a huge white teddy bear once.

Jimmy St. Germaine: We set the huge white teddy bear up against the stage next to her, and everyone took turns fucking the teddy bear. We also had meat masks back then. That was 1996, which I believe was before Lady Gaga, right?

Charlie Void: Very *Texas Chainsaw Massacre*. With the tongue coming out.

Jimmy St. Germaine: I keep singing and licking the fajita meat mask in front of my face, and I was vomiting. It was sickening. It was raw meat. We made the masks at 1:15 p.m., so by 10:30, that meat was rotten. They were pissed because there was rotten meat all over the fucking stage.

Gerry Atric: Contrary to popular belief, drugs did not play a big part in the Blue Flamingo scene. It didn't matter who was playing. The Motards. The Bulemics. The Chumps. The Reclusives. It was all about music and beer. It was standing water and standing piss. Lumberjacks trying to fuck young punk rockers. It was a really good time.

Miss Laura: At one time, we had a policeman stand outside because we had so many drug dealers coming by and we wanted them gone. Some young kid got mad about that and offered to shoot us.

Then, somehow or another, someone let him in the back door. He told the police officer, "Oh, yeah I was in there. They served me Hennessy and Coke." The bartenders looked at him and said, "The officer knows you're lying because we're beer and wine. We don't have Hennessy."

One time an undercover police officer came in and was trying to ask me how he could buy some drugs. I gave him my drug lecture. "This is not something that you should do. You have so much going for you. Why would you do this to yourself with drugs?" Unfortunately, in my past I've had a person doing drugs that fell down dead in my house, so I made a point of giving that lecture to anyone who asked me.

Susan Shepard: Touring bands who needed last-minute shows could always play there. Steel Pole Bath Tub and Harry Pussy played there. It seemed like anybody who wanted a show could play there. Noodle and the Paranoids and all those bands would play there a lot.

Conrad Keely: I remember the first time I ever encountered Jon Toubin. Noodle were playing at the Blue Flamingo. And here's the difference between Olympia, Washington, and Austin, Texas. Everyone in Austin is drinking their beers and smiling and just getting into the music. In Olympia, you just fold your arms and you stare intently.

Jonathan saw me standing like that, smiled at me, took his guitar, and just whacked me in the forehead with his guitar. I staggered back and was like, "Okay that's cool. I get it." And that was our initiation. We loosened up after that. But he did it with such a smile on his face. "Wake up and have a good time, you fucker!"

Tim Kerr: Half of the crowd was in bands, the other half were doing fanzines and taking photos. It's just back to this community again instead of being *a show* that we've all come to.

Craig Koon: The Blue Flamingo album was done on Prole Art Threat machinery,[3] which was unfortunate because it was deeply flawed. It's another scheme in a tangled tale. I thought it would be this brilliant idea of workers controlling the means of production. It was a fifty-year-old means of production, and it worked like shit. You'd have to hit it with a board all day long.

Scott Gardner: Whereas we have this nicely recorded *Live at Raul's*, we have Craig Koon's . . . What can I say? Not the most listenable live recording. But it's nice that we have that as documentation.

Craig Koon: I wasn't sure if too many of the bands on that record would be happy about it because it was on my Walkman in the Blue Flamingo, which is one of the greatest nightclubs ever—the only rival to the Cavity in terms of importance to Austin. The Walkman would slow down and speed up as its level compression circuitry would work. So it's sort of like being drunk while you listen.

I didn't want bands to beat me up, so I made it a mystery. For a while I had people thinking Ryan Richardson put it out. But I'm really proud of it. The record from start to finish was sort of the usual half-ass, things flying in the air and Kinko's bad copies. The title of the Blue Flamingo compilation, *A Curious Mix of People*, is from Miss Laura herself. One of my prize possessions is a baby blue T-shirt with a setting sun and a flamingo on one leg. And it says, "Blue Flamingo: A Curious Mix of People."

Jonathan Toubin: The Blue Flamingo scene was the first scene since the Cavity that allowed legitimate underground bands that couldn't get into a place like Emo's—say a band like Turbonegro.

Scott Gardner: I was in Germany in '97. I saw Turbonegro at a German club. It was packed. At the end, Hank—the lead singer—pulls his trousers down and lights some Roman candle and shoots it toward the audience. The crowd loved it. Then they came to Austin. Somehow Ryan Richardson made contact and gets them a gig at the Blue Flamingo and sure enough, he does the same thing with the firework. That was insane.

The Cryin' Out Louds at Blue Flamingo. Photo by Sean McGowan.

Jeff Martin: If you saw them at the Blue Flamingo, you saw a band burn Austin to the fucking ground. Nothing compared. They walked through the crowd and split it like the Red Sea.

Andy Maguire: It was a mishmash of every kind of human being on the planet. And it became the only place that you could really do a sort of start-up band.

Graham Williams: It became *the* spot for all the garage fans forever. The Motards played there every weekend it seemed like.

John Spath: Maybe three or four years into Emo's, I was already kind of jaded, but I used to walk down to the Blue Flamingo because I discovered that it was easier to use the men's room there. The bathroom line was huge at Emo's, and it stank so fucking bad. It was faster to just go down to Blue Flamingo. When I first started going there it was strictly a gay club. But I walked in there once and the Motards or the Inhalants were playing one of their early shows, and I was standing amidst this whole new crowd that wasn't necessarily going to Emo's and a band that I had never heard of before, and they absolutely blew my mind. I remember running back down to Emo's and trying to grab a few of my old jaded friends to come down to the Blue Flamingo and see what was going on.

Every three years things change and the old guard becomes washed away, the new guard comes in, and that's how I discovered a lot of these up-and-coming bands. That mix of late seventies punk meets mid-sixties garage stuff which is indicative of the Motards, the Inhalants, the Cryin' Out Louds, the Satans, the Sons of Hercules, all those bands. All of a sudden I went from jaded to going out on school nights, staying up until two in the morning because the Motards are playing. I *got* to see the fucking Motards!

Jonathan Toubin: The garage rock scene would be the Cryin' Out Louds, the Motards, the Hormones, the Inhalants.

Tim Stegall: The Inhalants really prefigured what became the sound of Austin for two years. That whole garage rock inspired stuff—very much like the Sonics.

Lisa Rickenberg: The Blue Flamingo was definitely my favorite place to play. It was a blur of amazing shows with our friends. It was always nice playing with the Motards and the Cryin' Out Louds, and Sugar Shack when they were in town. I remember gigs when the bartender was trying to hold the bar up because it was getting pushed over by people. And having a group of six-foot-tall drag queens sachet through a show was just the coolest thing ever. There would be somebody bleeding on the sidewalk, but I never felt unsafe there. The frat boys and that whole kind of Sixth Street vibe was a lot scarier to me than the way Red River used to be.

Craig Koon: The most important one for the garage scene was the Motards. They sort of became *The Beatles at the Star Club*. It pretty quickly coalesced around a garage scene with the Inhalants, the Hormones, Jesus Christ Super-fly, and the Motards.

The Motards at Blue Flamingo (*left to right*): Dave Head (guitar), Johnny Motard (vocals), Toby Marsh (bass), Suzanne Bishop (drums), Paul Johnson (guitar). Photo by Scott Gardner.

Johnny Motard: Motard was an insult that Dave Head's friends used to say in elementary school, like, "You're a retard. You're a moron. You're a motard!" We thought it was funny. Later, we found out it means "biker" in French. People would look us up online and find websites of French bikers doing weird things.

Tim Kerr: The Motards were probably the closest to what the Dicks were like at that point.

Johnny Motard: We played shit hard, and fast, and cheap, and we recorded that way. We were just trying to sound punk rock. We would get lumped in with the garage rock shit. Don't get me wrong—we played with a lot of these garage kids, and I fucking love some of them to death, okay? They were sitting around playing fast Buddy Holly–style riffs, cranking them up really loud, and singing lyrics about getting in knife fights. I'm like, "No, fuck you. I've never even seen you in a fist fight. I've seen you *run away* from them."

That wasn't us. No matter how ridiculous the Motards' songs sound, we were fucking living that way. To me, that was the difference.

Conrad Keely: One time we were walking up the road past the Blue Flamingo. The window breaks and this guy comes rolling out, screaming into a microphone and it was Johnny from the Motards. He was outside just in this pool of glass and stuff. That was a really fun time because it was all about just how much energy and excitement you could bring to the live performance.

Melissa Bryan: If you'd go when the Motards were playing, it was like sardines. It was really uncomfortable and violent and dangerous. It just didn't feel like where I wanted to be, because it was a bunch of dudes yelling, "Fuck you! Fuck you! Fuck you!" Too many fists and arms and people flying around. It felt so contrived in a way.

Susan Shepard: Yeah, the Motards had the crazy, bad live reputations.

Jennifer LaSuprema Hecker: You'd get blood on you. I sustained injuries.

Susan Shepard: Definitely the craziest live act going then. Had the reputation for falling apart on stage, but they were also really nice people. When John was sober, he was nice.

Sean McGowan: If I had never seen the Motards I don't think I ever would be in a band. We played our first show April Fools' Day '94 at Carl Normal's house with Stretford. All of these great bands were coming up. There was a real community building. When these bands formed—our band and the Motards—you would see accomplished, seasoned punk rock guitar players lining up to see these guys do something that they could never return to.

We weren't always the most sensible people. It was just excess. So if you're [drummer] Mike Leggett, you're just like, "I am working with complete idiots." And I don't blame him. We were playing a show at the Blue Flamingo, and he just started to load up his equipment and take it out the side door in the middle of the set. And that was the end of that.

I ran into Sean Powell twenty minutes later. "Sean, do you want to play drums with the band?"

"Yeah, dude, totally!" But Sean was dealing with some issues. I think the last straw with him was that he showed up at rehearsal with a children's drum kit. He was just pin-eyed and—forever the salesman—he was like, "Dude this thing's going to sound great!"

At that point there was a disconnect. We were going to quit. We went to a party at Paul Johnson's house. Aaron [Fox] was always at the Chumps shows, so he went to each of us and was like, "No way! I'm your new drummer!" That was just a great fit because he loved the band. Aaron's always really good at hitting accents that set off my vocal. Everything in the Chumps has always been good but simple.

Tim Hayes: The little garage scene was blowing up, so there was a bit of friction for some of the underground community. That's where the cross-pollination needed to happen more. When you have a band like the Cryin' Out Louds or the Motards, it's like having a party with your buddies. And you want to invite everyone to that freaking party. They don't know the whole story so they might go, "Yeah, they have nothing to do with Sincola or Miss Universe." But we do have a lot to do with that. It's our community, you know?

Tim Stegall: I regret the fact that factions did pop up, and there wouldn't be a lot of crossover anymore. That factionalization was one of the deaths of everything. Eventually, a more fundamentalist punk scene came along that had its own merits. Lower Class Brats and the Dead End Cruisers, and even the Bulemics to an extent. There was a time when everything was fresh and innocent and new.

Chepo Peña: The Satans were at one gig Gomez played. They were our friends from Kid's Meal back in the day. Brock [Hoffman] threw a bottle at me because we were making fun of that kind of music. I jumped off the stage and got in a fight. We were definitely making fun of their music, and I think that grew out of us feeling like people were starting to treat us like we weren't cool anymore. And I was like, "What happened to all of us hanging out in Copperas Cove?"

Graham Williams: Copperas Cove had an active scene. Minority was the first band I knew from there. Lil Vegas was a pizza place with an arcade that had a stage. The first time Rancid played here was there. Gomez went up and played with them. Copperas Cove had a bunch of skaters, and a band of really active people who put on shows, recorded music, put out records, told all their friends, and started to build a scene.

All those folks got connected with Austin and moved here. Most of them still live here and have done so many other bands. Noble [Brown] had Brick, and I was in a band with him—New Year. Chris Hodge and [Mike] Gerner stayed together in so many bands. 100 Watt Clock. Carbomb. Prima Donnas.

Conrad Keely: The Prima Donnas were a big influence on us. We had a friendly rivalry going on because they were our friends. I was so jealous because they were such consummate showmen. They were practicing at the Duval House and were really secretive about this project. Mike Gerner had been in Carbomb, and Jon Rueter was in the New Girl Art Trend Band—an all-girl group except for Jon. I actually recorded their first single, "King of the Underworld." We played a lot of shows with them.

Jason Reece: Sound-wise, New Girl Art Trend Band was more electronic and more influenced by that Riot Grrrl DIY approach coming out of the Northwest. Definitely angular postpunk, like the Slits. It was art-punk.

Conrad Keely: That's our mutual influences. We weren't going to be a stereotypical band. We were going to make *art*. I remember spotting Chris Lyons [Prima Donnas] long before I knew him because he was so tall and had that Romulan mod cut. The joke was they were from England.

Jason Reece: And their British accents were terrible. If you thought these guys were from the UK, then you're obviously thick.

Conrad Keely: They played this electro-clash stuff that was way before what would ever become a mainstream sound. It had these cheap synthesizers, their lyrics were hysterical, and it just went off at the first show they played.

Tim Kerr: The singer was literally shooting this Roman candle in the Blue Flamingo and people are hitting the floor. I'm so short, I was standing near the back, up on a chair, watching all this and laughing, and then I realized, "Oh shit, I'm a really good target up here!" So I got behind the jukebox.

Jason Reece: There was a sense of danger. The shows weren't so safe. There was a period of time when we weren't getting any shows because we were kind of banned from everywhere. Blue Flamingo was taking us on and like, "Oh you can do whatever the fuck you want. You can trash this place." They loved it. We packed the place with fifty people, so they were excited the booze was selling.

Ty Pearson: I started booking the KVRX nights at the Blue Flamingo. One of Trail of Dead's first rock-'n'-roll shows was there on the free Monday nights. They were a two-piece: drums and guitar. The stack that they brought in was floor to ceiling and three cabs wide. It would have been too loud for Liberty

Lunch. They only had ten friends show up who all left in the first five minutes. It was just me and the bartender there with our fingers in our ears for forty minutes. I thought it was the worst thing I have ever heard in my life. I hated every second of it.

Also, I got a word in their name turned around on the flyer and they totally gave me shit. I was like, "Why do you have a fucking name that's ten words long? What a fucking joke. No one's ever going to see you guys!"

Ryan McDaniel: There was probably an inch of separation between you and the crowd. Throughout the night, your gear would be doused with beer and whatever fluids were going around the place. You didn't know if the PA was going to blow up on you. Those were probably the most exciting shows in terms of pure, raw energy.

Miss Laura: I remember having to take care of some riots. The Dogshit Rangers came with such a fury, and I remember pushing them outside because they started throwing everything around. If you want to see a large drag queen start pushing out some bands, I used to do it. Then the people was outside and the police came with the horses. Those horses *do* bite people.

Tim Stegall: One night the Cryin' Out Louds played the Blue Flamingo, and two heavy metal dudes came in. They decided they were going to get in the middle of this garage rock crowd and start a mosh pit. Of course, these surly people with Pabst Blue Ribbons don't want to be shoved into. So what happens? One of the heshers decides he's going to start a riot, and he slugs somebody. Every single person in the bar became security and started wailing on these guys, pushing them out the door. Angele [Moyseos] from the Cryin' Out Louds . . . I can remember her bass up in the air like Davy Crockett at the Alamo.

Johnny Motard: The most disturbing things I remember might have been the things I did, like when I puked up a fucking Rohypnol and picked it up out of my puke and fucking ate it again. The place was a fucking pit, man. How about the time the fucking urinal was backed up so bad it went to the fucking stage? I was rolling around in it while we're playing.

Sean McGowan: During the time the Chumps formed probably right up until 2000, there was a fair amount of illicit drug activity. Usually it was pills. Valium and Xanax. Rohypnol. For a lot of us, it's fun until one day it's not fun anymore. And that doesn't stop us from digging the ditch for a long, long time. I think it's hard to not fall into that when you're in an environment where it's almost the identity of the group you're working with. We were expected to be fucked up.

Tim Storm: At Blue Flamingo, the Chumps were getting ready to go on. Frankie Nowhere, the bass player, stumbles in the door, hits the bass, and falls on his face. Out. So the audience duct tape the bass around Frankie's waist, hold him up, and try to wake him up. Then he sort of plays through a couple of songs. Then down again. At that point the show was over. That struck me as a fantastic show. There was really no music involved, but it was just so much fun.

Jimmy St. Germaine: We were opening for the coolest fucking band in town, the FuckEmos. A fight breaks out and some dude gets thrown out of the fucking window onto Seventh Street.

Johnny Motard: Yeah, it was a human being breaking the fucking glass out. I remember that night, but I don't remember it. People were throwing fists, but it was all good-natured.

Jimmy St. Germaine: And here's the great thing, our singer has a beer in his hand, and he leans out the window to see what's going on and the cop goes, "That's an open container, we're going to arrest you if you don't get back inside. Get back in there!" And he goes, "Hey I'm just watching, fuck you!"

Charlie Void: And you could tell a cop "fuck you" without getting beat and tased and then shot in the fucking neck. I am white, so I am not susceptible to getting shot by cops in this town, thank god.

Melissa Bryan: Everyone was sloppy. People didn't practice very often. I think that was one of the problems with Austin. There was kind of a stigma against success. When Spoon started to get popular, people were like, "Oh, they're trying too hard, they just wanna be famous. That's not cool." If you had goals, it was bad. If you wanted to be on a major label, or you wanted to put records out and do anything beyond Austin, it was looked down upon.

Miss Laura: Everyone said that SXSW was going to be pretty upset with us because we had really big South By So Whats.

Melissa Bryan: The Spoon thing was so random because they were discovered by Gerard [Cosloy] at the Blue Flamingo. But that's where they were headed whether it was Matador or somebody else. It was going to happen.

Britt Daniel: It wasn't an official South By Southwest show, but we played there during South By Southwest in '94.

Andy Maguire: Our set times got messed up with the Motards somehow. We knew Gerard was showing up to see us, and we got into it like, "No we *have* to be at a certain time!" So the Motards had to move for us, which was very nice.

Britt Daniel: That was where Gerard Cosloy from Matador saw us for the first time. That club has always been part of the Spoon story because it was where we were discovered.

Andy Maguire: We were negotiating with Geffen but decided to go with Matador because Gerard had been very helpful.

Britt Daniel: I think if Gerard Cosloy hadn't been a fan of the band I don't know if we would've kept going. At several points in this band's life, he was the one cheerleader who was very loudly trying to egg us on. He's a very smart, funny guy and has a history of putting out great records. For that guy to be interested in us, that meant something was happening. There was a lot going on at one point, and it felt like everything was exploding a little bit.

Andy Maguire: We already had our product—*Telephono*. It was recorded with John Croslin, and so we were basically trying to sell that. We were being flown to L.A. and doing the rounds with people. It was pretty intimidating. And exciting. We were presenting them with a finished product, which is unusual. That requires a different negotiation. We were meeting managers, meeting lawyers, doing all that stuff. But then I was no longer in the band. I was told that I was going to be replaced as soon as it was convenient. It's not a part of history I like to think about a lot. It's a little painful.

Melissa Bryan: We all want some guy to walk into the Blue Flamingo and go, "You! I want you! I'm gonna make you a superstar!" We all want that, so when somebody else gets it, it's like, "Oh, they suck. He's an opportunist!" I think Britt got a hard time about that. It was jealousy and this general attitude: "Don't send your stuff to major labels. Don't send your stuff to Warner Brothers."

Tim Hayes: There was South By So What with Au Go Go—one of the best fucking labels out of Australia. That compilation on Au Go Go was a documentation of what was happening in Austin amongst the little community we had back in the mid-nineties.[4] I can't remember all the bands on the bill but there was the Inhalants, Sugar Shack, the Cryin' Out Louds, the Motards, and probably the Satans.

Lisa Rickenberg: Au Go Go picked up Sugar Shack first. That show at the Blue Flamingo was one of my favorite shows ever.

Tim Hayes: The Blue Flamingo was right in the heart of SXSW that year, and it was packed to the freakin' nines. The streets were full. Everyone in SXSW has to wear a wristband so you can go in and see all the fucking hip fucking bands that are supposed to be playing. "Hip," my ass. Anyway, the only way you were going to get in to see *this* showcase was to snip your wristband. And I watched freaking Sub Pop's [Bruce] Pavitt snip his fucking wristband just to see what was really happening in Austin. It was chaos, man.

Rick Carney: I bet we had two hundred people in there. People kept going farther and farther back, and all of a sudden, the bar just imploded. No one batted an eye. No one started freaking out. It was just, "Okay, now we can get ten more people in."

Tim Hayes: It shows the importance of the mid-nineties scene in Austin, because there was that buzz. It was just starting to happen, and people were kind of coming from all around, really curious to see what that buzz was all about.

Ty Pearson: At SXSW 1998, Blue Flamingo did their anti–South By show. I think it was the River City Rapists' first show which of course was awesome and crazy. John Motard and Doug Didjit. The next band was Mondo Generator, which is one of Nick Oliveri's bands. All of a sudden I feel this huge elbow in my back at the Blue Flamingo, and I turn around and it's this dude who is like 6'3", bald, goatee, completely naked besides his guitar. He goes up to the front of the stage, turns around, and blows a fireball that encapsulates 50 percent of the club. People were just going nuts. The show finishes and the Dwarves get up on stage, play one song, and destroy everything on stage. The drum set was just tinder. They walk out the door and over to Emo's.

Tim Storm: Some of the bands got bigger. Lower Class Brats are a huge success story in terms of underground bands. The Bulemics became very popular.

Miss Laura: Unfortunately, I was going to sleep when the bands were playing. That's how everyone knew that I was really sick. I ended up having to let someone else take over, and they decided they did not want me a part of it. Our agreement fell apart and I lost quite a bit of money out of that deal. That's when it became the Blue Flame.

Dotty Farrell: At one point, when it was the Blue Flame, the homeless people smashed out the window and took all the alcohol. The electricity got cut off, and there was water all over the floor. This is not conducive to having a band play. We can't do this anymore if you're not going to pay the electric bill, and you can't close and lock the door anymore because there's people coming in the window. It was bad.

Tim Storm: Even though we played Emo's and other places, the Blue Flamingo was the heart of the scene. And Miss Laura was its heart.

CHANCES

WE'LL JUST ROCK FOR OURSELVES

LOCATED ON THE NORTHWEST CORNER OF THE intersection of Red River and Ninth Street from 1982 through 1994, Chances was a lesbian bar that backed into becoming one of Austin's most eclectic live-music venues by 1990. Its steadfast refusal to color within genre boundaries meant you could see anyone from a young Lisa Loeb on the brink of a number-one single to Day Glo–coated industrial bluegrass freaks Caroliner Rainbow from one night to the next.

Seen through the typically squalid prism of underground music club aesthetics, Chances was refreshingly picturesque. Entering the low-ceilinged building from Red River, you would find the bar to the right and a small stage to the left. But when the weather was nice, shows took place on an outdoor patio with a larger stage that backed up to a limestone cliff wall.[1]

Chances proprietor Sandra Martinez initially moved to Austin to attend nursing school at UT before side-barring into club ownership. When Martinez and her business partners first bought the club in 1982, it was a gay men's bar. Their first move was to open Chances up to nongay clientele, which hastened its transition to a nonexclusionary lesbian bar.

When her partners dropped out in 1986, South By Southwest was just around the corner. Soon there would be a demand for more downtown stages to house the nascent music festival's showcase acts. Although Chances was three blocks from Sixth Street, it was close enough to make adding live music a solid commercial proposition. Former Hundredth Monkey drummer Laura Williams was hired to book, and it was off to the races.

Not all the club's 1980s regulars welcomed these changes. In a 1998 *Austin Chronicle* profile written by Spike Gillespie, Martinez recalled the resistance to removing the window coverings that offered patrons privacy from potential outing.

"A lot of the original regulars said they wouldn't come back because they could be seen," Martinez said. "A lot of people challenged me. I felt strongly and said, 'It's important that we open the windows and the whole environment.' We were opening up our little secret, opening up a look inside the club. I thought it was a survival tactic for both the bar and the gay community."[2]

In some respects, Martinez's insistence on opening things up can be seen as a corollary to the way Randy "Biscuit" Turner of the Big Boys and Gary Floyd of the Dicks fostered LGBT acceptance within the greater Austin punk scene by being openly gay frontpersons from deep East Texas with undeniable stage presence.

Women were also central to Austin's punk history from its inception. In January 1978 a Chicano music venue at 2610 Guadalupe called Raul's booked the Violators in what has since become recognized as the city's first local punk bill. The Violators were three-quarters female, including a teenage guitarist named Kathy Valentine who would soon move to Los Angeles and become the bassist for the Go-Go's. Lorenda Ash (F-Systems), Shona Lay (Standing Waves), and Sally Norvell (the Norvells) would follow.

By 1985, when MTV's *The Cutting Edge* profiled Austin's underground music scene, two of the marquee bands—Zeitgeist[3] and Glass Eye—had gender parity in their lineups. Houston émigré Gretchen Phillips cut her teeth in handmade art-punk outfit Meat Joy before her lesbian folk-rock band Two Nice Girls got popular enough to get them signed to Rough Trade. Phillips ultimately got name-checked by Kathleen Hanna alongside Gertrude Stein, Billie Jean King, Angela Davis, and Joan Jett in Le Tigre's 1999 song, "Hot Topic."

If third-wave feminism wasn't as overt in 1990s Austin as it was in Hanna's environs of Olympia, Washington, the primacy of women in every aspect of Chances' operations exemplified many of the movement's key goals. By integrating Chances into the overwhelmingly male local rock circuit, Martinez helped modulate the hypermasculine and heteronormative attitudes endemic to rock music while also providing a friendly base for adventurous all-woman punk bands like Girls in the Nose, Handful, Olive, and Power Snatch.

Like the Big Boys and Biscuit's nineties-era band Swine King, Power Snatch made every gig a production. One of their more memorable Chances shows was backing a Cher female impersonator with vocalist Cindy Widner donning a mustache to play Sonny. Then, on April 16, 1994, there was the Punk Prom and Little Debbie-Taunt Ball, an homage to Austin's first Punk Prom held May 16, 1980, in the waning days of the Armadillo World Headquarters.[4] The Power Snatch iteration at Chances was thematically truer, with balloons, tin-foil decorations, hideous formalwear, a prom court, and a hickey contest to accompany sets from the Hormones, Stretford, Sons of Hercules, and emcee Phillips.

Power Snatch had a yin and yang relationship to the Pocket FishRmen. Both were theatrically inclined big-rock juggernauts with a predilection for the absurd. So when the FishRmen issued "Intellectuals Rocking for Women," a self-referential, tongue-in-cheek anthem celebrating the band's antisexist stance with an offering to let women pee in the men's room, Power Snatch borrowed a page from Kitty Wells and wrote an answer song. The result—which Widner called "an homage and a critique"—was called "No Thanks (We'll Just Rock for Ourselves)."

With this artistic push-and-pull as a backdrop, preconceptions about what a lesbian bar should be were nullified upon entry into Chances. It was a unique space at a unique time that reconciled its lesbian and punk clientele with equal hospitality. In expanding the venue's reach, Martinez facilitated connectivity and alliance among the marginalized. During the 1990s Chances hosted benefits for everything from AIDS Services of Austin to Texas Abortion Rights Action League to labor-of-love zines like *ArtCore*.

Punk has long been the province of castaways, but there's a difference between rejecting convention and being told you have no place in it. And despite its veneer of liberal, laid-back friendliness, '90s Austin was a mixed bag in terms of LGBT rights. Rep. Lloyd Doggett, who represented most of Austin throughout the decade, joined the entire Texas Democratic delegation in voting to ban federal recognition of same-sex marriage with 1996's Defense of Marriage Act.[5] Closer to home, Austin's city council voted to extend benefits to domestic partners of municipal employees in September 1993, but a referendum led by an antigay group called Concerned Texans to rescind these benefits passed with 62 percent of the vote in May 1994.

While some organized, fundraised, and lobbied to advance the cause of LGBT rights, the Austin chapter of the Lesbian Avengers resisted in a key redolent of the more extreme music emanating from Chances. When a local Baptist church proclaimed, "Don't be deceived, homosexuals commit the most heinous crimes in America" on its marquee in 1994, the Avengers responded by dumping a pile of horse manure on their lawn. Somewhere beyond the argument between what constitutes legitimate political strategy, Martinez's inclination to provide a "look inside" helped build a broader coalition for LGBT rights through creative association.

By the summer of 1994 the stressors of running a bar for twelve years had taken their toll, and Martinez decided to close Chances. "I never thought about what Chances had done for the community until after we'd closed," she told Gillespie in the 1998 *Chronicle* interview. "I kept hearing, 'Would you ever consider doing it again? Do you realize what we lost when you closed?' over and over."[6]

Martinez's lasting mark on Austin goes beyond Chances. In 1993 she opened Top Drawer, a venerable thrift store benefiting Project Transitions, a nonprofit providing housing and support for people living with HIV. She also served as executive director and volunteer coordinator for the Austin Gay and Lesbian International Film Festival.[7] Martinez declined to be interviewed for this book, but her legacy can be heard loud and clear in the accounts that follow.

Sandra Martinez: It was a gay men's bar when I bought it. My partners and I didn't know the gay bar business, so we left it as a men's bar for a couple of months. When I lost my partners in '86, I was faced with the questions: "Do I close? Can I really do this by myself?" I wasn't feeling very confident about which direction to take the bar.[8]

Laura Williams: Everything was so fluid and that's where Chances comes in. It started out as a neighborhood lesbian bar and then it was just Chances— this huge neighborhood club. And I mean it was *totally* fluid. Everyone from every possible walk of life, gender, sexuality.

Kerthy Fix: It was much more than a lesbian bar. It was good times. You got to be half naked on stage in bondage wear. Where else would we get to do that? To me, Chances was really the epitome of where everything met together in the Austin music scene.

Gretchen Phillips: There was a kind of music that is the lesbian bar band that you guys don't know nothing about. That is these women bands that would do some originals and some covers, and they're often very sprawling and large. There's the girlfriend on the cowbell and maybe she plays the tambo. Between the Therapy Sisters and Nancy Scott and Two Nice Girls and Girls in the Nose and His Boy Elroy, that would be enough to book Chances

Mrs. Fun playing Chances. Photo by Lisa Davis. Courtesy of Austin History Center.

pretty consistently. And my recollection is that after SXSW, there were more bands with men in them.

Laura Williams: You came to Chances to hear really good music and come to a really cool bar. It was perfect.

Gretchen Phillips: Whoever's coming to see the band at Chances are like, "What is this club? I fucking love this club! That stage is so nice, it sounds so good. What is this?" And I'm like, "This is a lezzie bar and you have not been invited, except for now you *are* invited. Check it out!"

Laura Williams: When I was booking Chances—and you've got to consider other people's perception—I never thought of it as like they are coming into another territory. I was just like, "I want all of you here!"

Melissa Bryan: There were so many women who were hanging out there who started bands that would play there. It was so normal. It wasn't like, "We're *girls* in a band!"

Susie Martinez: One of my very first bands was called Pumphouse. We started playing at Chances and it was such a cool scene because it was like what Cheer Up Charlie's is now. It's the same venue. It was predominantly gay women that were there, but you would have this nice mix when these bands came. It was actually a *scene* because a lot of the bands weren't just gay bands.

Laura Williams: The impact it had on the community was big because when I was booking for Chances, everybody came. It wasn't like, "Oh hey we're going to the lesbian bar." They're going to Chances because Pocket FishR-men's playing and the Wild Seeds are playing. It would be Friday, Saturday, Sunday—jammed.

Cindy Widner: Sandra [Martinez] booked everyone. It really didn't matter as long as you weren't like actively homophobic or a misogynist or whatever.

Laura Williams: I think Sandra is very compassionate and invested. Sandra had the capacity to rally the troops and the patrons. During SXSW everyone would just come in and help. People would work the door, we'd bartend, we'd build whatever we needed to build. Put the fences up, take the fences down. There were lots of moving parts, but Sandra just knew how to put it together almost effortlessly.

Laura Creedle: It was a wonderful place to play, but I do think that Sandra made it a warm place. I remember her carding me. I was like, "Really, Sandra?" And she was like, "Yep. TABC are gunning for me all the time. So yeah, you better have your ID on you." At that moment she looked at me like, "What do you *think* TABC are doing with Chances?" So a little education there for me. To be able to make it such a wonderful place and still be fighting the good fight is pretty amazing when I think about it like that.

Dotty Farrell: There were other queer bars like, say, the Crossing. That was a male gay bar. We would go out dancing at the Boathouse. We would go to different queer bars to go dancing because no guys would hit on you and you could just dance all night. Ninety-nine-cent drinks and we'd just go crazy. There was this terrible place called Dirty Sally's. They'd have ten-cent drink night.

Jonathan Toubin: Chain Drive was a club that played a little bit of a part in punk. Not only was there a band that named themselves after it [Chaindrive], but everybody went there sometimes for a drink. We always felt comfortable around the good old leathermen, who were all, actually, despite looking tough, really sweet.

Dotty Farrell: And then there was the Hollywood. That was a lesbian bar, and they were really serious lesbians where you had to have on a starched western shirt or a button-down shirt and they all had dry-cleaned, pressed Levi's on. And so they didn't want any mess coming up in there. They didn't want girls that looked funny and weird that had shit tied all over them. And they didn't want punk rock.

Gretchen Phillips: I've been to many lesbian bars in my life, and I would play at different lesbian bars, but Chances was the arty dyke bar. I might actually get threatened to be beat up at the Hollywood because I'm doing my Deborah Hay dance and some girl is like, "I hate how you dance," and she kicks me in the head. That's never going to happen at Chances because there's just too many grad students there.

Laura Creedle: I liked playing the Cavity, but I felt like Chances was home. And that's because everybody was welcome at Chances. One of my favorite memories was the Madonna Hoot Night in the '80s with Happy Family.

Dotty Farrell: I remember we [Swine King] did a Jesse Helms hoot night there to help raise money for AIDS Services of Austin. Biscuit did a poetry reading that night.

Cindy Widner: It was a huge time for gay activism and gay art. ACT UP was happening. Lesbian Avengers was political protest in a creative form.

Dotty Farrell: One night, Kelly Linn and Susannah from Moist Fist got married. Biscuit was the preacher. It was a very big elaborate to-do and it was outside, and it was about 30 degrees out.

Kelly Linn: I remember the Wedding Show clearly. We brought in mannequins as the bridesmaids and groomsmen. We wore wedding dresses and leather motorcycle jackets and veils and all of that.

Susannah Simone: Sometimes it would piss off the guys in the band because we would spend $47 on costume material and some candles, and now we're getting reimbursed three dollars each for the show. I think they had fun though. We had costumes for them too.

Kelly Linn: We put as much energy into getting ready for the show as performing. We did like just being strong women up there. We also both had the same idea of the visual concept of it, with parts of it being humorous in a way.

Susannah Simone: We had a theme and new costumes for every show, and we dressed identically. We always wore sunglasses so that we looked a little more alike. When Kelly Linn cut bangs on her hair, I was like, "Whoa you can't do that! That means I have to do it too!"

Gary Chester: At first you want to do some music that doesn't hurt your ears like Ed Hall does. We played some quiet music. Some Bach. Some Satie. And then it turns into this horror fest where there's disco and girls dressed exactly the same all around me.

Susannah Simone: There was one show outdoors at Chances we called "Running Through the Woods." It was supposed to feel like a horror movie, like somebody being chased through the woods. We had these incredible long brown yarn wigs, and diaphanous floaty gowns. That was the show that Peter Frampton came to for just a few minutes. We were so excited!

Dotty Farrell: I was in a play there called "The Well of Horniness." It was a Big State production, and it was supposed to be a '40s radio play. I played a guy called Rod. Anytime we would say "the well of horniness," everybody in the audience had to scream, kind of like *Pee Wee's Playhouse*. "The well . . . ahhh! . . . of horniness." The homeless people that were up on the cliffs started yelling, too. And you could hear somebody peeing off the cliff while we were on stage. I love the realism of downtown Austin.

Kerthy Fix: That weirdo sensibility was really goofy and funny rather than *hard rock*. There was a playful quality.

Jonathan Toubin: We [Noodle] had a gig at Chances with Power Snatch for their Career Night show. These leathermen that worked at the IRS approached our drummer [Lance Farley] who they worked with and said, "I have this idea for your band. Why don't we just loan you our leatherman wear, and you can wear it on stage?"

Gretchen Phillips: Power Snatch were wearing office wear. They had thrift-store power suits, and I totally stole that look. I got a good SXSW review that was, "It looked like this substitute teacher was playing this lezzie rock weird thing." And I was like, "Yes, I look like a substitute teacher. Yes! Perfect!"

Jonathan Toubin: Half the audience was leathermen, and half of it was lesbians that are regulars and there to see Power Snatch. It looked like a middle-school dance—the men over here, the women over there. But by the end of the night, it worked out really well and we had a blast.

Kerthy Fix: In Austin the queer female collaborations with straight men and gay men were not so political or angry. It was about goofy fun and art.

Gretchen Phillips: Those were my dreams from punk rock times, which was completely mixing it up. I went to Michigan Womyn's [Music] Festival, where it certainly wasn't mixed up. I had my women-only things, but my dream really was about men and women being together.

Brant Bingamon: When we were coming up, the lesbian presence in Austin was strong. It was beautiful. And one of the coolest things about the lesbians was they liked to rock 'n' roll and they didn't mind if hetero dudes came around. They let us come and rock out and be really stupid in their club.

Laura Williams: In Austin, when you saw female musicians, it's just as natural as you would see anybody else. Everything was just a wall of music. Happy Family and Girls in the Nose and all of those. . . . It was just music. That's who we were.

Gretchen Phillips: To me, a very real legacy is a kind of normalized lesbian visibility. Chances didn't brand itself as, "We're not a lesbian bar because Stretford's playing." They didn't rebrand as that. It was a lesbian bar where Stretford's playing. That is not a small thing.

Cindy Widner: "Inclusive" is a funny word, though. It implies that there is some essential, central group to be excluded from. In this case, that group is assumed to be composed of young, white, cis, straight men. But the thing is, that's not the group that formed the core of outlier music in Austin.

Kathy McCarty: Almost every band had a girl in it here. It was just normal. Sometimes there would be an all-girl band like Buffalo Gals[9] and it would be a little notable that it was all girls but—for the most part—it just really wasn't a thing. And then we went out touring the rest of the country and it was a *huge fucking deal* out there. People would do things—I'm not kidding—people would do things like not do your sound right because you had girls in the band. Just things to sabotage you. And it was so alien to me.

Carrie Clark: The minute that you left Austin, I would be with my Marshall amp and my guitar on me and my guitar effects pedals in front of me, and the sound guy would come at me with a bass D.I. It was just a reaction: if you're a girl, you're the road manager, you're somebody's girlfriend, or you're the bass player. That happened a lot.

Gretchen Phillips: You've got to talk about music stores as a woman in Austin, Texas. I hear Strait Music advertising on really fucked-up homophobic radio which was such a heartbreak because I wrote them a fan letter in the '80s. As a woman going to buy a pick and some strings, the degree to which my entire life I've been ridiculed by the men at the music store for purchasing what they're selling, you know? And Strait was not condescending. They were nice as though you were part of things. And that was an anomaly.

Laura Creedle: A lot of people were very supportive, but there's always these moments it felt like an uphill battle. I just hated music stores back then. They were a very dude-bro kind of place. I went into a music store with my boyfriend and a guy came up and he was like, "Hey dude, what can I do you for?" And Henry went, "I don't play guitar. My girlfriend plays guitar." And he's like, "Well, what does your girlfriend need?"

Cindy Widner: Women had been on stage and in Austin's music mix since anyone could remember. Janis Joplin, Sue Foley, Sarah Brown, Buffalo Gals, the Delinquents, the Violators, Meat Joy in the 1970s and '80s. Two Nice Girls or the Butthole Surfers or Moist Fist or Girls in the Nose or Glass Eye or Eloise Burrell or the Reivers or Lucinda Williams. Or Dotty Farrell, Terri Lord,[10] and Darcee Douglas[11] everywhere. And that doesn't even get into genres like country and soul and jazz and blues.

Carrie Clark: I think the '90s were really important for girls in bands. Everything changed. In the late '80s and the early '90s, there were the Kims—Kim Deal and Kim Gordon. Then, as the early '90s came around, there were the women in Stereolab and My Bloody Valentine. Then there was the Riot Grrrl scene. Even though Austin is a woman-friendly town, it was hard to get in a band, especially as a guitarist.

Lisa Rickenberg: I never felt handicapped by the fact that I was a woman in bands. I'm sure I enjoyed the extra attention and credit I got for being a woman in a band, but I never really thought of myself as a "Woman in a Band" at the time. All the other bands we played with—the Motards, the Cryin' Out Louds, Sugar Shack—all of these bands had women in them, and it wasn't really like a *thing*. But I also never got stuck in the kitchen talking about babies.

Power Snatch, Wet—a lot of the bands that were about LGBT sexual identity—those are people who could play their instruments and wrote their own songs. In the garage rock scene, there were a lot more short skirts, bouncing up and down, playing dumb, pretending you couldn't play even if you could kind of thing. Having guys carry your equipment for you. That kind of stuff really got under my skin.

Kathy McCarty: Sometimes when girls go to play music—rock music particularly—they have an idiosyncratic take on it compared to the guys who have been sitting around noodling with Led Zep all the time. And a lot of times people see that as a disqualification, that you're coming out of left field in some way. But I never heard that here. No one was ever like that here.

Rebecca Cannon: It didn't matter if you were a girl or a guy or very well gifted or not gifted. You just had to really want to be part of it and bring something creative and different or shocking or fun or silly. I don't remember the discussion of male or female. It was more like, "We can now do this because it was leveled because of the DIY thing." Anybody could do it.

Kathy McCarty: In a lot of ways, the biggest voice or influence on our scene was Biscuit. You know—Randy Turner. He was a feminist.

Dotty Farrell: He was happiest when he was on stage and performing. Or being the host of the art show. He just liked to surprise people and see them laugh and see them have a good time. He was an entertainer.

Roger Morgan: He was influencing people in a lot of ways. He would stop by Sound Exchange and buy up all of these local cassettes before traveling to San Francisco. Five or six of each band. He would take them and give them away in San Francisco. So I was thinking, "Wow, this is kind of a cool network of artists and musicians."

Kerthy Fix: I don't think you can underestimate the influence of Big Boys and Biscuit. To project a queer sensibility onto punk rock and to have punk rock be fun was very different from the L.A. scene, right? Or the New York scene. Biscuit—he's beloved, but I'm not sure he gets his due as a visual artist. A hilarious queer man. In terms of what you get permission to do, when that's part of your world, there's this huge latitude for every goofy performance art weird thing I want to do on stage. And people will love it. Or not. But it doesn't matter.

Dotty Farrell: One of Swine King's first shows was on the outside stage at Chances with Snoopy [Melvin] and Rob Cooley both on drums, me and Darcee on basses, Mark [Kenyon] and Skip [Hiatt] on guitars. Randy could hardly stand up for very long at the time, so we found this ridiculous, elaborately carved wooden throne and he sat and sang from atop it. The theme was Mama Cass, and we all wore mumus stuffed with pillows—which kept falling down as I jumped around playing—and wigs. Before we started, I dressed Skip up in an apron with a folded paper hat and an over-the-shoulder concession box full of ham sandwiches which he handed out to the audience. After playing "Monday, Monday," on cue, we all—audience included—ate and choked together on ham sandwiches.[12]

Kerthy Fix: Swine King was really part of the greatness of the Austin music scene. They were always very flamboyant and really poppy and funny. And the queer scene here was very inclusive because it wasn't being attacked. It felt very open.

Gretchen Phillips: These guys are gay and everybody loves them. That's kind of amazing. I came from a town with gay radio shows, gay bookstores. It was a lateral move. I always thought that all punk was also gay. Then I would meet people from other scenes, like this friend of mine, Ria Pell, in Atlanta and she was like, "Our scene was very macho and it definitely wasn't gay, so you were really lucky."

Cindy Widner: Queer folk like Biscuit and Gary Floyd and Gretchen Phillips and Meg Hentges[13] and Teresa Nervosa/Taylor[14] and Terri and Darcee weren't "included" in the scene—they were the core of the scene!

Gretchen Phillips: I had been here for a year, and so I was starting to play with people and put things out and think about writing and think about my adult life and how am I going to do it and am I going to be out? Do I dare

Gretchen Phillips Experience (*left to right*): Phillips, Andy Loomis. Photo by Lisa Davis. Courtesy of Austin History Center.

to be out? And *The World According to Garp* had this very terrifying scene where Glenn Close gets assassinated for being out, and it was very real for me because of Harvey Milk being assassinated not very long before. I had to spend a week thinking, "Am I willing to be killed for unequivocally being out?" And I thought, you know, yeah, because what am I living for?

I think that's what it meant to have Gary and Biscuit and Chris Wing[15] and David Stain,[16] who was a dear friend of mine. I didn't feel isolated. I felt like I was part of something and that this would be a good idea actually to put this forth. There wasn't enough of it going on nationally or internationally in terms of a punk version of lesbian expression. There was plenty inside of women's music—which I also completely had my foot in that door and loved—but it wasn't a means of musical expression that was energetically interesting enough to me.

Kelly Linn: Gretchen Phillips—Two Nice Girls and Meat Joy—is a total powerhouse woman. She's an amazing musician. At first she was just so bizarre

Darcee Douglas, Power Snatch. Photo by Lisa Davis. Courtesy of Austin History Center.

to get to know. She seemed very hard, but she ended up being one of the most amazing people that I've known. So talented. So intense. Just smart. I loved the Meat Joy days. They made the record and got all these blank record covers and had record painting parties. So each cover is different.

Melissa Bryan: As the '90s went on, there was a really big scene of women who were playing music. Doing their own thing, not really attached to the Riot Grrrl thing going on in other parts of the country.

Rebecca Cannon: Now the playing ground was leveled because it wasn't just special people that were gifted or glamorous that could be in bands. It was *everybody*. It was us girls that didn't maybe feel confident previously. And now we're like, "I want to do a punk rock band. I want to do a nerd rock band," but I don't remember gender being a big part of the discussion. Today, people are very *gender*. Gender is high up there. It's very present. It was just an environment where it wasn't really talked about.

Cindy Widner: It was true that Austin didn't have a game-changing network of Grrrls that formed a neu-feminist movement through zines, music, meetings, and manifestos like the ones that emerged out of the Pacific Northwest and D.C. Austin *also* didn't have the kind of punk scene that aggressively excluded women, as I've been told was the case in Seattle. Women were always part of the various scenes here—onstage, in front of the stage, in the pit. It could be that women musicians and fans didn't feel the need for *revolution girl style now!* A friend once told me, "Other places had Riot Grrrl, but Austin had Power Snatch."

Laura Creedle: When I was in Power Snatch and things were shambolic, I would turn around and look at Terri [Lord] and go, "Yeah, I can't believe I'm playing with her!" I kind of worshiped her from afar. I mean, who didn't? Amazing drummer.

Cindy Widner: My favorite show was the Punk Prom at Chances—a callback to the one the Dicks and Big Boys headlined at the Armadillo once upon a time. That was a lot of prom realness, down to the awkward prom-court pairings to the awesome sight and sound of Terri drumming full-on in the puffiest '50s dress I'd ever seen!

Laura Creedle: This was Terri's idea because she didn't go to prom. It was not a time that you could be an out lesbian at prom. And so we were like,

Terri Lord, Power Snatch. Photo by Lisa Davis. Courtesy of Austin History Center.

"Let's have a prom where everybody wears a dress or a tuxedo!" And then it was all a scramble of getting our costumes together and corsages and it was delightful. I had this ridiculous pink-and-orange dress that I found at a thrift store, and I put my hair up in sausage curls. Gretchen got Chepo and my husband Henry to dance together and serenaded them. It was a blast.

It was just one of those uncomplicated fun moments. And that's another thing about the '90s. We just did fun silly stuff.

Cindy Widner: The theme nights and goofy antics—another thing that has a rich tradition in Austin music, from at least the time of the Uranium Savages, running through the Dicks and Big Boys era through Ed Hall/Pong and Pocket FishRmen, Swine King, and every band Greg Beets has ever been in—all of whom we admired and loved.

Laura Creedle: I think about how much time we spent with the Lesbian Avengers and Lisa Davis. One of the only recordings of Power Snatch is one of our very first shows. Lisa Davis was wearing a foam tongue. Someone else had the foam vulva. Lisa was around me and stepping on all my boxes and

knocking into me, and I was just trying my best to make it through the songs. It was a crazy thing. Lisa taught me how to breathe fire. That's something to share with your children, right? I miss her so much. She was an amazing person. Definitely one of the big reasons that we were always just kind of crazy chaos on a stick.

Kerthy Fix: I remember the Pocket FishRmen song, "Intellectuals Rocking for Women," and then Power Snatch had an answer song, "We'll Rock for Ourselves." Of course, Cindy, the lead singer of Power Snatch, had been in a band with the singer of the Pocket FishRmen's wife, and the Power Snatch/Pocket FishRmen/Horsies/Happy Family little nexus was just kind of enmeshed. That kind of pop humor—intellectual kookiness—was functioning side-by-side with this kind of hard dude rock element—Agony Column or FuckEmos or Crust—the whole Trance scene.

We were all functioning together and there was a little bit of overlap, but there was a lot of respect. I think that what Power Snatch and Pocket

FishRmen did was anchor what could've been an über masculinity. They really humanized both sides and kept the music scene from imploding for a long time. There was a sort of collegial balance that existed in that '90s Austin music scene with women and queers and super dude-y dudes.

Cindy Widner: Power Snatch wasn't a Riot Grrrl band, but it did foreground things like gender, sexual orientation, sexuality in general, queerness, misogyny. But we were *women*—neither girls nor Grrrls. Representation was important, but it was also just a fact that we are powerful, grown-ass women. We'd all been in bands before, and Terri and Darcee were already legends. Plus, there were tons of other all-woman bands largely unrelated to Riot Grrrl by then: L7, Babes in Toyland, Seven Year Bitch, Lunachicks, my faves Calamity Jane and Frightwig. Women in Austin were integral members of great and beloved bands from the Inhalants to Sincola to Stretford to the Cryin' Out Louds to Swine King to Sixteen Deluxe.

Rebecca Cannon: I loved that Sincola was three women and two guys. I also loved that two of the women were lesbians because when we would go play at Chances or Electric Lounge, there would be so many girls and girlfriends there. That was really fun to be a part of that scene and to have a group of people in Austin supporting us. I was really proud of that.

Kris Patterson: I really like having a mix. I think that just represents how we are in real life. But none of this was planned. It just happened to work out. It wasn't like the Runaways.

Rebecca Cannon: I was kind of confused about my sexuality at the time, so I would be like, "I'm a lesbian! Oh wait. I'm not." It was just fun to be a part of all of that, and I would say that we were all fluid before we knew what fluid was. And we were gender queer. It's interesting how semantics spell it out. There was only a couple of little boxes, but really we didn't fit in those boxes. So I'm glad for the spectrum now. There was a lot of gender fluidity and spectrum stuff going on. Gender queer without having the words.

Laura Creedle: Coming from the '80s, I didn't feel like that dialogue was quite there, you know? The '90s was really a time when it was a dialogue between all parts of that music scene, where people were just like, "No—*this* is who I am." And it did feel free. It did feel like more thought was going into what the music scene was and what we were doing and why and who we were including. And a lot of that has to do with Chances.

Rebecca Cannon: I think Austin was very inclusive. All Freaks Are Welcome. You didn't quite know where you fit in, who you were, or what your sexuality was. I think the theme that's run through punk rock was inclusivity for the freaks and outcasts. "Okay, they don't want you? We do. You're welcome to come here! We love you."

SWEATBOX STUDIOS

SWEATBOX IS BURNING (OR, HONK IF DICK CHENEY SHOT YOUR LANDLORD IN THE FACE)

AUSTIN'S CACHET AS A MUSIC EPICENTER RESTS squarely on live performance. From backyards to supermarkets to laundromats, musicians set up and play all over town seven nights a week. Without the "live" qualifier, it's difficult to imagine music as a thing Austin would stake its cultural reputation on.

Among those political and business leaders looking to maximize the economic impact of music in Austin, a common concern is that the music industry is *too* focused on live music. Unlike Nashville, Austin never had a Music Row of record label offices, publishing houses, and recording studios.

It's worth noting that many of Austin's most significant records weren't actually recorded in town. The 13th Floor Elevators went to Houston to record "You're Gonna Miss Me" in 1966. Willie Nelson's *Red Headed Stranger* was recorded in the Dallas suburb of Garland in 1975. While some of Christopher Cross's 1979 Grammy-winning debut was recorded at Austin's Pecan Street Studios, it couldn't have become the embodiment of yacht rock without the full L.A. studio treatment.

Despite not being known as a record-making town, Austin had recording studios. Most significantly, Willie Nelson owned Pedernales Recording Studio in the village of Briarcliff near Lake Travis. Opened in 1979 in a converted golf clubhouse, Pedernales attracted big-ticket clients thanks to its Nelson association, relaxed vibe, and proximity to a golf course.

145

In November 1990 the IRS seized the recording studio and golf course when Nelson was unable to pay back millions in back taxes, penalties, and interest. Although the property was worth millions, no one offered the minimum bid when it went up for auction. In March 1991 former UT football coach Darrell Royal purchased the property for $117,535 and held on to it until Nelson could afford to pay him back. Sublime recorded most of their multiplatinum 1996 self-titled major label debut at Pedernales with Butthole Surfers guitarist Paul Leary producing. Sadly, guitarist/vocalist Bradley Nowell died of a heroin overdose in San Francisco shortly before *Sublime* was released.

Founded by Freddy Fletcher and named for his father, Arlyn Studios opened in 1984, just off South Congress in the same former motor lodge complex housing the Austin Opera House (also owned by Nelson for a time). Major artists like Neil Young and Willie Nelson recorded there, but local artists like Sincola also recorded at Arlyn during the '90s. Lucky Tomblin's Fire Station Studios was housed in San Marcos's former city hall and firehouse, hosting everyone from Doug Sahm to the Dead Milkmen.

Without vanity money to throw around, recording a full-length album at these studios typically required label support. Cedar Creek Studios and Music Lane were more common destinations for indie or unaffiliated bands. Happy Family recorded 1990's *Lucky* at Cedar Creek, while Mineral recorded their 1997 emo touchstone *The Art of Failing* at Music Lane.

Further down the food chain, some took matters into their own hands. Crust rented space in a poorly maintained office building just off North Lamar and turned it into their own Butterylicious Studio. Pocket FishRmen guitarist Cris Burns put his Radio-TV-Film degree from UT to good use by opening Stupendous Sounds Studio in West Campus with fellow engineer John Hancock. Burns even tried his hand at vertical integration by starting a record label called Austin Throwdown.

Others didn't even bother going out. Ex–Stick People guitarist Craig Ross performed and recorded an idiosyncratic solo album for MCA, 1996's *Dead Spy Report*, almost entirely by himself at home. Likewise, Fort Worth post-rock transplants the American Analog Set recorded 1997's *From Our Living Room to Yours* in the rent house they lived in, much to the consternation of their landlord, who threatened to evict them for making too much noise.

For anyone else in a band with no money and no clue how to record even with entry-level technology like the Tascam Portastudio four-track cassette recorder, there was Sweatbox.

Opened by budding engineer Mike Vasquez in 1992, Sweatbox Studio was purpose-built for capturing the noise drifting over from clubs on Red River.

The studio was located on the second floor of a run-down building at the corner of Fifth Street and San Jacinto. Instead of golf, onsite recreation at 304 East Fifth consisted of choosing between lugging equipment up the stairs or taking your chances in a dodgy, slow-moving elevator. Answering nature's call meant subjecting oneself to the stinkiest urinals in town.

During the 1920s the building housed cotton brokers and exporters. By 1992 sketchy loan peddlers occupied the ground floor storefronts while rehearsal spaces occupied the upper floors. The building also housed the Green Room, which morphed into East Fifth Street Market, a short-lived cooperative venue primarily run by band members like Glorium vocalist Paul Streckfus, Gut bassist Brandon Crowe, and bassist/guitarist Paul Newman, who played in Yuck and Gomez in addition to his namesake math-rock quartet.

When Sweatbox opened, studio time was $12.50 an hour—less than you'd pay to sing over a soundalike Whitney Houston track at the mall. Even if a band only made $50 a night, they could save up enough to cut a single over the course of just a few shows. The result might not be commercial radio–friendly, but that was sort of the point.

Just because it was cheap didn't mean Sweatbox couldn't yield great recordings. The angry wall of noise conjured by the Cherubs and engineer Paul Stautinger on 1994's *Heroin Man* showcased the studio's sonic potential, as did subsequent high-water marks like Glorium's *Cinema Peligrosa* and El Flaco's *Thub*. When Alejandro Escovedo and ex–Doctors' Mob drummer Glenn Benavides decided it was time to record their cathartic glam/punk combo Buick MacKane, Sweatbox was a sensible landing spot. Most of 1997's blistering *The Pawn Shop Years* was cut there with ex–Big Boys/Poison 13 guitarist Tim Kerr producing.

In addition to playing in blues-tinged punk outfits Jack O'Fire and the Lord High Fixers, Kerr was Sweatbox's best-known resident producer. He was prolific, recording hundreds of sessions there. Kerr produced vital works for local garage punk heroes the Motards and the Inhalants as well as artists from further afield like Houston's Sugar Shack; the Makers, from Spokane, Washington; and Pittsburgh's the Cynics.

Cheap rent was a key to Sweatbox's longevity. That came courtesy of Harry Whittington, a prominent local lawyer who owned the building.[1] Some might call Whittington a slumlord for letting the building fall into neglect while waiting for the right time to sell out, but the capital outlay required to fix up such an ancient property would've destroyed the air pocket that allowed economically marginal tenants like Sweatbox and KOOP to lease space in the middle of downtown Austin through the '90s and into the mid-aughts.

ABOVE The Inhalants recording at Sweatbox Studio. Photo by Sean McGowan.
RIGHT Tim Kerr observes as Mike Vasquez runs the board at Sweatbox Studio. Photo by Sean McGowan.

While any casual observer could've predicted the collapse of this tenuous arrangement, few would've imagined how dramatically it went down. On January 5, 2006, the building caught fire. Over at Emo's, where Attack Formation was performing a free show on the patio, bandleader Ben Webster announced, "Sweatbox is burning."[2]

According to the Austin Fire Department, the cause was "improperly discarded smoking materials." While the fire itself didn't destroy Sweatbox, the studio sustained extensive smoke damage. Vasquez and engineer Bryan Nelson temporarily moved operations to Nevele Eleven Studios and plotted their next move.

Then it happened again. In the early hours of February 4, 2006, a four-alarm fire broke out at the adjacent Taste nightclub and spread to 304 East Fifth. This fire effectively totaled the building for good.

But February 2006 wasn't done with Whittington. On February 11, Vice President Dick Cheney accidentally shot him in the face during a South Texas quail hunting trip. According to an incident report prepared by the Texas Parks and Wildlife Department, "Whittington downed a bird and went to retrieve it. While he was out of the hunting line, another covey was flushed and Cheney swung on a bird and fired, striking Whittington in the face, neck and chest."

Whittington unwittingly gained national fame because of the incident, especially when he issued a public apology to the vice president after recovering from his wounds at a Corpus Christi hospital. "My family and I are deeply sorry for everything Vice President Cheney and his family have had to deal with," Whittington stated on February 17. "We hope that he will continue to come to Texas and seek the relaxation that he deserves."

A few months later, what was left of 304 East Fifth was razed. A nineteen-story Westin Hotel rose in its place in 2015. Although the hotel paid homage to Austin's musical legacy with related decor and a meeting room named after Willie Nelson, it wasn't adequately soundproofed, which meant guests on the hotel's north side were kept up until two a.m. by the incessant low-end thumping of a Sixth Street nightclub called Nook. The hotel owners filed a nuisance lawsuit against the club, but the two parties ultimately settled out of court in 2017, with the hotel agreeing to pay for a sound mitigation system at the club.[3]

As for Sweatbox, Vasquez moved the studio to East Austin, where he operated for another six years. In 2012 he closed Sweatbox and moved to Oregon to work on wind turbines. After two decades of operation, Vasquez estimated the studio had recorded about two thousand bands.[4] What follows are just a few of the stories from the many sessions that took place there.

Mike Vasquez: I moved here in 1989 with a band called the Dorks from New Hampshire. We had a dirt-cheap rehearsal space that was right downtown. Hundred and ten dollars a month. Every time it rained, the floor would be filled with eight inches of water. So finally the band broke up and I inherited the space and they fixed the roof and I was like, "Man, I can record bands here!" But the main reason I wanted to do it is because I went to another studio that was here, and I paid $600 for eight hours. He charged us so much money for three songs, and he erased our favorite song by accident, and I was like, "Man, I'm going to record bands myself." I just started buying equipment and trying to teach myself.

Michelle Rule: It kind of seemed like you were going into a rundown office building. It was old tile with a long hallway. Everything else in Austin seemed fancier. So yeah, that was definitely gritty.

Mike Vasquez: I started charging $12.50 an hour, and a lot of bands would help me learn. The Cherubs taught me a ton. They were one of the first bands that really showed me how to make things sound better. First I had an 8-track half-inch. And then ADATs came out. I bought those. They were really expensive. It was really stupid. I should have just stayed analog. But we made some good records with those things. The Cherubs' *Heroin Man* record was one of them.

Brent Prager: That was just the best experience ever. They were a new studio, and they were very open to the idea of letting us max out the sound board to the point where some damage could occur, and this was their only sound board. We were just really grateful because nobody else wanted to let us do that. We had asked around a little bit and they were like, "No! Fuck no, why would we do that?" So that was cool. The people had a relaxed attitude. It's like Cavity was to hangout, Sweatbox was to record.

Owen McMahon: We distorted the ADATs. That's what gave *Heroin Man* a real fuckin' gnarly sound—digital distortion. It's not the most pleasant thing to most ears, but that's what made it work.[5]

Mike Vasquez: Tons of awesome records—the El Flaco records—were done on the ADATs. It sounded good. Digital was a brand-new thing and you could get more channels, and the tape was like a VHS tape. Analog tape was pretty expensive, and nobody had money so it was all a matter of trying to do it in a way that bands could afford.

Bryan Nelson: I'd heard a Gut record that was recorded by Paul (Stautinger) at Sweatbox on the ADATs. It sounded awesome and that's how we wanted to sound. We loved Nomeansno and wanted that kind of harder raw sound. I started playing bass with Mike in his band Sisterunaked, and then he kind of tricked me into working at the studio.

I was interested in learning because I'm a musician and I wanted to know how to make good sounds. I didn't want to just trust the person behind the curtain. I had all this free time because I'd knocked some teeth out skateboarding so I couldn't work, and I was on painkillers. Mike talked me into running a four-track. I rented a four-track from Rock 'n' Roll Rentals and just sat there for a month and mastered it. I can do tons of shit on a four-track and it's awesome. And—basically—if you can do this on a four-track, you can do any of this stuff. I mean, it's the same signal path.

Mike Vasquez: I remember Tim Kerr wanted to bring in his band Jack O'Fire, and he kept telling me to listen to Billy Childish to get ready for it. I think he liked the whole feel of the studio, and so he started bringing in other bands and producing.

Bryan Nelson: Tim started recording more and more bands at the studio. Then he got in really well with Estrus producing records, so bands would be on tour and come down and record. They would come in and do a single or something in the middle of their tour.

Mike Vasquez: Tim's great because he takes the role of helping the bands put their songs together and really kind of changes tempos and changes parts and comes up with cool ideas. He has things in his mind that he wants to translate to their music—his own ideas. And he can do that because a lot of bands really respect him.

Tim Kerr: I started recording bands kind of in the late '80s, but then it really got going during the '90s. At one point I literally could've stopped working and just done this for a living, but I never ever wanted to be in a position where money was going to dictate something with any kind of self-expression. I basically told bands, "You pay me with whatever you can afford."

Lisa Rickenberg: The Inhalants' first single was recorded at Lone Star Studios, where I interned. I wanted to learn engineering, but mostly it was just sitting there answering phones. But they gave us some free studio time, so we recorded that. Glorium recorded their second single there, too. It's where Woof Gang Bakery is now—on Lamar just up the street from Waterloo. It's a little building on the corner, and it was apparently designed by the same guy that built Electric Ladyland. It was super nice. You could clap your hands in the middle of the room, and you wouldn't hear any echo. It was the worst possible place to record a garage rock single. It was completely sterile sounding, but it was free. Austin had a number of really nice recording studios at the time, but they were prohibitively expensive for, you know, crappy punk bands.

Tim Kerr: The [Sweatbox] room was actually really great because Mike built stuff. It was this wooden room, and it just had a real good sound in it to begin with. And it was more community and family. It was just as important as anybody's high-falutin' $25,000 for two hours. It was just as good as that. And everybody at that time was a lot more open to just "Let's try this, let's try this . . ." And I'm one of those people where the community and friendship and all that stuff is a whole lot more important to me than anything else.

Lisa Rickenberg: Sweatbox was great because suddenly there was this recording studio where it was a really low hourly rate. They wouldn't try and polish things up too much, and it sounded really raw and you didn't have to stress out about how much time it was taking you because it wasn't costing you that much money.

Tim Kerr: I don't use headphones. It's the way they used to record all those bands in the '60s. To me, the music is a musical conversation with people and the friends you made this band with. I don't care how many times you've been in that studio, it's completely different when you put those headphones on. Take those headphones off! It'll come out through the music. And if you can get that, the rest of it is easy. We just learned how to baffle and turn things. If you figure out how to turn things, you don't get much bleed at all on the overheads on the drums.

The other thing that's really funny is a lot of people will try to get everything as clean as possible, and then they put reverb in and make it sound like you're in the room. What the hell? You didn't even have to do any of that. You could have used the room, too.

Scott Gardner: Tim kind of dabbled in a bit of lo-fi I guess. A lot of bands back then were actually intentionally going for lo-fi. It wasn't because they didn't have the right equipment, but they actually were trying to get a lo-fi sound.

Tim Kerr: We've done everything from the Basement to Joe Nicolo, Joe the Butcher, who did Will Smith and Schooly D and all that kind of stuff. So I've just learned through osmosis. But I also learned a lot from Spot. I liked being around him all the time. I really learned the whole idea of "It doesn't matter what's on that board. What matters is what's coming out of that amp or coming out of the voice." Put that microphone in a certain place and find that spot where it sounds the best, where the person playing is real happy with it. You don't need all these bells and whistles after that.

Mike Vasquez: Spot asked me to record his solo record, which was a high point for me. He's my hero of recording guys. He did all my favorite bands, so that was pretty intense, and it was really awesome. It was half–banjo record and half–Jethro Tull. He's an amazing musician.

Tim Kerr: My favorite band that I've ever been part of in the '90s is Lord High Fixers. That changed every single one of us that was in that band and changed all the people that were close to that band. It's fairly corny to talk about because bands say this kind of stuff all the time, but we didn't know where Mike [Carroll][6] was when the whole Monkeywrench thing first happened. He could have been dead with all that had been going on.

And so when Mike came back, it was like getting a second chance with somebody that you thought you lost. So with that in mind it kind of grew because you started realizing this could be the last time the three of us are sitting here. Something could happen easily as soon as you walk out that door, so you better celebrate. You better hug. It just really changed all of our outlooks. We were all older when we were in that band so none of us really cared about anything else other than just the friendship and the fun of it.

Gerry Atric: Me and Ray used to cut the Bulemics demos at Sweatbox. Every two songs we wrote we went straight to the studio and cut demos because that's how it was done back then. And we mailed them on a cassette tape in a fucking white envelope to record labels.

Ray Ject: Sweatbox was awesome, what can I say? The first Bulemics album, we got kicked out of there by Mike Mariconda because we were too drunk.

Gerry Atric: The first Bulemics album actually sold six thousand copies. This is before downloads. And one thing I can say about that album—it was the last album of the '90s recorded in the Red River scene. It really was. *Old Enough to Know Better* was the last full-length album recorded by any of these fucking old-school bands. But you had to *buy* it. You couldn't fucking download it. You had to know someone or you had to blow someone. Your average dipshit off the street with a studded leather jacket and a fucking Hot Topic fucking haircut could not just say, "Oh yeah, I downloaded that from my fucking butthole and plugged the fucking bullshit into my ear and I know the words."

Bryan Nelson: I engineered a record for the Bulemics where Mike Mariconda was producer. He produced a couple of their records, and it totally got rejected by the record label because it was so gnarly. We used the worst mics we could find. We kind of did what the Cherubs did times ten so you couldn't even barely understand anything. But then the producer was taking it to another level.

Gerry Atric: We finally found three record labels that wanted to sign us at the same time. It was Junk Records, Man's Ruin, and TSB Records. It was a bidding war.

Rob Patterson: The studio was recording these little Austin bands for labels like Rise and Unclean.

Michelle Rule: "When the Well Runs Dry" was recorded at Sweatbox [with] Mike Vasquez and Rick Carney. David Yow was there that day. One of our heroes!

Rob Patterson: Eventually it grew to be this national garage band/punk band mecca by recording all these very cool bands out of Austin. Vasquez knew how to build a community, capture music, and build a great room for people to play in.

Tim Kerr: When I was recording all those bands in the '90s, I was constantly trying to get people to put "guidance counselor." Don't put "producer." Just put "guidance counselor." I may feel strong about something, but the bottom line is I'm working for you, so you get final say because I'm working for you guys.

Lisa Rickenberg: I met Tim at Sound Exchange when I was working there. He took a real interest in us and helped us a lot in the promotional realm. He almost always engineered or produced our singles and got us hooked up with Estrus. Because he recorded us, Dave Crider was like, "I'll check them out."

Graham Williams: Tim is interesting because he's such a young-at-heart person. He's like, "This is *your* scene!" Big Boys had that tagline, "Now go start your own band." He truly believes that philosophy. He's an artist and it's no different. I don't think playing guitar or bass or producing bands is any different than making paintings and murals on the side of buildings.

Johnny Motard: Tim was great to us, man. Tim helped us out a lot, dude. To be walking off stage at your first real show and have Tim Kerr shake your hand and tell you you're doing a good job—that's some pretty heavy shit. I grew up a suburban punk kid in the fucking '80s. I listened to the Big Boys. Poison 13—that's the fucking shit.

We put out that little tape with the three songs on it that ended up being our first single. We just went to the 99 Cent store. You could buy ten tapes for a buck, and the things would play once and then fucking fall apart. We made a million of these little fucking demos and we gave them out at shows. Lisa Rickenberg from Inhalants took a liking to it. She was hanging out with Tim Kerr, and he was teaching her studio stuff. She played him the tape. He was having a big New Year's Eve show at Emo's, which was really our first show. New Year's Eve with the Makers, and the Mono Men, Jack O'Fire, and a bunch of bands. Got on stage, did our thing, the crowd fucking went crazy! I don't know why, because we couldn't play.

We basically learned how to play in front of this town, man. When we started playing shows, we had no idea what we were doing. None of us had ever been in a band before. We walked off the stage and Tim Kerr's standing there with that big, goofy-ass grin on his face, like, "You guys were great!" A week later we got a call from him, and I think he actually paid for us to go in the studio and record everything we knew, which didn't end up being our first album. We took two songs from that and put out a split with the Cryin' Out Louds. He paid for it and everything.

Mike Vasquez: Things were starting to get pretty busy. A handful of clubs were opening up. There was the Cavity, Blue Flamingo, Flamingo Cantina, Emo's. There were at least four clubs that you could play in easily. There were tons of good bands popping up, and it was starting to get really exciting. The Green Room was downstairs from Sweatbox.

Bryan Nelson: They have the same owner. Same landlord.

Mike Vasquez: Our landlord was the dude that Dick Cheney shot.

Bryan Nelson: Harry Whittington . . . His building burned on January 6, 2006. It was wounded during that first fire. And then the second fire was February 4, 2006. It was insane.

Mike Vasquez: It took out the whole block.

Bryan Nelson: He had a nightclub that was next door. That's where the fire started. And then a week after that second fire is when he got shot in the face by Dick Cheney. The first fire happened, and the fire department came and kicked every door in, smashed all the windows and everything got hosed.

Mike Vasquez: But after the first little fire, I had a big session coming in, so I pulled most of my equipment out of there. But after the second big fire, we had to sneak in at night through the ceiling. We had to dig through it to pull out tapes and microphone stuff. It was kind of crazy.

Bryan Nelson: Yeah, there was that month between fires. We could only get in there at certain times during the day, and there was no electricity and we had to kind of lock it up as best as we could.

Mike Vasquez: The whole thing was ready to collapse. In fact, the whole front façade on the corner fell out into the street and trashed three cars.

Bryan Nelson: Yeah, that was awesome.

TV AND VIDEO

RAW MEAT IN THE STUDIO

ONE OF THE MORE PROLIFIC UPSETS IN Austin Music Awards history took place in 1995, when *CapZeyeZ* topped perennial PBS favorite *Austin City Limits* to win the award for Best TV Show.

While *ACL* was—and remains—Austin's most significant televisual export, it had almost nothing to do with the local bloom of underground rock music in the '90s. Fastball was the only band even peripherally associated with that bloom to appear on *ACL* during the '90s, and that was only after the trio had a platinum-selling album. For the musical denizens of clubs like Emo's and the Blue Flamingo, *ACL* might as well have been produced in Idaho.

Over on MTV, the closest '90s equivalent to 1985's Austin music episode of *The Cutting Edge* was the 1997 premiere of *Austin Stories*. Local comedians Laura House, Howard Kremer, Brad "Chip" Pope, and Johnny Hardwick pitched the initial concept for the low-budget sitcom in 1994.[1] By the time MTV's programming brass got back to them in 1996, Hardwick had been tapped by sometime-Austinite Mike Judge to star in *King of the Hill* as the voice of Dale Gribble.

Borrowing thematic elements from *Slacker* and subsequent '90s quarter-life crisis films like *Reality Bites*, House, Kremer, and Pope starred as three young adults tooling about town in various stages of comedic inertia and irresponsibility. Because the show was set in Austin, music wove its way into the narrative. Scenes were shot at Sound Exchange, and Sixteen Deluxe performed the theme song.

Despite receiving mostly positive national notice, *Austin Stories* got a mixed reception in town that paralleled the underground music scene's reflexive tendency to regard commercial success with suspicion. Some flagged dramatic liberties such as making the fictional alt-weekly where House's character worked much more button-down than the real-life *Austin Chronicle*, while others groused that spotlighting Austin on MTV would further diminish the city's way of life.

As it was, the show never had a chance to find its legs. MTV scheduled it erratically and promoted it poorly. *Austin Stories* was canceled after thirteen episodes, but not before establishing the town-centric template that would be utilized to more popular effect by Fred Armisen and Carrie Brownstein for *Portlandia* in 2011.

With smartphone cameras, inexpensive video editing applications, and streaming video still years away, producing and distributing music videos was a tall order in the '90s. Even so, some Austin bands managed to make music videos through a wily combination of anemic independent label budgets, a large body of potential volunteers willing to work for experience, and friend-of-a-friend access to production facilities.

Trance Syndicate was the rare local label that packaged and sold a VHS tape of its music videos. *Love and Napalm: The Video* (1992) featured clips from Crust, Ed Hall, Drain, and Pain Teens that visually reflected the label's high weirdness aesthetic. A few years later, a small cadre of Austin directors that included Heyd Fontenot, Kerthy Fix, Matthew Richardson, Walton Rowell, and John Spath formed The Administration. This loose production collective made music videos for several local underground acts, including Texas Instruments, Dumptruck, Olive, and Sixteen Deluxe.

Aside from its intriguing allusions to Vaseline-coated kink and violence, Fontenot's 1995 video for Sincola's "Bitch" pegged the hometown-interest angle with cameos from fellow scenesters like Darcee Douglas (Power Snatch), Dotty Farrell (Swine King), and Bill Jeffery (Stretford). Richardson's 1995 video for Starfish's "Runaround" captured the shambolic vibe of the city's musical subculture by juxtaposing black-and-white footage of a woman swimming in a Hill Country creek with color scenes of the band playing in a cramped practice space festooned with Christmas lights, Kiss posters, and an Elvis tapestry.

Directors Scott Calonico and Rob Timbrook squeezed an impressive amount of attitude out of 1998's *The Collegians Are Go!* The short film functioned as a long-form music video for local garage punk combo the Collegians and their archrival band, Los Tigres Guapos. Utilizing grainy black-and-white film, appropriated footage of Dallas's Dealey Plaza, and cooked spaghetti for innards, the duo posited the Collegians as academic rock-'n'-roll superheroes who vanquish a George Romero–inspired zombie John F. Kennedy. Despite its nonexistent budget, *The Collegians Are Go!* rivals the Butthole Surfers' 1996 video for "Pepper" in shlock value—even with the latter's cameo from *CHiPs* star Erik Estrada.

For bands without a proper music video, the most likely avenue for video exposure was public access television. Austin made the most of the public access requirements imposed on the city's cable television franchise. You never knew what you would find when scrolling past Austin Cablevision channel 10, which was founded in 1973 and remains the oldest continually operating public access channel in the United States. Before his conspiratorial bromides found a national audience, Alex Jones was just another strange public access TV show host in Austin.

Lighter fare included Carmen Banana, a Carmen Miranda–inspired drag queen who proffered an entertaining mix of cooking and safer sex tips. Finely sequined bleach-blonde Jordan Thomas warbled stream-of-consciousness songs to Casio synthesizer arrangements as family members dressed like Elvis wandered in and out of incongruent green-screen backgrounds of the Golden Gate Bridge and Wembley Stadium. In the days before YouTube, Charlie Sotelo's *The Show with No Name* (1995–2005) was the only way non-tape traders could see things like Todd Haynes's *Superstar: The Karen Carpenter Story* or John Heyn and Jeff Krulik's *Heavy Metal Parking Lot.*

A number of public access producers focused on music. Tim Hamblin and Hank Sinatra were two of the most prominent. Hamblin's *Vidiot's Choice* started in 1982. He also directed a raucous video for the Big Boys' "Fun, Fun, Fun" and a hilarious one for El BJ's "Gomer Pyle Is God."

In 1991 Scott Spurlock's *Dull-A-Vision* interspersed music videos with footage of sexual congress and suicide, prompting protest and city scrutiny of public access operations. Then there was *CapZeyeZ*, the show that made producer Dave Prewitt—who went from doing single-camera shoots at clubs with suboptimal straight mic sound to multicamera video productions under Sinatra's tutelage—the unsung hero of '90s Austin music.

Every Saturday at midnight following a viewer discretion disclaimer, Prewitt and his crew of volunteers would broadcast in-studio performances live and uncensored over Austin cable channel 10. When he wasn't doing *CapZeyeZ* or its companion show *rAw TiMe* at the public access studios on Northwestern Avenue in East Austin, you might also see Prewitt schlepping video equipment in and out of nightclubs to tape live shows. *CapZeyeZ* ran

CapZeyeZ crew at Austin Access Television, 1998 (*left to right*): Dianne Whitehair, Leg, Dean Truitt, Dave Prewitt, James Laljer, Bambi Saunders. © John Anderson/*The Austin Chronicle*. Courtesy of John Jack Anderson.

from 1990 to 2007 and featured all types of music during that time, but Prewitt tended to focus on metal bands from the Back Room and freak rock acts like Squat Thrust, ST 37, the Pocket FishRmen, and Crust. Prewitt also conducted the last televised interview with comedian Bill Hicks in 1993.

After the bands played, a cohost would interview the bands, and callers could dial up the studio to insult them with fusillades of profanity since FCC indecency rules held no sway over public access TV. Then Prewitt would play videos into the wee hours of the morning. Over the years *CapZeyeZ* amassed a definitive archive of '90s Austin bands in action, many of whom would have otherwise only been videotaped by a friend holding a camcorder with

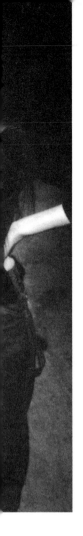

a low-quality microphone. While chin-scratchers debated the health of the scene, the *CapZeyeZ* crew materially supported it week after week.

On August 29, 1991, Austin's city council approved a resolution declaring the city "The Live Music Capital of the World." Beyond adding that tagline to convention and visitors' bureau marketing materials and "Welcome to Austin" signage at the airport, what additional role or responsibility this conferred upon city government wasn't immediately clear. For many musicians, the declaration rang hollow if you were getting ticketed for being double-parked while loading in for a gig downtown or cited for putting up flyers on the Drag.

A few years prior to this declaration, Hamblin and Sinatra began lobbying to have a future public access channel dedicated to promoting local and independent music. During the 1988 edition of South By Southwest, Hamblin helmed a de facto proof-of-concept effort by airing a four-day SXSW video festival of music programming on an existing public access channel.

"The South By Southwest video festival jelled a lot of the music video community here and brought a lot of regional and national prominence both from record companies and from other producers and we now have the potential of developing that into a major video festival that can be internationally known," Hamblin said at a 1989 Austin Community Television news conference announcing a feasibility study for an all-music access channel.[2]

At the same news conference, Sinatra—who had videotaped over 180 musical artists in the past year alone—said he thought an ACTV-run music channel would be in "real good shape" with $500,000.[3] It took a few years, but the city council ultimately recognized the channel as an opportunity to back up its slogan with an actual deed. They appropriated $200,000 in franchise fees paid to the city by the cable company to jumpstart the channel. While Sinatra had warned against making the channel a commercial venture, the council envisioned its investment as seed money for a channel that would ultimately be self-sustaining.

The one-of-its-kind Austin Music Network launched on April 1, 1994, with a four-hour block of programming that preempted Country Music Television, leading to many angry phone calls from country music fans wondering where their Wynonna Judd videos went. AMN soon moved to its own dedicated channel and began broadcasting a twenty-four-hour schedule.

Though the concept of a TV channel solely dedicated to local music was audacious, its execution was botched out of the gate. When the city's initial contract award went awry, AMN was instead launched as a department within the city itself. As a result of this course change, manager Ronny Mack had just forty-five days to hire staff and put the channel on the air. He quickly tapped Kent Benjamin—an *Austin Chronicle*/SXSW veteran whose personal music video collection rivaled modern-day YouTube—as program director. Although they could share production equipment with the greater pool of public access producers, AMN only had one dedicated camera. The channel's video editing system ran on Amiga, a non-PC/non-Mac operating system that lacked compatibility, spare parts, and extant support.[4]

Moreover, AMN's standing as a city entity made showcasing controversial genres like rap, punk, and metal a more dicey proposition. A lilting acoustic number from Tish Hinojosa was less likely to prompt an angry constituent call to the city council than, say, the FuckEmos' 1996 video for "Barf Baby." While Prewitt worked for AMN, he wisely kept *CapZeyeZ* and *rAw TiMe* on the regular public access channel to avoid just such a scenario.

If you look back at the AMN footage that the Austin History Center has archived, much of it is done with a single camera, suboptimal lighting, and no real direction to speak of. For every engaging episode of *Check This Action!*, the weekly music news and show preview program cohosted by Margaret Moser and Tara Veneruso, there were hours of cheap-to-produce footage of pedestrian singer-songwriter festival performances that would be rerun interminably. Unlike MTV, there was nothing slick about AMN, but the same could be said of Austin itself in the 1990s.

Throughout its history, city council support for AMN was tenuous at best. Its line item in the budget was conspicuous enough to get tagged as a boondoggle yet inadequate to meet the production demands for a twenty-four-hour channel. Plans for AMN to generate revenue via third-party productions never materialized because the channel would've needed to divert scarce resources that were necessary just to stay on the air, not to mention the thicket of rules and regulations related to a city government entity doing for-profit business.

In 1998 the city council voted to contract out AMN's operations to Rick Melchior's Music Management Company. Ads began appearing on the channel, but the new model never came close to meeting revenue projections. In 2000 the council turned over the AMN contract to Threadgill's owner Eddie Wilson. Two years later the city council had written AMN out of the budget and the channel was set to shut down when city manager Toby Futrell identified couch-cushion money from hotel bed tax revenue to keep the channel alive on a drastically pared-down budget. SXSW cofounder and former director Louis Meyers took over AMN and tried to turn things around to no avail.

With the combined legacies of the Armadillo World Headquarters and

SXSW failing to make AMN thrive, the channel left the air in 2005. As for Prewitt, he continued producing music on public access until 2019 and can still be found shooting live performances of local bands for his *rAwTiMe* YouTube channel in 2023.

"You either go to shows or you stay home," he says. "The music is always there."

Tim Hamblin: When I was involved with Louis Meyers, Roland Swenson, and Louis Black, we went to the New Music Seminar to promote Austin music. Then the New Music Seminar guys decided they were going to do a version in Austin. But a few months before it happened, they changed their mind. So Nick Barbaro and Louis Black all went, "What the hell, let's us do it!" So they did it in 1987.

I taped the Huey P. Meaux keynote address on a black-and-white camera. And after the first one, Louis Black said to me, "What did you think?" I said I thought it was great, but where was the video?

Louis said, "Well, you can do something." So Ronny Mack, Hank Sinatra, and I got all the people who were doing music video stuff together. We had about twenty-seven hours of music on video. At that time, Channel 33 was a showcase channel. I booked this big chunk for that, and they said, "That was great! Why can't we have that all the time?"

Dave Prewitt: I picked up cable access in Austin on channels 10 and 33. There was a show called *Rockline* where they were all very sprayed hair and tight pants. Very cheesy. But that's what I had to watch for local music entertainment because things like MTV and *USA Night Flight* were just a little too commercial.

Tim Hamblin: I was on the board of ACTV and said, "Why can't we have one channel that has just music on it?" And let's program it so that on Sundays let's put some gospel on. You know? Let's put metal and rap on after midnight so the good God-fearing country folk don't freak out.

Buckner Cooke: Ronny Mack, Kent Benjamin, Hank Sinatra, and Tim were the leaders of the charge in getting Austin Music Network off the ground.

Tim Hamblin: Ronny Mack and I lobbied the city council, and I was amazed we got this contract! I donated most of my library and already had relationships with all the record companies. Ronny took over as manager and it became a city department. I was artistic director, Ingrid Weigand was production. Kent Benjamin, who sadly passed away, was great at programming. An encyclopedia of all types of music.

Dave Prewitt: Austin being what Austin is, created the Austin Music Network. If we're the Live Music Capital of the World, where else are you going to have a TV channel devoted to music? That was a big passion piece for me in the beginning. I had to be part of it. I remember April 1, 1994, hitting "play" on the tape and switching it on the bar. And we were live.

Tim Hamblin: So we start and we get a four-hour slot on CMT—a twenty-four-hour national country station. We would start off with Billy Joe Shaver and Flatlanders—that kind of singer-songwriter stuff. We'd play W. C. Clark and people would leave messages on the request line, "We don't want to hear none of that n***** music! We want country!"

Buckner Cooke: Going from four to twenty-four hours, you don't really have a plan.

Tim Hamblin: I was desperate to make this all work. I was working through the night, watching every video that had come out. That was a hell of a thing. Sometimes the cleaner would come in and I would be sleeping on the floor, and she thought I was dead. And on top of all that, the people wanted live shows filmed.

Dave Prewitt: We'd always try to get the key good gigs in advance. At access, the biggest part of getting the gear that was cool was being advised so we could reserve it early. So we'd plan it. I'd get my camera people all in file and it would be like, alright, we're going to do this thing! I'd have a truck or a van or a station wagon, and I'd have a couple of grunt workers come with me. We'd load these iron cases that were made of lead, it felt like.

Buckner Cooke: The thing is, the lighting for a club for the audience is completely different than what you need to have for a video television presentation. We couldn't go into Antone's or any club and really change the lighting grid to better serve our purpose. We were really just lucky to be in the room. In most clubs, the red light becomes saturated, and it didn't look good.

Dave Prewitt: You had your cables on a clean floor, and you'd roll these cables out across the floor with anticipation that maybe people would respect and see what you were doing. Then you'd come back at the end of the night and [makes slimy noises]. Oh man! You'd pry it off of the stuck floor with the drinks spilled all over it. I remember two a.m. closing time, I couldn't wait because I knew we'd have to stand with the rag and pull the cords through and then wipe the [cables] clean.

Buckner Cooke: Dave can go up to the manager of Steamboat, Danny Crooks, and say, "Hey, can we change this light and this and bring this up here?" Dave got to do that because he had known these people for years. He was a fan. He did everything he could to promote the clubs and as many local bands as he could. There was a respect for that that came out of the musicians and the clubs.

Dave Prewitt: Lots of work went into it. Again, all free. Maybe I'm crazy, but none of us really were too concerned with that. Of course, if you had the opportunity to drink for free or maybe take home a twenty on some special gig from a club that got a sponsorship that night, that might happen once in a blue moon. But really it was all about that passion. And we worked our butts off.

Frenchie Smith: We happened at a time right before you could have all these digital archives of our existence. It was all kind of analog. You went to the record store. You went to the show. If you videoed us, you were Dave from *Dave TV*.

Buckner Cooke: *CapZeyeZ* and *rAw TiMe* definitely played a major role in the scene because you had a place to promote your music video, and it didn't have to go to MTV or VH1.

Dave Prewitt: Anybody could do the access programming. I always had a camcorder or something to document my live-music experiences beyond seeing a band. At two [a.m.], the bars close, so you're going to go home to drink. Do you want to watch infomercials, or do you want to see some more music and keep the party rolling? So I said if I'm going to do a live show, it's going to be in the heart of the time people are going to care about seeing it. Porcelain Grind was the first band. They brought in the amps, we put a couple of mics in the room, they played live in the studio, and all of a sudden, I'm a venue.

Richard Whymark: We would arrive at the studio to set up just as Alex Jones was finishing his weekly show. He was exhausted from all his ranting about the Branch Davidians and Waco and the ATF. *CapZeyeZ* had a live band play for an hour and then take abuse from the audience on the telephone—with no delay. If it wasn't Dave hosting it, it might have been Dean [Truitt, Seed guitarist], or Bambi Saunders—who is Rebecca Cannon's cousin—taking abuse from people who were getting home from the bars. You could hear them firing up their bong in the background.

Susan Shepard: The public access documentation is really amazing. It's really astounding that there was that level of television presence for all those bands. I was in high school and these bands were on TV. That was awesome. I mean, where are you going to find those kinds of bands on TV anywhere?

Dave Prewitt: I remember Squat Thrust playing on the show. My good buddy Wade [Longenberger]—rest in peace, man—he would always play his Fender Tallywacker—his bass shaped like a penis painted pink and have a section of raw meat hanging from the top. And as good as we cleaned up, I guess we didn't clean up all of it, and I got a call on Sunday morning from the church program that came in after *CapZeyeZ* on Sunday morning. And they were really wondering why there was raw meat in the studio.

Russell Porter: Dave would let anybody play on the show. It was great. I made them so mad when we played on there, but it was beautiful. They don't want you to smoke in there so of course I was turning around and smoking, and they would come and grab my cigarette away. It was really funny. They forgave me and figured it was a *rock moment.*

Dave Prewitt: Crust—one of the amazing Trance Syndicate bands from the 1990s. The Reverend[5] came in dressed in Scotch tape and a couple of ladies' garments covering particular areas. Well, even though we're on access, we can't show certain things. Especially when they're erect. And if you're the Reverend, why would you be anything else? He was beaten with roses until he was bleeding. He had the entrails of some animal pulled from a stuffed doll that looked like the girl that was dancing in the studio. People will never forget that.

Fawn Li: I was on the TV a lot and people would stop me and say, "Where do I know you from?" And I'd say, "Sometimes I'm on the TV." But really what it was is I found people who were of my tribe. I was finally safe.

Dave Prewitt: Then we had *Austin City Limits*, which was the next level up and a major thing and has become even more indifferent than it ever was with the festivals. It was a TV show I never considered competition, but I look in the *Chronicle* early on in doing my show and right there, I'm number five and they're number one. So I keep telling people to vote next time.

Then next year, I'm third. *Austin City Limits* walk out on stage at the awards show and say, "Thanks a lot for this award. I know there's not a lot of other competition, but we come first every year and get this award and thank you so much."

So, yeah, man, the next year—twentieth anniversary of *ACL*—*CapZeyeZ* took that award. That was a proud moment for me. I'll never forget that. We go from having fun, chilling out and going to see bands, to walking out onstage at the *Chronicle* awards and beating *Austin City Limits* for Best Music TV show. And then taking home a *Billboard* magazine award two years in a row for *rAw TiMe*.

Ed Hamell: I would always make sure I did Dave's show at SXSW so the industry people would see it and say, "I saw you last night!" It was a huge help.

Dave Prewitt: I always refused to do *CapZeyeZ* on the Austin Music Network. It was nice to be able to flip through your local TV channels and see something different. That doesn't mean you liked it, but you had to look. AMN was like driving by an accident, but it never went beyond being another access channel.

Buckner Cooke: Austin Music Network was at a point where they didn't know if they were going to continue. There were certain people in the community—and certain people on the council—that didn't see the value of what they were getting for the $200,000. This was the last gasp. They're going to kill it off or they're going to give it to a private entity.

Dave Prewitt: Every time I've seen anyone talk about it from the city council, it's kind of like they had to. I'm supporting this 'cause I don't want to look like a jerk. No one's ever gotten behind it. They kind of have done what they had to do to keep it from looking negative in the press.

Tim Hamblin: Some of the music commission didn't like it because they wanted to see, they wanted it to be like *Austin City Limits* and it's like, you know, *Austin City Limits* could do four shows for what we got for a year.

Buckner Cooke: In kind of retaliation for his ill feelings about how the whole thing was going, Tim started the live noon show *Reality* and tapped me to be the director. Tim and Darcie Fromholz hosted.

Darcie Fromholz: The great irony about it is we were in the basement of the city council.

Tim Hamblin: If we fucked up, we fucked up. And I fucked up plenty of times. But Darcie was great.

Darcie Fromholz: That was one of the many times that the Austin Music Network was on the ropes. I don't think it was ever off the ropes. Our backdrop was basically a chain-link cage that the tapes were stored in. It was very grungy and very DIY. Tim has always been a bit of an anarchist, and it just came from this very genteel rage.

Buckner Cooke: Darcie gave it credibility. She not only had a family name[6] but had been involved in the Austin Music Awards and was part of the scene. And we did have some spectacular moments on that show.

Tim Hamblin: When we had Darcie's dad on the show, he sang "Dear Darcie." That was obviously dedicated to her, and I was in tears. It was beautiful.

Darcie Fromholz: You could just see not just the love but the affection and the genuine pleasure that we took in each other's company and that's what came away from that show.

Richard Whymark: Then, before the city sold the network, Buckner and I did another live show, on Friday evenings—*Live & Interactive*.

Buckner Cooke: Part of the impetus was having a call-in show to gauge whether or not we really have an audience. Are we just throwing money away and taking up space on this channel?

Richard Whymark: I asked Andy Langer to host. I felt he would be good on camera. He will deny this until his dying day, but I was the first person to put him on television.

Andy Langer: I'd been on Prewitt's various shows, even an MTV *Week in Rock* segment, but never as a regular host.

Buckner Cooke: Andy showed up and said, "This is a one off. I'm never doing this again." And then he beat up Morningwood—which is another great sentence—live on the air. After the show was over, he was like, "Same time next week?"

Andy Langer: I remember for a lot of the run I was toying with what I guess was the really amateur equivalent of roast interviewing.

Buckner Cooke: I don't remember specifics, but he was just rude. He was very rude, and they openly were talking at breaks about leaving and then started muttering about it on the air. I think Rebecca Cannon was the next week's guest, and Andy was kind of pulling the same thing with her, and I remember her famously saying, "Well, now I know why Morningwood almost walked off."

Richard Whymark: Andy got into it in a good way. Because of his contacts, he was able to bring on bands that were far more famous than anyone Buckner or I knew. We knew the local bands. We knew Rebecca Cannon, and we knew Morningwood. But he brought Goodie Mob, for instance.

Buckner Cooke: He would be a little confrontational. We have Alejandro Escovedo on the show, and Andy's like, "So you're on tour now and you're selling albums. Oh wait, you don't sell albums do you?"

Buckner Cooke: Jon Dee Graham, Alejandro, Wammo—those shows were like watching a street fight.

Andy Langer: Alejandro famously fought back, either calling me "Chevy" [Chase] or "Magic" [Johnson] or both throughout the interview, referencing bad and short-lived hosts.

Richard Whymark: I asked Paula Nelson—Willie's daughter—to come and cohost and kind of rein him in a bit.

Andy Langer: Paula was a guest initially, and then I had to leave town on a couple of occasions and left it with her because she had great dad jokes and could hold her own. At some point, we cohosted for a while.

Buckner Cooke: The volume of calls we were getting showed us there were actually people watching.

Tim Hamblin: We got an award from the *Chronicle* for the Best Way to Spend $280,000. Some people thought it was a waste of money, but we always tried to sell it as promotion for the city.

Richard Whymark: It sounds like a lot of money to the layperson, but for video or television production that's the tiniest of drops in a big bucket.

Tim Hamblin: It was disturbing when Rick Melchior came to town and said, "I can do this *and* make money!" I talked to Daryl Slusher[7] and said, "You know, you really need to look into that because he's promising you stuff, and he's not going to be able to come through with it." He convinced the council that if he got that money from the city, he would be giving money back to the city within three years. And then he used *three times* that budget in the first year!

Richard Whymark: Melchior won the contract and moved us from a very low-ceilinged dingy basement under the old city council building on Second Street, to an actual proper television studio.

Nevie Owens: The Seventh Street studio was in a basement downtown. People were running around and doing their thing and there were musicians everywhere, so it had a fun feel to it. It was an indie sort of TV station.

Dave Prewitt: It went from the passion to the budget. And at that point, you can pretty much say the passion part was broke. The Austin Music Network has always been the bastard stepchild of the Austin music scene.

Buckner Cooke: Walking into that studio on Seventh, I was like, "Wow, this is a step up!" And then of course you realize that nothing worked. Over time, it kind of got better but it never really came to fruition. And we would play those stupid McDonald's ads early on.

Richard Whymark: They were an experiment. They weren't being paid to play them. The experiment was if we put on fake commercials, it will look like we have commercials. Therefore, people will want to put commercials on our station. It was good logic. Danny Crooks from Steamboat was a great supporter. He went on record saying that—after he started advertising—he got more people through the door and bigger bar tabs and the bands got more noticed. But no one else really advertised there. What Melchior didn't realize was that no one actually supported Austin music in Austin.

Buckner Cooke: I don't think he counted on that. Being an outsider, he bought into the whole "Austin is the live music capital of the world," and everybody must *love* the music scene.

Richard Whymark: To kick everything off, they did what I thought was quite a good idea, which was the *24-Hour Music Marathon*, where they did have two performance stages in one studio. And they had the best local bands at the time. Don Harvey, who used to run the Austin Rehearsal Complex, programmed most of it.

Buckner Cooke: But it was a complete nightmare technically. I have Spoon playing and I have no communication with anybody, so I'm knocking on the dividing window, "Your camera's live!!"

Richard Whymark: Even though we were under this new privatized regime, we could still play music videos from indie labels or unsigned bands.

Buckner Cooke: You have some fantastic music videos that were produced by local video talent. The bands were so good that the quality of the video could have gotten them on MTV. And actually did several times.

John Spath: Most of us were watching public access television and there was a ton of shows showing videos by bands that we liked. Sonic Youth and Dinosaur Jr. and just any number of cool bands. At some point I realized, that's not just happening in Austin—that's happening at every major little city around the country.

Buckner Cooke: The Administration in the early '90s was cranking out some of the best music videos I had seen. Kerthy Fix and Heyd Fontenot produced Sincola's "Bitch" video.

John Spath: We all had connections to free equipment. A lot of us were working on commercials, and at the end of the day there would be a little leftover film in the mag—a hundred feet, two hundred feet. We started absconding with that, so a lot of our videos were made with hundred-foot spools, which is about two minutes of film. Also, we had a soundstage, so the Sons of Hercules video was shot in there and a lot of the Sixteen Deluxe stuff from "Idea" was shot in there.

Kathy McCarty: "Rocketship" was done by me in Brian Beattie's kitchen. I'd made the record and Bar/None said, "We want some videos." I said, "Can I have some money?" They said, "No."

But then a very lovely thing happened. Clark Walker, who was a cameraman for Rick Linklater, came over with his Super 8 camera. I had made these silvery spacesuits for me and Peter LaFond to wear, and he just got roped into being in it, and I told him, "You're going to play my boyfriend from Planet X."

I had this idea that a giant streetlight bulb looked like a space helmet. I made some little puppets out of socks and made them look like little frogs. A great big piece of black velvet covered in golden stars was space. Brian made a rocket ship out of clay. We tried to be as creative as possible to make it work.

And then I had to edit it, and I didn't have any idea about that. Heyd Fontenot from the Austin Film Society stepped up and said, "I have a card to go down to Austin Access Television. We can just go in there and use their editing bays when they're not around. So we ended up going there late at night, and staying up all night for a couple of days editing it together.

John Spath: In that post-Nirvana period, I guess it felt a little disingenuous for a lot of the punk bands to be making a music video because it looked like they were shooting for a record deal as opposed to staying with the little indies and playing music for the people. So music videos were always sort of weird for a period there.

Darcie Fromholz: Austin music was changing a lot at that point. We'd moved from the Raul's old guard. Red River was starting to come up, and there is a different kind of music being made in Austin. The goal was to find interesting stuff and interesting people, and a lot of these kids had never been on camera. It was fun and fast-paced. It was DIY done with as much professionalism as we could muster.

Nevie Owens: We had a show on AMN—*Breakin' In*. It had live performances and music videos of lesser known indie bands.

Richard Whymark: On *Breakin' In* we went through lots and lots of hosts because the management didn't like anyone we hired. We hired Mark Rubin from the Bad Livers. I thought he was fantastic. Rolee Rios was great. Doe Montoya, too. She was fantastic. Flowed well, knew her music.

Nevie Owens: Melchior found out that I had been directing a few of the *Breakin' In* shows, and so he called me into his office one day. He said that he didn't want me to direct shows anymore because I didn't look like a director. Because I was a woman. And so I gave him my two-weeks' notice right then and there.

Richard Whymark: Many years later, Buckner thought about making a documentary about the history of AMN, but the city quashed it.

Buckner Cooke: Spencer Peeples and I actually got someone who was going to fund it. We went to the Austin History Center, and I talked to Tim Hamblin about this. He was now the city's video archivist. Tim said, "They're not going to let you do it. You can use any of the footage you want, but you cannot say Austin Music Network. And if it has an AMN logo on it, you can't use it." This was not something that the city itself really wanted to talk about. They are embarrassed by the amount of money that was spent, particularly on Rick Melchior's plan.

But the point of the documentary was that this period of time for about fifteen years has been archived. No other city in the United States came close to doing that in terms of documenting their music scene.

Tim Hamblin: It still does kind of irk me that, in the Live Music Capital of the World, we couldn't keep the music network going.

ZINES, FLYERS, AND THE PRESS

PUTTING THE WORD IN THE STREETS

THE 1990S WAS THE LAST DECADE IN which the printed page was the primary channel for promoting, hailing, or criticizing underground music. Not that anyone walking down Guadalupe across from UT in 1994 would've guessed. Utility poles were covered in band flyers for upcoming shows, the daily newspaper launched a simulacrum of an alt-weekly to compete with the city's actual alt-weekly, and the windowsill at Sound Exchange was cluttered with zines.

One of the earliest known music-related activities on what would become the internet began in the early 1970s when artificial intelligence researchers at Stanford and MIT used ARPANET to trade Grateful Dead tapes.[1] By 1990 the internet remained the provenance of early adopters. The World Wide Web was still a year away, and the first commercial provider in the United States offering direct connection to the internet only started serving customers the year before. As late as 1999, only 2,754,286 US homes had fixed broadband connections.[2]

The 1990s promulgation of underground publishing had plenty of local precedent. In 1887 William Sydney Porter—better known as O. Henry—got a government job at the Texas General Land Office. When not drafting maps, he developed characters for short stories. After getting a teller job at First National Bank, he began self-publishing a literary humor magazine called the

Rolling Stone in 1894. It didn't make money, which may be why Porter found himself imprisoned for embezzling from his employer.

About seventy years later, Jack "Jaxon" Jackson went to the Texas State Capitol print shop after hours and ran off about a thousand copies of *God Nose*, now acknowledged as one of the first underground comix. In 1966 editor-activists Thorne Dreyer and Carol Neiman launched *The Rag*, a weekly underground newspaper. *The Rag* covered issues the "straight" press tended to shy away from, including gay liberation and the fight for access to birth control. Staffers came from the ranks of the UT chapter of Students for a Democratic Society. There was no pretense of journalistic objectivity in their coverage of the war in Vietnam or the war on dissent at home.

In 1967 Vulcan Gas Company art director Gilbert Shelton drew a comic promoting a screening of a short film called *The Texas Hippies March on the Capitol*. This was the first appearance of the Fabulous Furry Freak Brothers. By 1968 Shelton's franchise-to-be was a strip in *The Rag* that was ultimately reprinted in other underground newspapers around the country.

For a '60s underground paper, *The Rag* had a long life, finally folding in 1977. A shorter-lived but still influential '70s publication was the *Austin Sun*. Published by former SDS organizer and *Rag* alum Jeff Nightbyrd from 1974 to 1978, the *Sun* was less polemic and more a chronicle of what would come to be known as alternative culture, including an obligatory road trip south to San Antonio to see the Sex Pistols perform at Randy's Rodeo on January 8, 1978.

When the *Sun* folded, three staff—Big Boy Medlin, Ginger Varney, and Michael Ventura—moved to California and became the inaugural core staff of the *L.A. Weekly*. Music writer Margaret Moser stayed and became the first music columnist for the *Austin Chronicle*.

The *Chronicle* was founded in 1981 by Nick Barbaro and Joe Dishner. Editor Louis Black was their first recruit. Dishner exited early in the paper's history to become a successful film producer, leaving Barbaro and Black to cultivate their vision of a paper that covered local culture and politics in ways a traditional daily newspaper couldn't or wouldn't.

Barbaro and Black were both graduates of the *Daily Texan*. Like many of their alt-press forebears, they came into their journalistic roles as active participants rather than arm's-length reporters. Barbaro was one of six people arrested at the debut performance of the Huns at Raul's on September 19, 1978. The show, which drew coverage from as far away as London, ended in a melee when an Austin police officer got onstage to stop the band and singer Phil Tolstead responded by kissing him.

Meanwhile, New Jersey transplant Black helped run CinemaTexas, a film programming unit that screened classic, foreign, and obscure films in the days before home video. Black and others wrote copious program notes on each film shown that were copied and handed out to moviegoers. In the absence of a dedicated revival house like New York's Film Forum, Cinema-Texas became a key link in making Austin a film-friendly town.

Film was also in Barbaro's blood. His mother was Marilyn Buferd, an actress who beat out Cloris Leachman among others to win the 1946 Miss America pageant. He arrived in Austin by way of UCLA in the mid-seventies to attend grad school at UT's Department of Radio Television and Film. Barbaro served as film critic for the *Texan*. As was often the case with *Texan* staffers, the student newspaper work got in the way of his graduation.

"Nick Barbaro and Louis Black were slackers before slackers were cool," opined their *Texan* colleague Mark McKinnon, a folk musician turned journalist turned political adviser who played a key role in getting George W. Bush elected president.[3]

Despite that assessment, Barbaro and Black were running a business. Unlike much of the underground press of the '60s, the paper sought to sustain itself through profit. Because it was free to readers, the *Chronicle* needed advertisers to survive.

The early years of the *Chronicle* were lean. The paper's first office was a climate-challenged loft space above a dry cleaner. Once Buferd's seed money ran out, slow ad sales and cash-flow issues threatened to make every biweekly issue the last. The *Chronicle*'s advertising manager in the early '80s, Ramsey Wiggins, described the environment as "like being on the set of an Andy Hardy movie, only with sex."[4]

The paper started finding its footing when ad reps like Carolyn Phillips, Lois Richwine, and Jerald Corder developed mutually beneficial relationships with businesses that catered to what was emerging as the alternative demographic. Beyond the usual suspects of nightclubs, record stores, and head shops, this might mean a barbecue restaurant serving hormone-free brisket (Ruby's BBQ), a place to buy Doc Martens boots or Manic Panic hairspray in the days before Hot Topic (Atomic City), or a women-owned sex toy store (Forbidden Fruit) operating one step ahead of Texas state laws regulating "obscene devices."[5]

It would be difficult to pinpoint when the *Chronicle* crossed the line from upstart to establishment. Some might say it was when the paper's longtime political reporter Daryl Slusher got elected to city council in 1996. Others might say it was on August 8, 1992, when voters overwhelmingly passed the *Chronicle*-supported Save Our Springs ordinance (drafted in the wake of the June 1990 all-night city council session covered in the first chapter) despite well-funded opposition from real estate and business interests. Then there was the time the *Chronicle* took on beloved Texas supermarket chain H-E-B—and won.

In October 1989 conservative pastor Mark Weaver of the American Family Association got H-E-B to remove the *Chronicle* from their Austin stores. Like most alt-weeklies, the *Chronicle* ran personal ads in its back pages, including those seeking same-sex partners. Weaver deemed this content unacceptable for a family grocery store, and H-E-B—a privately held family company run by Chairman/CEO Charles Butt—initially agreed.

As Weaver publicly celebrated, *Chronicle* readers responded by boycotting H-E-B. Although this often meant shopping at stores that were less convenient or more expensive, enough Austinites took their business elsewhere to make the San Antonio–based grocer reconsider. The *Chronicle* was back in H-E-B by early November.

"A few months after this, the *Chronicle* began to experience unprecedented growth, and advertising became very robust," wrote Black in the paper's fifteenth anniversary issue in September 1996. "There were many reasons for this: the longevity of the paper and ongoing, excellent editorial content, a recovering economy, and increasing internal reorganization and sophistication. The most important aspect was that for a few weeks everyone in Austin was talking about the *Chronicle*, and one of the things they realized was that everyone was reading the paper."[6]

As the *Chronicle* and SXSW grew from speculative grassroots endeavors into thriving businesses, backlash was inevitable. As early as 1988 Ed Hall was setting the contrarian tone by printing "SXSWSUX" T-shirts (which many SXSW staffers could be spotted wearing the following year). Some began referring to the *Chron*/SXSW power base as the "Granola Mafia." The vast majority of blowback was confined to barbs, though there were odd exceptions. Right after SXSW 1991, someone set fire to a stack of newspapers outside the *Chron*/SXSW offices at the corner of West 28th and Nueces, causing considerable damage to the entryway.

On the south shore of Town Lake, the powers that be at the *Austin American-Statesman* were paying a different kind of attention. While the *Statesman* already devoted resources to local arts and entertainment coverage via a solid roster of writers like Don McLeese, their primary vehicle for this coverage in the early 1990s was a traditionally designed weekly pullout called *Onward* that was unlikely to woo alt-weekly advertisers.

In 1994 the *Statesman* decided to shake things up. They brought popular ex-*Chronicle* music columnist Michael Corcoran back to town from Dallas and remade *Onward* as a de facto alt-weekly, complete with free distribution at many of the same restaurants and shops where the *Chronicle* was distributed. If imitation is the sincerest form of flattery, the *Chronicle* brass were surely beaming.

Then there was the name—*XLent*. This attempt to capitalize on the emergence of Generation X through a tortured play on words proved dated and mockable right out of the box. Nevertheless, writers like Corcoran, Marc Fort, and Chris Riemenschneider made the resulting alt-weekly war a fair fight. Few realized they were living through the last heyday of print media.

Even with two alt-weeklies, much of the underground music scene remained under the radar. The *Chronicle* started the '90s by publishing a comprehensive, year-end list of all known local releases. The sheer volume of releases emerging from Austin in the underground rock genre alone soon made this endeavor prohibitive. For acts that couldn't garner ink in the *Chronicle* or *XL*, a bumper crop of fanzines helped pick up the slack.

Though closely associated with 1970s DIY punk, fanzines have even earlier roots in the science fiction subculture of the 1940s. As the "fan" part of the appellation implies, most "zines"—as they were known by the 1990s— were passion products. Unlike the *Chronicle*—let alone the *Statesman*—most weren't intended to generate a profit, and even fewer actually did.

The key factor in the explosion of zine culture in the 1990s was ready access to photocopying machines. After first becoming ubiquitous in offices during the 1960s, self-service Xerox machines began appearing in more publicly accessible spaces like post offices and convenience stores during the 1970s. The first Kinko's—named in honor of owner Paul Orfalea's coiffure—opened in 1970 in Isla Vista, California. A similar company, Ginny's, started in Austin a year later.

By the mid-1980s Kinko's had locations all over the country, often in proximity to universities. Many locations were open twenty-four hours a day. By the '90s a typical mix of Kinko's patrons in the wee hours might include grad students churning out last-minute papers on pay-by-the-hour Mac Classic desktops, band members running off handbills for their next gig, and zine publishers making copies for distribution at coffee shops and record stores.

The zine renaissance that accompanied the '90s underground music scene in Austin could not have occurred without sympathetic copy shop workers and office drones who surreptitiously photocopied zines on someone else's dime when no one was looking. Despite Kinko's attempts to crack down on shrinkage through the use of copy-counting "auditrons" and security cameras, the ability to float free or cheap copies to friends served as a de facto perk of the job.

"Copy machines not only helped to forge social bonds but also arguably changed who could be an active participant in the making of culture," writes Kate Eichhorn, chair and associate professor of Culture and Media at New York's New School. "After all, as long as the city was a bulletin board and the bulletin board was everywhere, in a sense we were all living *in* our communication platform."[7]

The epicenter for zine distribution in 1990s Austin was the windowsill at Sound Exchange. While music was the fulcrum upon which local zines like *No Reply, Apathy Trend, Adventure Seekers, U-236, Yet Another Fanzine,* and the indispensable *Austin Show List* spun, subject matter ran the gamut. One of the most eclectic zines was *Show Us Your Butts,* which featured grainy, photocopied pictures of local scenesters displaying their posteriors. A few notches up the food chain, ad-supported periodicals like Luann Williams's pure pop music digest *Pop Culture Press* and Benjamin Serrato's arts/culture broadsheet *15 Minutes* occupied the middle ground between zines and the *Chronicle.*

The other means of print promotion for an unheard local band was putting up posters or flyers. By the 1990s Austin already had a rich music poster history. Shelton's psychedelic split-fountain inked posters for the Vulcan Gas Company between 1967 and 1968 begat the even more far-reaching work of Jim Franklin and the Armadillo Art Squad—a coterie of artists including Guy Juke, Kerry Awn, Micael Priest, and Bill Narum—who collectively created hundreds of posters for the Armadillo World Headquarters during the 1970s.

The democratizing forces of punk rock and photocopying greatly decreased the entry barrier while increasing the number of music posters and flyers. From the 1980s up through the mid-nineties, every telephone and electric pole on Guadalupe across from UT was covered in layer upon layer of band flyers. In the 1980s the term "poster band" emerged to describe a band that put up posters for months before actually playing a gig.

Often working under cover of darkness, band members or their friends would move up and down the Drag with Kinko's sacks full of flyers along with one or more means of affixation, such as staple guns, packing tape, or homemade wheat paste. If a band could scrape together a little extra cash, they could hire Fritz Blaw, who started Motorblade Postering Service in 1989 to post flyers on bulletin boards in restaurants, shops, and other "legal" locations.

A simple cut-and-paste band flyer might include show details scrawled in Magic Marker under an old magazine ad or photo of someone's grandmother. Led by future Orange Mothers bandleader and visual artist Ethan Azarian, Vermont transplants the Hollywood Indians created manifesto-style flyers in the early '90s that raised the band's profile through stunts like challenging the Butthole Surfers to a drinking contest.

While virtually all band flyers were artistic, a few proved to be legitimate art. At the start of the 1990s, Madrid-born Frank Kozik was the preeminent poster artist in Austin. Initially working in photocopy-friendly black-and-white for '80s punk bands, Kozik's signature style was comically imprudent transpositions in fiery, full-color screen prints. One of his more emblematic works, a poster for a 1991 Jesus Christ Superfly show at the Cannibal Club, featured Barney Rubble reimagined as a Black Panther against an American flag backdrop.

Kozik moved to San Francisco in 1993, but by then a new generation of local poster artists had emerged. Jason Austin may have been the most prolific of the lot, successfully channeling a freaky mélange of psychedelia and B-movie exploitation. Lindsey Kuhn coupled making punk flyers in his native Mississippi with toiling at a screen-printing shop in Austin to become one of the most sought-after rock poster artists in the country. Local musicians with a flair for poster art also got in on the action, including Ed Hall drummer Lyman Hardy, Sincola drummer Terri Lord, and Rockbusters guitarist Richard "Dicko" Mather.

Yet even as Austin poster artists were celebrated for their creativity, the form's efficacy as a vehicle for enticing people to come to shows was waning. In 1993 the city amended its Land Development Code to make it a Class C misdemeanor to post signs on utility poles.[8] Starting around 1995, the city started enforcing the ordinance in earnest.

That year, Do It Now Foundation guitarist Tom Cuddy was fined $500 for putting up flyers on the Drag, and Flamingo Cantina owner Angela Tharp received a citation for a FuckEmos poster that happened to have the club's name on it (prosecutors ultimately dropped the charges).[9]

"I want everyone to know that this is the third time they've done that," Micael Priest told the *Austin Chronicle* in 1997. "About every six years or so, they would come along and come up with some new ordinance to bother us with. One of them was that you had to register the posts you wanted to use, and you then had to pay them in advance. *For the telephone poles!*"[10]

Even so, enforcement remained consistent enough on Guadalupe to make flyering a risky proposition. Unlike the city's previous saber rattling, this one stuck. By 1997 utility poles on the Drag were no longer covered in layers of show flyers. Eichhorn's notion of city-as-bulletin-board became a thing of the past. The primacy of the printed page would soon follow.

Britt Daniel: When you'd go to Sound Exchange, there was three new fanzines there a week. You were finding out about local bands, and then you'd go see them at house parties.

Bones DeLarge: Fanzines were kind of the lifeblood of the punk rock scene. You could write a review of the show you've seen, lay it down at the local music shop—Sound Exchange or something—and go, "There's my two cents." Then it gets feedback. It brings people together and the people start communicating over that.

Melissa Bryan: Most of them were free. There were a lot of people doing stuff about the local scene.

Paul Streckfus: And not just local bands, but the good thrift stores, the cheap restaurants, the vegetarian spots, places where the cops are fucking with people.

Robert Zimmer: People would literally do some of these zines by hand in their garage. It was a really powerful, grassroots way to spread the word. We had our own mini-zine at the radio station [KTSB] called the *Call Letter*.

Susan Shepard: If you had an opinion and you wanted to express it, you had to go all the way down to Kinko's and learn how to run a copy machine. It was a lot harder to have an opinion back then.

Rebecca Cannon: I worked at Kinko's right out of college, so I made a lot of people's zines and posters for very little money. Kinko's was a big part of the whole '90s culture. All of Sincola's posters were being printed up in 11x17" color for very little money.

Carrie Clark: There are so many cool posters. Frank Kozik did some, but by the time we came around, he was already doing the Amphetamine Reptile stuff. That's when Jason Austin, Lyman Hardy, and Billy Bishop came in and took over the punk rock poster art thing.

Jonathan Toubin: In Austin everybody needed these flyers. It was the only way any of us had to tell people what was going on.

Melissa Bryan: It was all cut and paste. Kinko's at that time would be this haven for musicians. There was always a musician behind the counter. I got so many free copies. Man, those were the days! It was before they had cameras in their stores. Jonathan Toubin worked at that Kinko's over by campus, so everyone went there.

Jonathan Toubin: I had the ability to make an infinite amount of flyers for the arts, so I set aside a certain amount of time and effort and I created a system around the security cameras and the blind spots.

Carl Normal: I'd visited Austin in the early '80s, and it was a totally happening punk scene. So when I returned in '89 to live here permanently, I was a bit disappointed because that scene had died off quite a bit. I thought, "There's gotta be some like-minded people here. How to connect them?" So before I even started putting a band together, I did a fanzine. My own spew, typed up on 11×17", photocopied, folded in half and distributed for free. I had a little box by the front door. It was *the* place to get *No Reply*.

Jonathan Toubin: When you were eighteen and into a different kind of rock and roll, it was very frustrating to read the local weekly. There wasn't much for you. We had one fanzine called *No Reply*, but *No Reply* was focused on 1977 punk rock. Later on it started to include what was happening around town.

Craig Koon: The DIY thing had gotten lost in Austin. You're waiting for someone to do something for you. Austin's always had a problem with statis. You know, the velvet coffin. It's easy to live here and you raise to a certain level and you have your friends and you can call up a venue and get a gig and you can get guaranteed meals and beers, but that extra effort to go further was kind of by the wayside in the late eighties/early nineties. Then people realized, not just in Austin, but all over, this isn't going to work unless I get off my ass and do it.

Tim Stegall: Craig came to town and did not have that slacker ethic. He was very driven and had very definite ideas about what music should be and how it should be presented. He wanted a scene, but he wanted a different scene than what was happening at that time.

Craig Koon: The Pocket FishRmen were actually doing fun, energetic shows, and they were *it*. Then I met Mary and Edith and Dana in Pork. I was like, "This is the stuff that I like about music. It's just having fun. Not caring about what anyone thinks of it. If you can make some bucks and get some beer, that's great." That actually inspired me to start the fanzine.

Carl Normal: When I started *No Reply*, I don't remember any other fanzines in town. But shortly after that, Craig Koon moved to town and did *Yet Another Fanzine*. The first thing he wrote about Stretford was that we wore mod suits, and he accused us of being Jam copyists. Which wasn't accurate. We were never good enough to be anything like the Jam! So I wrote back and said, "So we wear suits? So what? Bands have been doing that since the '60s and '50s in all genres. Why don't you write about the music?" I think he liked people who threw it back in his face. The next thing he did was ask us to put out a single. We made up fast.

Tim Stegall: It wasn't very nice of him to find my resumé that I'd filed at Waterloo Records when I was trying to get a job, and posting it on the back cover of his fanzine. All water under the bridge now, but I was pissed at the time. After a time, he and I grew to respect each other and helped each other out. It took me getting the Hormones going before he finally did.

Craig Koon: I did the first issue and had people just stare at me, and say, "Why are you doing this?" It was baffling that there was all this inertia to getting anything going in Austin. Then three or four bands just started to say, "Fuck it", and do stuff.

Rebecca Cannon: The zines didn't have to be about music. They could have short stories and poems and cartoons. When I was in Sincola, I did stories for *FringeWare* about music. The technologies that are so taken for granted now were new then. Websites. The internet. Email. Promoting your band online. This magazine, *FringeWare*, was about virtual reality and all the new technologies that were coming up in pop culture.

Travis Higdon: Another great zine was Chris Lyons's *Pocket Pack*. It was about this big. Another favorite was *U-236*. He [Dave Nickerson] only published reviews about garage rock and punk rock that he absolutely loved.

Richard McIntosh: Greg Beets and Buzz Moran put out *Hey! Hey! Buffet!* They would go to shitty buffets around Austin and make these really dumb, well-written reviews of them.

Chuck Trend: What else? *All The Rage, Make Room, Page Boy, Yet Another Fanzine. Arthur's Cousin* was all about Chris Cornell. *Asian Girls Are Rad. Let the Guilty Pay. Humbug Volunteer. The Minus Times. Beat Up the Poor. At Least We Don't Have Earthquakes. Lost Armadillos in Heat.*

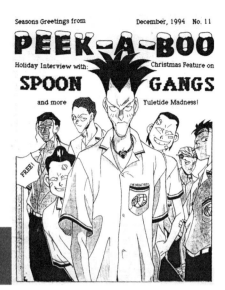

Peek-A-Boo fanzine holiday issue, 1994. Courtesy of Travis Higdon.

Britt Daniel: I read the *Peek-a-Boo* fanzine and there were these pictures of them drinking, and everybody had their shirts off and girls were in their underwear. I was like, "Who are these people? They look like they're having fun. I really want to meet these dudes!" Within six months we were friends.

Travis Higdon: Some friends and I did *Peek-A-Boo* in '93, partly just wanting to be part of the scene. Zine culture was huge at that time in the sort of punk/alternative underground. We were writing about music and movies and pop culture.

Britt Daniel: Travis and Phillip [Niemeyer] both ran the fanzine, but I think Travis was the only one that ran the label. He was really ambitious and really detailed and had a great graphic eye. You'd go over to his house, and there'd be a big row of all the mail orders that he was going to send out. He was always on top of it, so I wanted to do something with him.

Travis Higdon: Other punk rock zines would intentionally try to make it look real sloppy and Xerox it a hundred times to get that really contrasty effect. My mindset was coming at it as an outsider from zine culture. I would really try to get the layout perfect, pull the tape off, and try to get all the edges straight. I guess we felt like outsiders in the punk culture. We never really felt welcomed and so we used the zine—used humor—to kind of deflate the scene in certain aspects as well as praise it, 'cause we were fans.

Carl Normal: In the '80s there wasn't really a name for music that wasn't mainstream and wasn't hardcore punk. They used to call it college rock. That's how I felt about *Pop Culture Press*. They covered the independent rock scene, not the real heavy side of it. I wrote for them a little bit. I did a Buzzcocks interview and a Motörhead interview.

Luann Williams: One of the reasons I wanted to do *Pop Culture Press* was because there was just this fantastic local scene going on, and I thought the *Chronicle* was only covering it some. I fashioned it after this big tabloid magazine called *The Bomb*.

I found this whole crew of people to write for the magazine. And KVRX was how I met Naomi Shapiro and Robin Longman and Jason Cohen and Peter Blackstock. After a while I thought, "Well we have to put out music too." So we started putting out these flexi discs. The very first one we did was with Stretford. Carl was a big catalyst in making that happen.

Carl Normal: We did a split single with Stretford and Sincola on a seven-inch flexi disc, which was pretty cool.

Luann Williams: Then we started doing CDs. I asked Roger Morgan at Sound Exchange, "How do you put together a CD?" After much talk, we put out this little sampler and had a few local bands on it.

Michael Toland: I did skew the magazine toward local stuff because we only had so many pages. Usually the major label stuff got kicked out first because we figured they were getting coverage elsewhere.

Luann Williams: We did features on Stretford, Sincola, Fastball, the Wannabes, Spoon. And Daniel Johnston. Atlantic supported him and that was one reason we put him on the cover. That's one of my favorite covers. And we reviewed the very first Spoon single. Naomi Shapiro put it out on her label, Fluffer.

One of my favorite bands from that time was Cotton Mather. I'm such a Britpop fanatic, so I loved all that. At the time there just really wasn't very much pop music in Austin, so they really struck a chord with me because it was so Beatles-esque.

Mark Fagan: Jeremy Rueter put the *Punk Yearbook* together—a collection of people who were in the scene. It's total DIY. Not the best print job, but this was one of the coolest things ever. It shows you how large the scene was. It has the "Scenester's Map of Austin" with Tower Records, Quacks [Captain Quackenbush's coffeehouse], Ken's [Donuts], Hole in the Wall, Post Office, Sound Exchange, Wheatsville [Food Co-op]. Stashus Mule—an old record store. Star Seeds [twenty-four-hour café], which we used to go to all the time. Kerbey Lane [Café]. Mount Bonnell. Blue Flamingo, Emo's, Flamingo Cantina, Liberty Lunch, Electric Lounge, the Cathedral House, the Eco Action Warehouse.

Travis Higdon: Jeremy started a zine library. It was a very meticulous library of every zine he was able to come across.

Britt Daniel: He started a fanzine library in his house. The house was just open, and anybody could come in and go to his library where he had every zine that he could collect. I thought that was something else . . . His house *is* the library.

Richard McIntosh: Jeremy Rueter also did a zine called *Boys in Trouble on the Interstate*. Paul Streckfus—the singer of Glorium—would get his dad to review music in Austin. He wrote the weirdest reviews and analogies.

Chuck Trend: Jeremy did an issue of his fanzine that was called *Girls in Trouble*. He made the whole issue nothing but contributions from girls in the scene. It was a big deal. I think he felt female voices in the scene weren't represented enough.

Mark Fagan: There's still an ongoing debate about music journalism being a boys' club. Jennifer Hecker and Susan Shepard have a different voice, and that voice needs to be heard just as much as ours does.

Chuck Trend: *Geek Weekly* was Jennifer's zine, and she was friends with Susan who did *Hope You Die*. Susan did a lot of garage rock type stuff. She interviewed the Satans, and they were big fans of Goner Records. It was cool too because the hardcore scene during the '80s was male-dominated. There was a lot of testosterone. And in the '90s there was a lot more involvement.

Jennifer LaSuprema Hecker: We met the Satans because they dumpster-dived our sofa. I was like, "Hey, enjoy the sofa!" And we ended up becoming friends. They had this copy of *Maximum Rocknroll* on their coffee table that featured an article mentioning Susan, and it blew their mind. The girl that they had just read an article about lived two doors down from them!

hope you die

(A SLOW PAINFUL DEATH)

Number One
Spring 1994

$0.00

TAKE A SPOONFUL

CORPOR...

STIR...
BEND
MELL...

in me:
SXSW:
 a punk poser
 tells all
Grifters:
 shows, records,
 sleep-over
 reviews

Texas Travel

Pavement

and maybe
a little more....
excerpts from
"Hope You Die
Before I Grow UP" (#0)

↑ Drawn by
Brien Hindman, 18.
Brien is a senior
at Westlake High
School. He does
not play any sports
and he does not
"mosh"

Hope (You Die) fanzine cover, 1994. Illustration
by Brien Hindman. Courtesy of Susan Shepard.

Susan Shepard: That *Maximum Rocknroll* cred.

Jennifer LaSuprema Hecker: We were in high school, and I was a couple years older. We both had lots of freedom. She also had very adventurous taste.

Susan Shepard: We went to high school with Chepo Peña. He was in some great punk bands and got us to go out and hear more stuff. I did my *Hope You Die* fanzine for a while and Jennifer did *Geek Weekly* for a while. Then we collaborated on a South By Southwest preview fanzine.

In 1994 I had been asked to be on this panel at South By Southwest because I had written something for the *Chronicle* about being a teenage girl and going to shows. It was moderated by Mike Flaherty from *Sassy* magazine. I put together a fanzine for the panel called *I Hope You Die Before I Get Old*. It was teenage ranting and stuff about how old people sucked. I guess other teenagers related to that. Yeah, I was seventeen and I had put our address right there, not really thinking that people would try to show up or look me up in the phone book.

Travis Higdon: I read *Geek Weekly* all the time. Another one was *Apathy Trend*, which *Peek-A-Boo* had kind of a mock rivalry with. He would publish insults about us and our zine, and we would publish insults about him and his zine. It was all very serious and also not serious at all.

Chuck Trend: Reading the *Chronicle*, I was like, "Well this doesn't seem to reflect what I see going on." There was a void that needed to be filled. It was a long time before Ed Hall got the recognition that they deserved from the *Chronicle*.

The point for me was to write about stuff I liked and not write negative things because there's no point. You're wasting space. You would react against bands that were being talked about in the *Chronicle*.

Mark Fagan: You mean like Sincola? Why is Sincola getting all of this publicity and not Gut?

Chuck Trend: You would react. Starting the zine was just, "Fuck the *Chronicle*." They have a certain point of view that they're trying to get across, and it's based upon what they like. Not what you like.

Chepo Peña: It seemed like earlier in the '90s, it was always Alejandro or Robert Earl Keen or whatever.

Chuck Trend: Austin music has always been defined by this kind of Americana mishmash of country, folk, blues-rock. So if you are a punk band, you're always fighting an uphill battle. You were never going to fit the stereotype of what certain media outlets thought Austin music should be. At the time, "alternative" was kind of a dirty word. That was a way of soft-selling punk rock. And we were very much Dead Kennedys, Black Flag. If your background was Flatlanders or Alejandro or what-have-you, then you were kind of speaking a different language.

Mark Fagan: But the *Chronicle* has to cover the *entire* music scene, and you're going to focus on the FuckEmos and the Motards and Gomez and Gut and Glorium and all these bands. And those are the bands I'm interested in. And bands that have come out of Austin—like Spoon and Trail of Dead and the Sword—those are all dudes who would be standing next to us at the punk rock clubs. And so even though those bands are all completely different, they all come from this same scene.

Kerthy Fix: In terms of music, the *Chronicle* was not respected.

Cindy Widner: They would jump on stuff way too late or not get it. Tim Hayes worked at Sound Exchange with the garage rock purists. They thought the *Chronicle* didn't have a clue about music.

Tim Hayes: I can definitely say for myself that the reason the Cryin' Out Louds existed was a reaction against what the *Austin Chronicle* was always talking about.

Kerthy Fix: But our generation has a suspicion about making money and the mainstream point of view.

Chuck Trend: We had such a screwed-up idea of what should or shouldn't be commercially viable. In my mind, when I heard the Motards or Gut or Glorium, I was like, "This is fucking awesome!" There was no reason why that band couldn't continue to grow and be more successful if they were nurtured in the right way. And so writing about bands in fanzines was a way of validating at a grassroots level what that band was doing and hopefully gave them some positive feedback so they could think, "Okay someone heard this record and liked it and took the time to write about it."

Chepo Peña: It's funny though that a lot of bands wanted to be in the *Chronicle*, but once they were, people would criticize them.

Susan Shepard: Yeah, it's hilarious . . . the capacity that people have for pettiness and bullshit in a scene. It's a bottomless capacity. The fact is, you can't expect a general-interest publication to take an interest in your scene.

Rob Patterson: I worked with Brent Grulke at the *Chronicle* when he was music editor. I took over music and did that till August 1994. I think I did a pretty decent job covering new bands. "Ready or Not" was about whether new bands were ready. Or not. I was in a state of transition, but the second wave of punk underground was really starting to happen and blossom.

Tim Stegall: By the time I arrived at the *Chronicle*, the Raul's punk rock days were long gone. The Big Boys were all split up and off into various projects. King Coffey from the Butthole Surfers was doing his Trance Syndicate label—a very strange, acid-damaged form of art rock. This was three months before "Smells Like Teen Spirit" hit.

As a rock journalist, I wanted to be Lester Bangs. I wanted to have that crowbar to help out bands that I loved. Maybe we could show there's this really cool scene going on in Austin, Texas. That was hard as hell at the *Chronicle*. It seemed like I had to pound my head against a brick wall just to get the Motards or Gomez or Sincola in there.

Marc Fort: I'm working at the *Statesman*, writing about music and arts and entertainment, and the editor is like, "Hey, we're going to start this new entertainment tabloid. We're going to call it '*XLent*' or '*XL*.' We don't know yet." It came out on Thursdays and looked an awful lot like the *Chronicle* in its size and what it was covering and the advertisers that it was aiming for.

From the get-go, the paper was very specific that it was not going to be a *Chronicle* knock-off. But it was. They specifically wanted to cover the music that was bubbling up from the underground that was going into the mainstream—that 1991 post-Nirvana culture that permeated everything.

Chepo Peña: What's ironic is one of the first stories *XL* did about a band was the FuckEmos.

Marc Fort: I'm at a party. Someone hands me this brown cassette tape. It says "FuckEmos" on it. Already I'm intrigued. It's these songs that are just ridiculously catchy, beautiful punk rock. And it was raw, too. The vocals were distorted. There was nothing like the FuckEmos. I was writing for the *Statesman* and they were like, "What band is doing well right now in the scene?" "Well, there's this band called the FuckEmos."

First of all, the *Statesman* can't print the word "fuck." So how are they going to contend with that? I was just stoked that I was somehow getting away with writing about this amazing little Punk Rock Band That Could that had the most memorable songs. I learned from Russell that his trick was to listen to love songs on the oldies station so he'd have these beautiful pop melodies going through his head. Combining that with the rawness and the energy of punk rock . . . Who had done that before? No one.

My pitch to my editors was, "This band is unlike anything you've ever seen. They have these beautiful punk rock songs. They're filling clubs." What was going to be a short little story about them quickly turned into a cover story for the *Statesman*'s new entertainment tabloid.

Keep in mind there's no cell phones. There's no internet. The newspaper still had a cachet and a penetration where the majority of people saw it. So the FuckEmos being on the cover of the *Statesman*'s weekly thing—that is normally talking about Willie Nelson and Lyle Lovett—was something unique.

Kerthy Fix: This is the pre-internet era. There's no social media. There's no way to really communicate unless it's in person or through zines or flyers or running into somebody at Quack's coffee shop and Les Amis [restaurant].

Britt Daniel: Bands seemed big because some of them had tons of flyers up everywhere. You'd get to know their name really quickly on the Drag.

Carrie Clark: It was just completely involved, and it was such a physical process. You screen-printed your flyers with your hands. You could spend a whole day walking around with your flyers, talking to people, making that contact.

Britt Daniel: It wasn't tons of fun, but I felt like I had to do it because all the cool bands had flyers up. It was a lot of build-up for that show, and then you'd go to do the show and—especially in Skellington's case—there'd still only be twelve people there. One person for every fifteen flyers that you hung up. Then at some point they started cracking down, and they wouldn't let you flyer anymore.

Kerthy Fix: I was arrested once for putting flyers up on the Drag. There was a photograph of me in the *Daily Texan*. It was before "Make Austin Weird." Sorority girls were like, "Quit putting that trash up on the Drag!" So it was that era, and they were arresting people.

Travis Higdon: I would go to the UT stacks and pore through the library, trying to find the perfect image for a flyer. And then buy all these font books at Half Price Books and Xerox them and cut and paste all night. And then that law was passed. No more flyering on the light posts. So everyone was like, "Oh no! Where are we going to put our flyers?"

Carrie Clark: You'd get this stack of posters that you screen-printed in your kitchen or your garage and a spray bottle of condensed milk—the best glue in the world—and some wet sponges. You needed at least two people because one person looks out for the cops and the other person slaps up the poster and sprays the condensed milk.

Gary Chester: Crust put up a poster, got fined a lot of money, *and* they won Best Poster of the Year simultaneously.

Lyman Hardy: It was illegal to put up posters, but there was an Austin Poster Day. There was a resolution that was signed. Kozik and Jason Austin and I and Carrie and a bunch of people got in this limousine and rode down for the big proclamation of Austin Poster Day.

Tim Kerr: If there was a poster up, they pulled it down. The club got fined. It just turned into this crazy thing where the only way you could have posters was put them up in the record stores or whatever. Then loading equipment in—if you were double parked for a while on Sixth Street you would get a ticket while you're loading into a club. Live Music Capital of the World!

SOUND EXCHANGE

BITTER PEOPLE WITH NO FUTURE SELLING MUSIC

'CAUSE YOU KNOW YOU'RE THE ONE AND THAT THAT HASN'T CHANGED
SINCE YOU WERE NINETEEN AND STILL IN SCHOOL WAITING ON A LIGHT
ON THE CORNER BY SOUND EXCHANGE.

BRITT DANIEL, "ANYTHING YOU WANT," SPOON

IN 1999 US RECORD SALES PEAKED AT $14.6 billion, the vast majority
(87.9 percent) of which came in the form of full-length compact discs.[1] The
top three selling albums of 1999 in the US—the Backstreet Boys' *Millennium*, Britney Spears's *. . . Baby One More Time*, and Ricky Martin's self-titled
English-language debut—racked up a combined year-end SoundScan tally of
$23 million.[2] If record buyers resented having to pay for a full-length CD to
get one or two hit songs, the widespread discontinuation of single releases
didn't leave them much choice.

Between glacial speeds and poor sound quality, the notion of downloading—let alone streaming—music online was still largely a concept without
proof. That changed on June 1, 1999, when Shawn Fanning and Sean Parker
launched the file-sharing service Napster. Though legally dubious, Napster
clearly demonstrated that a robust market for singles still existed if the price

point—in this case, free if you had a computer and high-speed internet connection—was low enough.

At its peak in February 2001, Napster had 26.4 million users worldwide[3] who were freely sharing hundreds of millions of songs. The original iteration of Napster would ultimately be shut down in July 2001 as part of a legal settlement, but the fate of the premillennial music industry was sealed. Physical sales of recorded music began a long-term decline in 2000. By 2009 US record sales plummeted to just $7.8 billion.[4]

Reaction to the collapse of the music industry within the shambling confines of underground rock initially hovered somewhere between shrugging ambivalence and outright glee. Band vans and instrument cases alike were commonly festooned with bumper stickers from trailblazing '80s punk label SST Records that proclaimed "Corporate Rock *Still* Sucks." No less an authority than Nirvana producer Steve Albini outlined how easily unsavvy bands could get saddle-bagged by recording contracts with insurmountable recoupable costs in his 1993 *Baffler* essay, "The Problem with Music." And who needed industry when you could tear a literal page from *Book Your Own Fuckin' Life*, a how-to guide on touring first published in 1992 by influential San Francisco–based punk zine *Maximum Rocknroll*?

Nevertheless, the postmillennial shift in how recorded music was discovered, distributed, purchased, and listened to had ramifications even for bands counting records sold on fingers and toes. A recording that could be easily accessed and endlessly duplicated online no longer had the same value. This devaluation posed a grave threat to the viability of record stores, decimating large national chains and small independent retailers alike. According to music retail trade group Almighty Music Marketing, more than four thousand record stores nationwide closed between 2000 and 2010. One of those stores was Austin's Sound Exchange.

Like Emo's, Sound Exchange arrived in Austin by way of Houston, where it was founded as the Record Exchange in 1979. As the name implies, the store's primary stock-in-trade was buying and selling used recordings. Many were gently used promotional copies. While promo copies came stamped with a warning that they were still the property of the record company and could not be resold, music critics and radio station employees regularly sold them for beer money, providing a thrifty way to build a music library. Once Record Exchange relocated to Montrose in 1980, it became an integral part of Houston's music infrastructure, employing local musicians and selling local singles such as Really Red's "Modern Needs" and AK-47's "The Badge Means You Suck."

The Austin location of Record Exchange opened in 1980 at 2100 Guadalupe, just across the street from UT. Though it had a distinct identity from its Houston parent,[5] it retained the emphasis on used records, underground music, and local artists. In June 1983 the Big Boys held their record release party for *Lullabies Help the Brain Grow* there.

As the '80s progressed, many local acts eschewed vinyl records for cassettes as a cheaper, more portable means of getting recordings out. The most noteworthy was Daniel Johnston, who was working at the Dobie Mall McDonald's catty-corner from Record Exchange when local tastemakers first took note of his songwriting prowess. Johnston's tapes with hand-drawn photocopied cover art were positioned prominently in a special countertop display next to the cash register. By 1989 CDs and cassettes had supplanted vinyl. Both the Houston and Austin stores changed their moniker to Sound Exchange in response.

As the '90s started, Sound Exchange was one of several record stores dotting the UT campus area. Competitors included national chains like Amarillo-based Hastings Music and fellow independents like Inner Sanctum and Technophilia. In the fall of 1990 a hulking two-story outpost of Sacramento-based Tower Records opened in the former Varsity Theater at the corner of Guadalupe and 24th. Closer to downtown, at Sixth and Lamar, Waterloo Records emerged as one of the country's premier independent retailers, becoming the epicenter for local music of all stripes and hosting frequent in-store performances from both local and national acts.

It's easy to imagine an alternate path in which Sound Exchange gets shunted to the margins by the likes of Tower and Waterloo, but that's not what happened. Thanks to the efforts of store manager Craig Koon and a motley-yet-learned gang of employees like Roger Morgan, Patrick Lemire, Lisa Rickenberg, Tim Hayes, Mark Fagan, and Lauren Robertson, the shop became the true north of Austin's '90s DIY scene—an erstwhile salon where new music was discovered, zines and flyers were distributed, bands were formed, and networks were solidified.

As the store's nineties-era advertising slogan—"Bitter People with No Future Selling Music"—insinuated, the characters in Nick Hornby's *High Fidelity* had nothing on the cast of Sound Exchange. Leading man Koon struck the perfect balance of caustic wit, abetting enthusiasm, and sausage factory know-how to give those around him more confidence in their contributions. Though his curmudgeonly demeanor preceded him, few were as passionately supportive of the emerging local scene. In addition to his Sound Exchange role, Koon had a show on UT student radio station KTSB, published a zine called *Yet Another Fanzine*, and helped many local bands get their first recordings out.

Few can say they got a job after comparing their prospective workplace to Hitler's bunker, but that's how Koon described Sound Exchange's ambience in his fanzine before successfully petitioning owner Mark Alman for a job there. If Koon was highly critical, he was also highly motivated to make things better. A more aggressive focus on supporting the new generation of local underground rock bands was key to Koon's vision.

Backing conviction with action, Koon released "Wanna Ride," the debut seven-inch single by all-female garage punk trio Pork, on his one-off Sub Par/Worthless imprint in 1992. Its four songs were recorded live to cassette on Koon's handheld Sony Walkman TCS-430 at the Cavity, the Austin Outhouse, and the Hole in the Wall. Packaged with black-and-white photocopied sleeves, the single was altogether unprofessional, but it successfully bottled the band's raw essence in a fast, cost-efficient manner. Within a couple of years, it became normative for Sound Exchange employees to have a cottage record label on the side.

As noted in our last chapter, zines and show flyers littered the store's front window-well. While this didn't directly contribute to the bottom line, it furthered Sound Exchange's integration with the music scene. The *Austin Show List* was a vital document for finding out about musical goings-on beneath the radar of established press outlets in the final days preceding internet dominance. The zine later expanded coverage to other Texas cities. Started by Jeremy Rueter and then turned over to Sound Exchange employee Mark Twistworthy, the *Texas Show List* was a photocopied, hand-curated compilation of the week's shows and house parties, along with announcements for pickup soccer games, Critical Mass bike rides, and free meals served by Food Not Bombs. By 1997 the store's fledgling website was hosting the online version of the *Show List*.

Despite rising rents on the stretch of Guadalupe locals call the Drag and new competition from Bob Coleman and Dan Plunkett's Thirty Three Degrees,[6] Sound Exchange made it through Y2K intact. In October 2000 Koon organized a twentieth-anniversary show with reunion performances from Poison 13 and the Motards in the alley behind the store. Despite this happy milestone, Sound Exchange was on borrowed time. In anticipation of attracting a better-heeled tenant, the property owner put the store on a month-to-month lease. In January 2003 Alman decided he'd had enough and chose not to renew. Sound Exchange liquidated its inventory and burrito chain Baja Fresh took its place.

Outside the memories of its employees and customers, the most tangible legacy of Sound Exchange is Daniel Johnston's "Hi, How Are You?" mural. Koon commissioned the mural in 1993, paying Johnston $100 plus store

credit. The mural is a variation on the photocopied cover art for 1983's *Hi, How Are You?* cassette, featuring Johnston's Jeremiah the Innocent character. The mural has since survived multiple tenant turnovers and vandal defacements to become an unofficial local landmark. In 2018 Mayor Steve Adler issued a proclamation making January 22 "Hi, How Are You? Day" in Austin to promote mental wellness. When Johnston passed away in September 2019 at age fifty-eight, fans of his music and art paid their respects by leaving flowers, candles, and notes at the mural.

Though its connection to the buying and selling of records is tenuous, the mural makes a convincing final testament to both Johnston as an artist and Sound Exchange as a facilitator of art. With no legal preservation protection as of this writing, its continued existence is at least partially dependent on the grassroots outcry and negative publicity that would ensue if a subsequent tenant destroyed it. In these respects, it cuts directly to the spiritual imperative that drove much of the DIY culture that swirled around Sound Exchange—lifting small but authentic voices above the squall of commercial cacophony for a million-to-one shot at timelessness.

Craig Koon: Sound Exchange was a really lame place for a long, long time. I had written an article in the fanzine about it, and I called it Hitler's bunker. Everyone's just waiting for the Russians.

The owner said, "What did you mean by that?" "Well, it's just depressing in here. Your employees hate music. They hate the store. No wonder no one wants to fucking shop here."

They had a shoe box with only the Xeroxed covers of seven-inch singles. You didn't actually look at the records. You had to ask, "Can I see the record that this Xerox goes with?" And they would bring it out, sullenly. Half the store was empty. The back was just decrepit records, faded shrink-wrap machines, unused desks, and T-shirts that no one wanted. Why a retail store had 50 percent of the floor space unused was a mystery to me.

Lisa Rickenberg: It was during a pretty bleak period at Sound Exchange that I was the indie buyer. The owner was not a very pleasant person to work for. He would search our bags before we left work.

Bones DeLarge: I had bright yellow hair and I got canned.

Brent Prager: I got fired for wearing a gazelle femur up in my hair.

Craig Koon: I thought, "This is *the* campus record store. It can't be like that."

Lisa Rickenberg: Roger Morgan and Roger Wilson were super great people. And my coworkers were great, but there was a lot of selling bad pop music to frat boys and being abused by them.

Roger Morgan: It did get a little more punk rock and independent. I always liked that. When I was traveling around to other cities, I saw a lot of their cool record stores were doing the same. I can't really take credit for any of that other than just letting it happen.

Lisa Rickenberg: After Craig Koon took over, things got a lot better. Suddenly the music scene opened up in Austin.

Robert Zimmer: People would go down to these record stores—including Sound Exchange—all the time. In some ways, it was the equivalent of going to coffee shops now. People would go not just to listen to music, but they would go to socialize. They would go to recommend music to other people.

Roger Morgan: Any time you've got a place where everybody can gather and exchange ideas—even if it's not music—just exchange politics and other crazy things, it becomes this hub.

Craig Koon: Sound Exchange started to seriously threaten Waterloo's domination of the underground scene. People began to realize, "Hey, there's actually a lot of stuff going on here." It's a nuclear reaction. The more you get, the greater the reaction.

Sean McGowan: During the '90s it was just thriving. We would all celebrate one another. It was this mutual admiration society that just built a really loving wonderful thing for a number of years. Sound Exchange was really a hub for all of that.

Jonathan Toubin: I worked there from 1991 to '92. During that period, we ordered almost every punk seven-inch from any local market. No matter how small a pressing, there would always be at least a couple. There was a wall with these singles. Most of these bands couldn't afford to put out a full LP. Almost every Austin band from the early '90s has at least one seven-inch, even if they had to put it out themself.

Melissa Bryan: That wall was so important. This is Austin. This is what we do and here it is on the wall.

Chepo Peña: I would buy every fucking single that was on that wall.

Lauren Robertson: They needed a girl working there because the two women who were working there both left. So I was it. Because it's so close to UT, it was the same people coming in asking the same questions a million fucking times every day, slamming their hand down and being like, "Do you have the new Beck?" You're like, "Not again! This again?"

You're in the middle of arguing with someone because you don't want to buy their fucking Billy Joel cassette, you know what I mean? Working in a record store is so weirdly exhausting. People bringing in their flyers and being like, "Do you have tape?" If we gave tape to every person who hung a flyer, we would just constantly be tape dispensers. People complain about the personalities of Sound Exchange employees, and I think a lot of it comes from that.

Travis Higdon: The Sound Exchange windowsill was always littered with all kinds of flyers, newspapers, zines, trash, homeless people, free CDs. Maybe giveaway records, posters. Local bands that were giving their product away, maybe because no one wanted to buy it. Just tons of stuff.

Lauren Robertson: We had a lot of very colorful characters. There were lots of Dragworms.[7] There were a few shoplifting incidents, and we would have to chase them down. I remember one guy flinging shit on Craig Koon. Just crazy.

Roger Morgan: Ryan Walker—Bad Mutha Goose bass player—had this "Fuck the Police" T-shirt he liked to wear a lot. One day we had an incident of somebody stealing something, so he called the police, right? The police showed up to interview him. We noticed he had the shirt on, and so he's folding his arms over his chest the whole time. The policeman's like, "Just relax man. You don't have to be so nervous."

We were heckling him from behind. "Hey! What's that on your shirt? Why are you crossing your arms? You never do that!"

Rest in peace, Ryan.

Susan Shepard: One of my first memories of shopping at Sound Exchange is Mark Fagan making fun of me buying a Green Day record in '93 or '94. But then, instead of just mocking you, they would be like, "You should listen to this over here." Tim Hayes would always try to get you to listen to all the garage rock seven-inches. Craig would always try to get you to listen to whatever weird band he was going to put out on Rise, like Moist Fist or Noodle.

Kerthy Fix: I was doing college radio and would go there to shop. It would always be a *dude* place. It was intimidating because you had to know your shit. And were you cool enough with what you bought?

Cindy Widner: People would make fun of you sometimes. But behind the counter that could be really fun because Patrick [Lemire] would just keep up a constant monologue under his breath that was hilarious.

Roger Morgan: At one point Patrick had brought in a little mixer and he ran these cables to the stereo. He would play a record of John F. Kennedy doing a speech, and then he would have a gunshot record that he would crank up really loud. People would be listening to this speech and right in the middle of it you hear this *crack!* and people would get so pissed.

Craig Koon: One employee, James White, was really into the idea of painting a hip-hop/graffiti-style mural, which we all liked—but we were fairly sure the owner wouldn't. One day, Daniel [Johnston] came in, bought some LPs and sold me a drawing or two. In a moment of rare lucidity, I asked Daniel if he would paint the wall on our store, and he happily agreed on the spot.

Roger Morgan: When they said they were going to give Daniel Johnston paint and let him paint on the outside of the building I was like, "Are you guys sure this is a good idea?"

Craig Koon: It took him less than two hours. He spent nearly as long grabbing LPs as payment. The next day, I walked in just as Mike McCarthy ended a phone call with "Ma'am, it's not Satan—it's a frog."

Roger Morgan: People from the little church across the street were not happy with those demonic frogs. And they demanded that I remove them. They were like, "This is really disturbing, and our parishioners are having to look at this when we come in."

I'm like, "This guy is famous . . ." They didn't even fathom that this guy was famous. I said, "Even if I *said* I was going to do that, this town would revolt against me."

So they kind of accepted that and left. But later they co-opted that into their promotions. They did their own Daniel frogs, "Hi, how are you? Come to our Sunday services." Which I thought was hilarious. And justice.

Cindy Widner: Being in Happy Family—the first band I was in—I didn't even really understand that there was an "indie." I would go to Inner Sanctum and buy indie local records, but I didn't really understand what a big corporation meant. And of course, Nirvana was when all of that stuff got swept back up into centralized, very vertically distributed conglomerates owning a lot of the product. So it was kind of a weird time.

Roger Morgan: In the early '90s when Nirvana started popping up, even before *Nevermind* came out, the younger people that I was working with were listening to these bands and playing them. The first time I heard one of those Nirvana records I was like, "What's the big deal?"

I think we all agreed once *Nevermind* hit that this record is really something different. You could play it in the store, and everybody would be like, "What the heck is that? I want that!" As buyers, we're dealing almost daily with people coming in from record labels like Elektra and Warner Bros. and CBS. Everybody on an indie or punk rock label was suddenly interesting to them.

But then a lot of people began getting signed that we thought, "Man there's no way that band is going to get signed—they don't even have a full set of songs." And they would be the next darling on CBS. I guess they figured out how to work that system.

Graham Williams: Nirvana's second record blew up when I was in middle school to high school, but then post-Nirvana—you know, Green Day, fucking Rancid—all these bands went mainstream. So it seemed like it was a trickle-down of the national interest in alternative—like Jane's Addiction and Pearl Jam—to a local level.

Tim Kerr: When Nirvana broke, you had a whole lot of bands basically starting up because they think they're going to be on MTV and make all this money. "We're punk rock!" And they fell right in line with all these labels.

Cindy Widner: I worked at Sound Exchange when Kurt Cobain died, and that was really interesting. People did come in and tried to sell their rare Kurt Cobain stuff because it was going to be more expensive. But then there were also people who were sincerely freaked out and sad about it. But Sound Exchange was almost a little bit resistant. Is it on a major label? Is it popular?

Roger Morgan: There was a lot of drama that went on at that buy counter. People were unhappy about the money they were getting. People spitting at us. It could get ugly. I usually tried to avoid those kinds of situations, but Patrick came from the G&M Steakhouse, and he was groomed to offend people.[8]

Lauren Robertson: You have people waiting for you to open the door on Sunday morning because they've been up all night. They need money and they need you to buy their Steely Dan cassette that's been on the floorboard of their car for fucking months. You know what I mean? It's so fucking dark.

They are just so desperate for money, and you're the person telling them "No." And they're just fucking crushed.

Cindy Widner: When I worked there they had a T-shirt that read "Bitter People with No Future Selling Music." At the time it was dudes, and they all had their dude things. I usually worked with Tim Hayes when the Seattle garage rockers all moved to Austin. They were very purist about garage rock, and they hated anything that had any whiff of pop or even anything that could shake your booty slower. But Tim is a great guy.

Sean McGowan: Tim Hayes turned me on to a lot of music. He was definitely opening up people's world to new music that he was familiar with. He was the first person talking about Dead Moon.

Tim Hayes: When I got hired, Craig and I built a rapport. "Hey Craig, can you pick up the new Crypt Records thing?" He would get it, and we would sell a butt load. Even some odd lo-fi punk rock bands that no one had ever heard of.

You had to turn people on to that shit. It takes work, but it takes a smile and a laugh and some kind of camaraderie with whoever you're talking to. It was like being a fucking pusher. "Man, I got something here for you. . . . Come over here. Check it out." Pop a record on and jump on the fucking counters and dance. And guys would look at me going, "What the . . . ? There must be something to this shit!" The next thing you know, they're walking out the door with it.

The thing is, if they see how unpretentiously fun the music is, they'll want to be a part of it. Because with all that singer-songwriter shit. . . . I don't even want to come near that. I want Austin to be fun again and not pretentious as all hell. And so that started a scene from ground zero and turned it into an alcohol-fueled fun fest.

Tim Stegall: Tim was literally putting singles from Estrus Records in young kids' hands and saying, "You need to listen to this!" He really groomed an entire scene that way. He is directly responsible for garage rock becoming so big in Austin. He started the Hormones with me and Ron Williams. At the same time, he had started his own band, the Cryin' Out Louds.

Scott Gardner: Tim Hayes just loved music. "Have you heard this band? You need to buy this!" And so I just started buying all the garage punk that was coming out. By that time, everyone was forming a band or a record label.

Tim Kerr: I don't necessarily think Austin is unique, but it was sort of a unique time in Austin. All of a sudden you had all these characters that came together and the hub of it was Sound Exchange. It seems like Tim Hayes and Lisa and all them were making sure people were hearing all these bands.

Tim Hayes: The Inhalants actually were the first band that kind of filled the void. They were this really raw garage gunk rock band. There was almost an element of the Electric Eels to them where there was just this primal ooze coming from these three people.

Scott Gardner: I met Lisa Rickenberg at Sound Exchange. She says, "Hey, have you heard my band Inhalants? You should come see our band! We're playing at Chances." She had a kind of loping bass sound and Dave [Haney] had snarling vocals. Richard [Skinner] was their drummer. Garage music. Three chords and melody. That drew me into that garage punk scene that was happening in Austin, especially once I got my show at KOOP.

Lisa Rickenberg: We played our last gig on the roof of Thirty Three Degrees. Bob Coleman, one of the owners, did the *Garage Show* with Scott originally, and then he did *Commercial Suicide* on KOOP for a long time. He was super into a lot of experimental music. And Dan [Plunkett] had a huge influence on the type of music sold at Thirty Three Degrees. The garage and the psych stuff was mostly Bob, and then the more ambient electronic kind of stuff was Dan.

Brian McBride: Thirty Three Degrees—your experimental record store. They were great about bringing different artists to their store. Great about putting on anti-SXSW shows. They would bring all of these interesting and weird artists to town. People like Illusion of Safety. There was a niche out there that actually cared about things that were different from your typical rock.

Travis Higdon: Thirty Three Degrees in-stores definitely had their own vibes. I clearly remember Sound Exchange had a lot of in-stores. I think Waterloo Records in-stores were viewed as a lot more legitimate. They actually had a little stage set up. They'd advertise them in the newspaper.

Roger Morgan: We were starting to get a little bit of attention through the work of some of these people like Craig Koon and bringing in bands like the Mekons. We even had an in-store with Pearl Jam. I remember saying out loud—maybe where they could hear—that I thought that was the stupidest name and they were never going anywhere. And that's me. If I said it's not going to work, it's probably going to be hugely successful.

Travis Higdon: Sound Exchange was the sweaty, hot, dirty, loud, crowded punk in-stores. Those were really the ones I always wanted to be a part of.

Chuck Trend: Between Sound Exchange and the Blue Flamingo, it was sort of a self-contained kind of thing. When we went to a show at Blue Flamingo, it was you shoulder to shoulder with all these people from Sound Exchange.

Mark Fagan: Pretty much every band—even bands like Spoon who you might not think of as a punk rock band—came out of the same scene. And you would see Britt at the same show that you would see Bones from Lower Class Brats. And those bands have absolutely nothing to do with each other but, we all hung out together. Like Bones and the guy from Fastball [Tony Scalzo]. They all worked at the bagel shop a block away from Sound Exchange.

Craig Koon: The Drag was lively. And the people that were on the Drag were university students. Malls were just getting started, so they hadn't lived their whole life in the fucking mall. They were actually used to walking outdoors.

Graham Williams: Austin felt smaller and safer. There was definitely a lot of freedom and a lot of interesting and odd things happening, and it was like a fertile ground for discovering interesting unique things by just being here. It wasn't such a career-minded city. It was this little creative city.

Jonathan Toubin: The ethics of the town—everything that I consider bohemian and the values that are instilled in me—all came from this weird Texas version of the underground. Uniqueness. Confrontationalism. All these different things that were from that culture of Butthole Surfers and whatever else from the Drag.

Robert Zimmer: When Tower Records bought that space [the former location of the Varsity Theatre at 24th and Guadalupe],[9] people were extremely upset about it because it represented the corporate direction that people didn't want things to go. People saw it as a sign of bad things to come.

Laura Williams: That mural on Tower Records, I painted that with Carlos Lowery when he first put it up. And then when Tower Records had taken over the Varsity and wanted it restored, we restored it and Sandra [Martinez] helped me.

Roger Morgan: Once Tower Records came in, it gave us this evil thing that we fought against. It really emboldened us. It was very worrisome at the time thinking, "I know how corporations work. I see how they roll over people." And it did affect us. And digital downloading was coming, too.

Craig Koon: The joke was that no chain stores made money on the Drag. I had a couple of spies that would feed me information on what business decisions were being made at corporate levels. I would tell people, and they wouldn't believe me.

Brian McBride: The mid-nineties is very conflictual for Austin. At the same time that Austin is really becoming corporatized, there is also an equal reaction to maintain its integrity. You have places like Les Amis that can't afford the rent, so they have to sell off their property to Starbucks. You're ultimately witnessing the death of culture in a lot of ways. There are these people that—even though they are slackers—are dead-set in defending what they believe is a culture that deserves to live.

Craig Koon: Punk broke in '91 and kids wanted weirdness, but they wanted their weirdness appropriately packaged. And so the T-shirt shop closed. The game room closed. Europa [Books] closed. It's part because people changed and didn't want to shop there, and part being forced out by landlords.

Brian McBride: People are fighting to keep culture alive. It's harder and harder to do, given things like rent going up. It's those kinds of people that should be appreciated the most. It shouldn't really just be bands that are ultimately important for documenting a time in Austin's history. It is also the people that facilitate that.

Craig Koon: The Drag suffered from the greed of everyone else in the real estate run-up, starting with Jerk [Kirk] Watson, the mayor who ruined Austin. By this time the university had gotten so expensive for housing that our customers had fled.

Debbie Rombach: With Sound Exchange leaving and Inner Sanctum closing, it kind of changed the entertainment feeling of the Drag. Things started closing. Like the Showdown. They were a cousin bar to Hole in the Wall. And when Antone's closed that location,[10] that was a real signal of change on the Drag.

Craig Koon: We were basically unable to keep buying many new releases, and that allowed Thirty Three Degrees to catch up and entrench themselves as the cool shop. That, and the shift from punk/garage to emo meant we never did get back up in front.

It was not the best record store as far as management went, but we were still the best used LP shop in most of the country, let alone Austin—but we weren't the leader anymore.

Jonathan Toubin: Everyone loved Austin, but the things we loved were gone. The Drag was now just a bunch of chain stores, and everything closed year by year.

Craig Koon: One day a big "For Sale" sign showed up next to the wrestler.[11] I wanted to have a dignified funeral and a wake. Instead it was, "Everybody's gotta get out of Vietnam! Last chopper out!"

In April 2023, the building that housed Sound Exchange was demolished to make way for a multistory student housing complex with ground floor retail. The wall section containing Daniel Johnston's "Hi, How Are You?" mural was preserved.

RECORD LABELS

BITTER PEOPLE WITH NO FUTURE STARTING LABELS

IF YOU WALKED INTO SOUND EXCHANGE IN the mid-nineties, there's no way you could've missed the Wall of Singles. Strategically situated next to the cash register and listening station, the Wall was a teeming pegboard-and-hooks display of locally released seven-inch singles. When MTV's *Week in Rock* profiled the Austin music scene in 1994, the Wall of Singles garnered screen time alongside established figures like Charlie Sexton and Alejandro Escovedo.

While other record stores also sold local singles, none displayed them so prominently. As a result, the Wall became one of the most salient indicators of a new groundswell of energy in Austin's underground music scene. Despite higher production costs and lesser utility, seven-inch singles quickly rendered local cassette releases passé.

There would not have been enough local singles to populate the Wall without local record labels putting them out. While none of the labels formed in the wake of King Coffey's 1990 launch of Trance Syndicate had the distribution or notoriety of their forebear, their emergence was a key element of the ecosystem giving new bands a new opportunity to thrive.

By 1992 Trance had already released albums by Crust, Ed Hall, Cherubs, and Houston's Pain Teens along with a slew of singles. Ryan Richardson founded the Existential Vacuum label in 1991, focusing on unearthing out-of-print or unreleased Texas punk recordings, including a full-length from

Dallas-based cowpunks Loco Gringos and an EP by Coffey's pre-Buttholes band the Hugh Beaumont Experience. Bob Coleman's Over and Out label started in 1990 with an album from psych-tinged New Orleans punk combo Skinsect before focusing energy on Austin by releasing ST 37's *The Invisible College* LP and the Pocket FishRmen's "Fantasy Elevator Ride" single.

It was against this backdrop that Craig Koon recorded, packaged, and released Pork's "Wanna Ride" single. Although he wasn't first to the game, his low-rent approach made it clear that the barrier to vinyl entry was entirely surmountable even for a nascent act. Because Koon also managed Sound Exchange, published a zine, and DJ'ed on KTSB, he was able to leverage a slapdash vertical integration of sorts in promoting the record. "Wanna Ride" came out on the SubPar/Worthless imprint, the logo of which was a parody of the familiar Sub Pop logo—a common artistic strategy for a generation raised on Topps Wacky Packages stickers. Despite—or perhaps because of—its rawness, the single sold out of its first pressing.

In mid-1992 Koon joined forces with local poster artist Frank Kozik to start Rise Records. The business plan for Rise was to have Koon focus on bringing in both local and national bands while Kozik created collector-bait cover art in his controversy-courting style. Serving as Exhibit A was Kozik's logo for Rise, which incorporated the visage of Charles Manson. Rise's first release was 1992's snarling "Big Shit" single by Jesus Christ Superfly. That was followed by a seven-inch from the Mono Men, one of the leading lights of the fervent garage rock scene in Bellingham, Washington.

Rise's alternating pattern of local and national releases continued into 1993. Local Rise product included a full-length LP from art-punk collective Moist Fist and a single from a four-woman rock combo called Wet that made an anthem of sorts out of the Texas Restaurant Association's slogan, "Eating Out Is Fun." When Atlantic Records signed the Melvins in the wake of Nirvana's success, they were astute enough to allow the band to release a Kozik-designed single for "Hooch" on Rise to promote the *Houdini* LP.

By 1994 Koon and Kozik's business relationship had fractured. Kozik moved to San Francisco and ultimately started his own Man's Ruin label there. One of his last acts at Rise was designing the cover of the FuckEmos full-length debut, *FuckEmos Can Kill You*. By the time of its official release, the album was almost a year old. The band had been dubbing copies onto discarded cassette tapes and giving them away for free when the album made its way into the Emo's jukebox, becoming an unlikely favorite.

If the FuckEmos were a malevolent band with a hint of pop, Sincola was a pop band with a hint of malevolence. The quintet already had a buzz when Rise issued their debut seven-inch in 1994, but the John Croslin–produced record spread that buzz beyond the clubs. Now high school kids could hear Sincola's signature song "Bitch" on the radio.

Not long after Rise started, Koon's fellow Sound Exchange employee Roger Morgan reactivated Unclean Records. Morgan started Unclean while living in Boulder, Colorado, in 1983. He and the label moved to Tulsa, Oklahoma, and then Austin in 1986. The early incarnation of the label released records from Tulsa's N.O.T.A. and El Paso's Rhythm Pigs before going dormant in the late '80s.

Unclean's second era began in 1992, when Morgan released the psycht-tinged debut single from Flying Saucers. A bevy of local singles from Glorium, Inhalants, Stretford, and Rig (later to be named Crown Roast) followed. The latter's "Warthole" garnered airplay on John Peel's BBC show.

At the end of 1995, Morgan moved to San Antonio, which dovetailed with Unclean's focus on Alamo City–based acts like the Sons of Hercules and the Dropouts. "All those bands have jobs," Morgan told Rob Patterson in a 1996 *Dallas Observer* story.[1] "That's kind of a nice change. Up here [in Austin], a lot of the bands I hang out with are bums. They don't have any money. They're bumming money off of me. I go down there, and everybody buys me drinks."

While Rise and Unclean were the most prolific labels run by Sound Exchange employees, they weren't the only ones. Christian Caperton started Undone Records, which released the first singles from noise-rock trio john-boy and garage-blues combo Jack O'Fire in addition to Glorium's 1994 epic full-length *Cinema Peligrosa*. Mark Fagan's Bunkhouse put out eclectic seven-inch compilations of bands from Austin and Houston, including Androm-eda Strain, Sad Pygmy, and Noodle.

Mark Twistworthy[2] migrated from Houston to Austin in 1996 and got a job at Sound Exchange, bringing his namesake label into the fray. Twistworthy specialized in local bands raised on the head-down intensity of hardcore that had moved on to more musically adventurous terrain. Paul Newman's 1997 single, ". . . Please Wait During the Silence," created a suspenseful atmosphere with spartan arrangements and odd time signatures. Society of Friends AKA Quakers also employed quick musical turns on their 1999 *Vol. III* EP, but their evolution from hardcore drove deeper into distorted chaos punctured by the throat-shredding screams of ex–Crown Roast vocalist August Alston. For a short time, a band might have two or three different projects in the fire with different labels, all run by Sound Exchange employees.

The post-Trance local label renaissance wasn't confined to the corner of 21st and Guadalupe. Poster artist Lindsey Kuhn borrowed a page from Kozik and started the No Lie label, releasing singles from Jack O'Fire and the American Psycho Band along with full-length albums from the Cryin' Out Louds and Jesus Christ Superfly. Musician/sound engineer Kurtis Machler started Monkey Boy Records, which released singles from Peglegasus and Big Horny Hustler and an album from Chaindrive. Glorium vocalist Paul Streckfus ran the prolific Golden Hour label, chronicling the more esoteric, avant-leaning wing of the scene on cassette.

Alums of UT student radio station KTSB/KVRX also got in on the action. Former hardcore show cohost Joey Edwards founded Little Deputy Records, releasing 1993's *3,410 Flavors* EP from youthful pop-punk trio Gomez along with singles by SAP and Plaid Retina. Ex–music director Naomi Shapiro started the Fluffer label in 1992 to release a single from local pop combo Balloonatic. Then she made history by putting out 1994's *Nefarious* EP, the very first release from Spoon.

Spoon also recorded for Travis Higdon's Peek-A-Boo label in their early days. So did Britt Daniel's solo alias Drake Tungsten. Higdon started Peek-A-Boo as an offshoot from the zine of the same name in 1994 to put out a single by his goofball garage quartet the 1-4-5s. Highlights of the label's catalog include Silver Scooter's melancholic 1997 debut LP *The Other Palm Springs* and the Kiss Offs' 1999 LP, *Goodbye Private Life* (which features Higdon on guitar).

Enthusiasm for the seven-inch vinyl format began to wane as the decade wore on. "Nobody is doing vinyl anymore," Craig Stewart of Trance Syndicate imprint Emperor Jones Records told the *Austin Chronicle* in May 1998. "Nobody is buying it either."[3]

Peek-A-Boo's Higdon echoed a similar sentiment later that year. "The stores are overcrowded because it's been really convenient to put out a record over the past few years," Higdon said. "Everybody starts a label, and the stores get flooded with records. Unfortunately, some of them aren't very good and they stay on the shelf. The record shop owner stops buying so many records, the distributors won't take them, so you wind up with all these records in your apartment."[4]

This scenario could hardly be surprising since these local labels were driven primarily by their owners' desires to promote music they loved rather than clear-headed analysis of market forces. But love only goes so far. Behind the romance of owning an independent label lay the mundane grunt work of fulfilling mail orders, servicing far-flung publications and college radio stations with promo copies, playing phone tag with manufacturers, and trying to get paid.

Against this backdrop, it's no wonder few of these labels dealt in contracts. A "record deal" with one of these labels was often a verbal agreement. This usually worked out fine since most releases failed to turn a profit for anyone. No money, no problem.

The salad days of Sound Exchange's Wall of Singles and the notion that anyone with $500 and a favorite band should start a record label to release a single by that band were short-lived, but the groundswell of interest in documenting this new music in its nascent stage was transformative. By the end of 1993, acts that had previously been relegated to house parties and the occasional Cannibal Club show had multiple clubs to book shows at, multiple zines that might write about them, and now, multiple local labels to potentially put out their records. Taken together, this conferred a whole new level of approbation on what was happening.

Roger Morgan: The very moment I went DIY was at the Sex Pistols '78 show in Tulsa—some brave people coming into our city and having beers thrown at them and yelled at. Some of the people that I went to that show with went on to be in bands. Immediately. Shortly after that, I was forming the label. Anybody can do this! And I think a lot of people feel that way.

I was playing in a band called the Lepers and we decided to produce a single. We needed a clever label name and Unclean kind of comes with the whole theme of the Lepers. That was in the summer of 1986.

Bones DeLarge: Roger used to do Unclean Records when I was a kid. He put out bands like the Rhythm Pigs. He put out N.O.T.A. He put out a lot of the Austin bands after that. I was doing a fanzine in San Diego and would write to him, and he'd actually send me records to review. That was one of the coolest fucking things. When I moved to Austin and started working at Sound Exchange, he was working there. I was totally enthralled.

Roger Morgan: We were always jealous of each other, but in the long run we realized everybody was helping each other. None of us were making a killing on it.

Mark Fagan: I had Bunkhouse Records. I worked at Sound Exchange and Roger had Unclean and Craig had his label, and Christian had Undone. There was a picture of us in *Billboard* magazine one time because we all worked at this little record store in Austin and all had labels. That was just kind of the environment back then. Everybody just created and put stuff out.

Britt Daniel: When I came down to Austin, the idea of putting out a record was way too expensive. A cassette you could just go get duped. Sometime around '92 I started noticing that people were putting out seven-inch records. Craig Koon told me where to get the thing made. This is before he started his own pressing plant.

Tim Stegall: Craig Koon's originally from Ohio. He knew the guys from the New Bomb Turks and had worked for a time at Dutch East India Trading Company, which was the big indie record distributor. He had been friends with Gerard Cosloy and people like that. Craig saw himself as the fly in the ointment of the Austin music scene.

Craig Koon: You had to actually physically make something and go shove it in people's faces. If they paid attention to it, great. If they didn't, well, you tried. But you were at least having fun. At that point, nobody was really doing a label.

Roger Morgan: I have to give Craig Koon credit for getting everybody fired up. At Sound Exchange, we had promoters coming in from all labels, and we started getting this lightbulb going off, "Hey! We are kind of in a unique position here . . ."

Edith Casimir: It was so cool. I don't think we had to give him any money. And I think we probably got fifty bucks apiece back. It was just a piece of cake. It was so nice how other people did things just because they wanted to see them done. Other people would go, "Is it okay if I record this?" Or Bill [Jeffery] making a comic book about us. "I hope you don't mind. I made a comic book about you." Cool.

Bill Jeffery: Every Austin boy had a crush on Pork, and it was an honor to be around them. I loved their pop songs. I loved their garage songs. Because of Craig Koon, I was like, "Golly, this single's great!"

Edith Casimir: Nobody had to promote themselves that much because everybody else was promoting you for their own wholesome reasons. But the guy we were dealing with at Elektra was a flake.

Craig Koon: After I'd done the Pork record, I thought, "There's so much stuff going on here, I've got to document all these bands." I was thinking how to do it and I had no money. I'd spent it all on the Pork single. What do we do? A coworker at Sound Exchange said, "Well, you know that tall guy who comes in and sells us posters? Why don't you talk to him? He acts like he's got money."

Tim Stegall: Frank Kozik was a local poster artist that was getting a lot of national attention. He really started that vogue for the silkscreened, fine-art posters for rock shows.

Craig Koon: Frank comes striding in and was actually very nice. He said, "Well, listen, dude. I don't have any money, dude, but I'm Frank Kozik. People want my stuff, so you will get my art. We'll make limited-edition records, and people will want to buy them. The bands are just along for the ride." I called up Dutch East India and said, "Everybody and their brother wants to do a distribution deal, but I actually have an edge. I've got Frank Kozik." They liked that idea.

Rick Carney: When Rise started, all of a sudden we don't have to call New York or Chicago. Obviously, we were trying to get the attention of Touch and Go. We were trying to get the attention of Dutch East, who ended up being our distributor with Rise.

There was a deal through Dutch East where they actually manufactured and distributed everything. We would sell some records and then—when it was time for the label to get paid—Dutch East would simply manufacture more, keeping Rise and us always in debt to them. That was my first taste as to how the record business is what it is. If somebody can take advantage of you, they probably will.

Craig Koon: Rise and Sound Exchange are two sides of the same coin. They're both the story of promising beginnings, missed opportunities, and a sad demise.

Rob Patterson: There was great Frank Kozik art on them, and on the back of one of them it says, "Rise Records—the sound of Rob Patterson's colon twitching." It's really not a twitching colon. I really wasn't the enemy. I was the music editor of the *Chronicle*, so I wasn't doing enough. Frankly, how could anyone do enough? We didn't have enough space. Didn't have enough writers. But that's what you do. You oppose whatever you think the establishment is.

Tim Stegall: Because I was published in national magazines and all that, I think Craig thought that I was some figure who could be bought and sold.

He questioned my integrity as a rock journalist. I think he felt like I was a sacred cow that needed to be taken down. Then he heard the Hormones at our very first gig. Right away he was just really into it.

Michelle Rule: Craig took us into the little side lounge area at Electric Lounge and offered us a record deal. That was our first seven-inch. He made the vinyl version of our first album at his press over on Fifth Street. It had some little bubbles in it here and there. Some of them sounded better than others.

When we got home from our first tour, we had a cease-and-desist letter from Madison Square Garden, LLP. It said we were infringing on the name of Miss Universe. Supposedly someone had complained that they went to a club thinking that the real Miss Universe event was going to be there. I don't believe this for a minute. What kind of dumbass thinks they're going to go to some shitty club and see some woman in an evening gown with a sash? We hired a lawyer who told us that if we had $10,000 and [would] fly him up to New York City that we could win and get to keep the name. But we didn't have $10,000. We didn't have two nickels to rub together between us. That's when we became Miss Galaxy.

Craig Koon: We wanted to do one national and one local. The Mono Men were on their twelve songs, twelve record labels, worldwide tour, so that worked for them too. They came out and actually sold well, much to the surprise of Dutch East India. Our next record was supposed to be a single with Moist Fist.

Gary Chester: Moist Fist was during the Ed Hall days. Ed Hall played really loud, and our ears would always ring and then afterwards we'd listen to the Carpenters. My roommate at the time was like, "Let's be in a band where we could play nice and peaceful music." So we learned some Bach and some Satie and then my girlfriend Kelly was like, "I will sing."

Kelly Linn: I was like, "You guys need some women energy vibe in this." They were like, "What about the name?"

Susannah Simone: I was reading a novel by Joyce Carol Oates, and the last words of a chapter were, *Her smell is that of something being crushed in a moist fist.*[5] It's a sign! So we put it on the back of our T-shirts.

Craig Koon: We made a record and that became one of the first points where I should've realized there was going to be trouble with Rise Records. Frank gave them a cover that they didn't like. Creepy school children in wheelchairs, quoting Manson, with a spider.[6]

Susannah Simone: The artwork that Kozik did on our album is kind of reflective of "Let's just be absurd and offensive because that's what people expect from this genre."

Craig Koon: They were like, "What the fuck? This has nothing to do with us." They were really angry.

Susannah Simone: I remember seeing the album cover and going, "Yeah, what does this have to do with our band?"

Craig Koon: Frank's like, "Dude. They don't like the cover, they don't have to put out the record. That's what they get, man. The bands are riding my coattails." He wouldn't do another cover. After that, things stalled for a while.

Mark Fagan: We [Noodle] finished the record and turned it in, and Frank's going to do the art in a month. A month goes by and he's got some *ideas* for the art. And then a couple more months. This happens for about a year. Eventually we just got Lindsey Kuhn to do it. He killed the cover, by the way. It's the picture of Charles Whitman as a little kid on the beach with a gun.

Craig Koon: I don't want to sound like sour grapes with Frank because Frank did a lot of great things. But it was bewildering to me why he wouldn't work. I finally had to talk to him. He's like, "Dude, it'll all work out."

While this was going on, Roger Morgan said, "Well, I'm going to start my record label up again." Then the kid that was working with us said, "I'm going to start a record label too." Everyone suddenly had record labels. It was the perfect time. It fed on itself, and people got excited again. People actually thought music in Austin was fun. The sun came out and everybody was getting drunk and having fun.

Roger Morgan: We all got fired up again and the scene started happening again. Lisa in the Inhalants—she worked at Sound Exchange with us.

Lisa Rickenberg: Any band who was playing for any amount of time would immediately get local labels asking to put out singles. The Inhalants put out like six or seven seven-inch records on different labels. We did a single with Roger. We did a single with Craig on Rise. We did a couple singles with Estrus who put out our album. Estrus was putting out runs of like two thousand seven-inch and several thousand albums. It definitely got us out there. And we did a single on a Seattle label called Bag of Hammers. My boyfriend put out a split single with Stretford. We did a split on Peek-A-Boo. We did one on a compilation album with an English label. *Maximum Rocknroll* hated almost everything we ever did. We got distribution and a lot of people in other countries heard it for sure. And we got to go up and play Garage Shock.

Roger Morgan: We did a Glorium single through Jim Bradford, who was also a Sound Exchange employee. What attracted me to them was that real dissonant Sonic Youth sound. Ernest [Salaz] and Linus [Streckfus] played incredible together. And that was kind of the beginning of my working relationships with San Antonio bands. And then of course they said, "You got to go check out this other band we play with called Rig." I went to see them one night, and the top of my head blew off. They were so good. The single got played on John Peel.

Scott Gardner: Roger put out that first Sons of Hercules LP on Unclean. It was garage in the traditional sense. It had kind of a '60s vibe but '90s music and it really holds up well. Frank [Pugliese] is one of the all-time great frontmen. He's tall, lanky, and he just oozes coolness. He's got that Iggy/Jagger kind of swagger. A great focal point for the band.

Tim Hayes: The Sons of Hercules. I mean, where to begin? They are the foundation of that whole Austin, Texas, garage scene. Even though they're from San Antonio, they were like *the* foundation because they have been doing it for so freaking long. And Frank has been doing it since the '70s.[7] You can't speak more highly of those guys.

Scott Gardner: They're one of the bands that Mike [Mariconda] produced. His engineering production was different than say Tim Kerr. Tim had more of a garage aesthetic. Mike was never into the garage aesthetic. He was more into full-bodied rock. He wasn't into lo-fi.

Roger Morgan: We were most proud of our Sons of Hercules and Stretford releases. We were starting to get our shtick down on how to get things done. Dino Reyes doing graphic design. Mike Mariconda producing. Distribution was being taken care of ahead of time. We were doing vinyl, CDs,

Sons of Hercules vocalist Frank Pugliese representing San Antonio at Emo's, 1994. Photo by Sean McGowan.

and cassettes. Plus we were planning tours. Sons of Hercules were willing to travel. We got interest from the New Bomb Turks. A lot of things were clicking at that point and there was a lot of press.

John Spath: The Administration did a lot of work with Roger and Margie [Morgan, Roger's wife] over at Unclean. My own philosophy with bands is

[that] I like to see the band play. The band's personality is the most critical part of any music video. What I saw as problematic—and I still see it today—is directors just wanting to make something for their director's reel, and so they make a narrative story and they fumble trying to explain the lyrics.

Scott Gardner: That scene was just really diverse. You had the punkier Motards bad boys, poppier bands like the Wannabes, and the one band that everyone could agree on is Stretford. If you had to draw a Venn diagram, Stretford would be in the middle for everyone.

Carl Normal: There was definitely a resurgence of seven-inch vinyl. Our first thing on any release was "Pogo on My Own," which was on *Texas Bashing*—a four-song EP.

Ken Dannelley: A guy from the Perturbed put it out.

Carl Normal: That inspired us to put out a seven-inch of our own—the *Target* EP. Then Unclean put out a version of it much later because we didn't get signed to Unclean until '94. So we put out four singles if you include the flexi disc, which *Pop Culture Press* put out.

Chuck Trend: Stretford were a really good pop band but still had a punk aesthetic. They were unique just because of Carl and his personality. They had horns but they weren't like a funk band. And their records were good. That first Stretford record—and that first single on Unclean—were two of my favorite records from that time. The songs were just so good.

Tim Storm: The Hamicks were a little different, but they were part of our crowd as well.

Jonathan Toubin: These two punk brothers, the drummer for Stretford [Ken Dannelley] and his brother [Ron Dannelley], were at a small coffeehouse in San Marcos, and they happened to come upon an open-mic night.

This guy [Hamicks guitarist/vocalist Bob Taylor] comes up, and he's a really weird, skinny kid with an odd expression and downturned mouth. He only plays guitar with downstrokes on his acoustic. Kind of like new wave music, but with an acoustic guitar. He's singing a song, "There was poop in her pants. There was poop in his pants," and telling this whole story about how this person didn't know he had poop in his pants.

These brothers thought, "This guy needs a band." These two brothers, one of whom played bass, the other played drums, they proceeded to record this guy and his record went pretty well.

Roger Morgan: They became part of the friendly group. I recall thinking, "Who the hell am I going to sell this to?" Bob made a promotional coloring book. It's hilarious. It's done just like a child's book. "Connect the dots to see Ken playing drums at his first gig!"

Jonathan Toubin: As Noodle was wrapping up, they asked me to join the band because I was at all their shows.

Craig Koon: Suddenly *everyone* had record labels and everybody could be distributed. It's like baseball cards. "You got to get all their singles!"

Ryan McDaniel: Our [Gomez's] first seven-inch came out on Little Deputy Records. We recorded four songs but didn't have a label. Joey Edwards[8] wanted to start a label and was like, "Hey I want you guys to be my first band!" The *Planet of the Apes* seven-inch is the record that started everything off. We recorded it at Music Lane. It's a totally *big-rock-star* studio. It felt weird at first because we were this rinky-dink band. Our friend Rick Carney—who is the singer and guitar player in Jesus Christ Superfly—produced it for us.

Chepo Peña: We weren't that great of a band live at that point, and going into this big recording studio made us sound really big and good.

Ryan McDaniel: We were able to record our first six songs, which turned out to be *Planet of the Apes* and *Growing Up Gomez.* Chepo and I were fascinated by this book *Growing Up Brady* written by Mr. Barry Williams, who played [Greg Brady] on *The Brady Bunch.* The album has a photograph of him after he got into an accident driving his Porsche. Susan Olsen—Cindy Brady—was promoting *The Brady Bunch Movie* by doing an autograph session at a Taco Bell. In my bag I had one of these records. I showed it to her, and she was like, "Hey, that's Barry with a busted lip!" Yes it is! It was pretty cool to show one of *The Brady Bunch* people that we actually did a *Brady Bunch* record.

So this record comes out and sounds bigger and badder than we had ever sounded. I think one of the reasons was because I used all the gear of my friend Bryan Christner, who was in the most awesome hardcore band called Intent.

Mark Fagan: It was a real solidarity. We all bought each other's records and played on each other's records. We were competitive, but it was friendly, you know? And then the competitiveness actually made us want to do more. If your band put out a record, it's time for my band to put out a record. If y'all opened up for SNFU, we needed to open for the Circle Jerks.

Conrad Keely: Paul [Streckfus] wanted to do this cassette label. He got all of our different friends' bands together. He did this one A-tape with all of the bands with As in the name. . . . And You Will Know Us by the Trail of Dead, Andromeda Strain . . .

Lauren Robertson: I think he was criticized a little bit because he would record live stuff and just put out cassettes. I don't even know if he had consent. He was just a super fan and loved music.

Paul Streckfus: Golden Hour was really inspired by Todd Ledford's Bobby J Records tape label here in town. He was doing weird noise improv home recording stuff only on cassette. I did comps at first to get things going and introduce people to a bunch of bands at the same time. Eventually we started putting out our own CDs and a seven-inch. It was just a Panasonic handheld recorder, so lots of those recordings are really kind of noisy. Now I have a digital recorder and I'm releasing stuff online.

Lauren Robertson: Bands were going crazy about that Prima Donnas cassette that Paul put out. It got so widely distributed around the country. I got a call at Sound Exchange from Ian MacKaye. "You got to tell me about this band! Who is this? This is amazing!" I was like, "They're this fake British band and that's their deal."

Jonathan Toubin: The Prima Donnas were the first band to bring an '80s analog synth. They were *the* big K Records/Kill Rock Stars crowd, so we [Hamicks] had a split single with them and toured with them.

Lauren Robertson: The funny thing about Prima Donnas is they would go on tour in character and never break their British persona. They would end up at someone's house trying to continue this fucking charade. It's very funny. I saw them in New York with the Donnas in the late '90s. So yeah, Golden Hour elevated them.

Travis Higdon: There was a lot of different scenes going on in Austin at the time. There was the more intelligent/art/alternative rock scene with Spoon and Sincola and Sixteen Deluxe and those bands. There was the garage punk scene with the Motards, the Inhalants, and the Cryin' Out Louds and all those kind of sloppy drunk punk bands. Those scenes didn't really overlap anywhere except for Chepo Peña, who somehow played in every band in Austin. I just followed my taste. The Peek-A-Boo sound was all over the map.

Tom Hudson: Being on a label definitely felt really good. Travis was a really honest guy. It was done with a handshake and all the money was fifty-fifty split after he recouped the costs of creating the album. I think some people were surprised that we were on Peek-A-Boo, but we loved it. We liked the idea that Travis was all about putting out Texas-based music.

Travis Higdon: It started as a vanity label to release one single for the very first band I was ever in—the 1-4-5s. Nothing but schtick. We were huge fans of all the garage rock that was going on, especially this one band called Supercharger from San Francisco.

We were joking around about how all garage rock is just 1-4-5 chord progressions. We thought it would be fun to use that as our formula and never stray from that. And a lot of this garage rock paraphernalia is this muscle car, gearhead stuff, so instead of muscle cars, we had songs about Volvo hatchbacks and a Dodge Caravan. Next thing I know, we've got a record and toured Japan. So it was far beyond any of my expectations.

Then I was in the Kiss Offs with Phillip [Niemeyer] from the Teen Titans and Gavin [Scott] from the 1-4-5s and drummer Dwayne Barnes and keyboard player Katey Jones. We were all ready to do a serious band, so we tried to actually write artful songs. It was a lot of fun as well. The Kiss Offs gimmick was debauchery and letting that kind of carry over into music. A seedy, Velvet Underground-y type of thing.

The Teen Titans were hilarious. They had a sound that I would describe as kiddie-punk. It came from a true appreciation of punk music but not actually cool enough to make cool music, so we made funny music instead. The songs were very childish and whimsical and literary at the same time. It was a lot of fun.

I put out Spoon, the Vidi Vitties, and Super XX Man—Scott Garred from Silver Scooter's solo project—a band called Poopiehead, Junior Varsity, and Silver Scooter.

DRAKE TUNGSTEN
"Six Pence for the Sauces"

SIDE A - 1. Do the Manta Ray 2. Cool It You Need
SIDE B - 3. Chicago @ Night 4. He Was Soon to Undergo an
Experience for which His Long Training as an Aristocrat, a Gentleman,
and an Officer Had Scarcely Prepared Him 5. I Could Be Underground

D. Tungsten, P.O. Box 684651, Austin, TX 78768
All songs by D. Tungsten except #1.
Thanks M. Daniel drums on Manta Ray.
©1996 Peek-a-Boo Global Industries

Drake Tungsten cover on Peek-A-Boo
Records. Courtesy of Travis Higdon.

Tom Hudson: There was a time when Crank Records in L.A. was trying to win us over. It just wasn't the same. We'd go out and visit with him, and he'd take us out to dinner and try to court us. But it didn't feel anything close to like what we had with Travis.

The Other Palm Springs was recorded with Dave McNair, who randomly just saw us at a show at Hole in the Wall and really wanted to record us. He had a history of recording all these top-name bands in the '80s. Horrible music. We absolutely did not want to work with him, but he talked us into it.

He set up a twenty-four-track inside his house and totally interrupted his life for about eight weeks. It was a learning experience for him to realize what indie rock is all about and what sounds are cool when you record an album. By the end of it, we ended up with this album and we all loved it. He loved it and we loved it. This album I would definitely say is the heart of Silver Scooter.

Travis Higdon: The whole idea with the label was trying to support the Austin scene. I put out one single for Drake Tungsten and he self-released a cassette. Then he dropped the Drake Tungsten pseudonym and played solo as Britt Daniel. I don't think he ever intended to do much with Drake Tungsten beyond the cassette, and I asked him to do a few songs for a single. I think it was a venue for him to demo songs for Spoon.

Britt Daniel: I just wanted to do some solo shows. I had all these four-track recordings, but they were never done for a band. They were just done for me—not what Spoon was doing whatsoever. So I gave it a more interesting name.

Travis Higdon: Some of the records I put out got better national attention than they did local attention. I remember having conversations with a bunch of people that Austin could be the next Seattle. Not in a cheesy, hype-y way, but hoping people would see there's this magical musical thing happening in Austin. Some people thought that was a good thing. A lot of people thought that was going to be the worst thing in the world and that we were just going to get descended upon by media whores and A&R reps and douchebags . . . industry people.

TRANCE SYNDICATE

LOVE AND NAPALM

YOU KNOW, IT'S A NEW YEAR. IT'S A NEW DECADE. LET'S DO THIS RECORD
LABEL THING.

KING COFFEY

DURING THE 1980S IT WAS COMMON FOR promising Austin musicians to pack up and move to major metropolises as a means of advancing their craft. Dicks vocalist Gary Floyd left town in 1983 and reformed the band with new members in San Francisco. Ex–Scratch Acid vocalist David Yow and bassist David Wm. Sims embarked to Chicago to advance the Jesus Lizard in 1987—home of Corey Rusk and the Touch and Go label. Newer bands like Nice Strong Arm and Miracle Room subsequently left for New York, which put them in closer proximity to their respective labels—Homestead and Bar/None.

The Butthole Surfers simply stayed on the road for much of the decade. When they decided they needed a base, they rented a small house outside Athens, Georgia. It was here—not in Texas—that they recorded 1987's *Locust Abortion Technician*. For a band constantly on tour, the move saved countless odometer ticks by putting them hundreds of miles closer to the majority of large US cities.

Any Austin band that ever tried to mount a tour knows just getting out of Texas is a hurdle. Heading west toward California, the closest likely place for gigs is El Paso, nearly nine hours away. In the pre-internet days when long-distance phone calls and snail mail were the only ways to counter the realities of geography, Austin wasn't the most strategic beachhead for a fledgling band to launch a national campaign from.

On a more prosaic level, one line of reasoning went that Austin had a great music scene but no viable way to transcend the big fish–small pond dynamic. Others invoked the so-called velvet rut argument—contending that the pleasures of Austin's easy life made it difficult to create work of consequence.

This was the gap Butthole Surfers drummer King Coffey stepped into when he made his New Year's resolution to start what would become Trance Syndicate Records on January 1, 1990. Coffey's association with the Buttholes gave instant credibility to the endeavor. It also helped facilitate a manufacturing and distribution deal with Touch and Go, the band's label for most of the 1980s. The Touch and Go deal gave Trance more of a financial cushion and greater reach than the other local labels that emerged in its wake.

While these factors were key ingredients in Trance's success, it was the artist roster that built the label's reputation. Between 1990 and 1998 Coffey and his partner—later to be spouse—Craig Stewart cultivated an eclectic cross-section of homegrown underground noise. Some of it was ear-bitingly loud, some of it was sparse and subtle, but it was all left of center, and it was almost all from Texas.

As such, Trance hoisted an aural freak flag over Austin that signaled a geographic hotbed of musical activity. Though Trance didn't have the same seismic impact on Austin that Sub Pop had on Seattle, the symbiotic relationship between label and local scene was similar. Not since Houston's International Artists label introduced the 13th Floor Elevators to the world in 1966 had a Texas-based rock label held such sway.

Coffey's first salvo was Crust's 1990 EP debut, *Sacred Heart of Crust*. The trio's industrial-strength noise assault employed homemade instruments and martial percussion alongside copious nods to scatology and sacrilege. In many regards they were cut from the same soiled vestment as the Buttholes.

Then came Ed Hall, another local trio that steadily worked their way up from Dong Huong to headlining Liberty Lunch. Ed Hall combined elements of punk, hard rock, and psychedelia with the abandon of teens raiding the parental liquor cabinet, then girded their concoction with a danceable bottom end. Their shows were multisensory extravaganzas thanks to projectionist Luke Savisky's kit bag of film loops and the band's proclivity to perform in nothing but shorts and Day Glo body paint.

The Cherubs' 1994 salvo *Heroin Man* was the most trenchant release of Trance's formative years. Lead cut "Stag Party" begins with the loud, incessant warning pulse that accompanies an off-the-hook landline receive before boring headlong into waves of hypnotic sludge and primal screams. Even more impressive, it was recorded right in the middle of downtown Austin at Sweatbox Studios.

Heroin Man should've made Cherubs mainstays on the national alt-club circuit that stretched from the 9:30 Club in Washington, DC, to Lounge Ax in Chicago, to Bottom of the Hill in San Francisco. Instead, the band broke up shortly after its release.[1] That same year Trance released johnboy's *Claim Dedications*—a sparse-but-potent prog-punk exclamation produced by Steve Albini—only to have that band split as well.

The first signal that Trance would transcend its noise rock pedigree came with the 1994 release of Bedhead's *WhatFunLifeWas*. The Dallas-based band led by brothers Bubba and Matt Kadane took a slow, quiet approach to crafting songs that served as a diametrical counterweight to the label's other artists. Even Trance's logo had to evolve to incorporate what Bedhead brought to the tent.

As 1995 dawned, Coffey had an honest-to-goodness buzz band on his hands. Barely six months old, Sixteen Deluxe released "Idea." This fuzzed-up pop confection—one of the strongest singles to come out of Austin in the 1990s or any decade—was a direct hit to the sweet spot between familiar and novel. Almost immediately, Sixteen Deluxe began accruing national press and major-label interest.

Trance's March 17, 1995, SXSW showcase was a high-water mark. Held at the 1,700-capacity Terrace,[2] it was a centerpiece of a festival that had all but ignored the local underground music scene just a few years earlier. Label first wavers Crust and Ed Hall shared the bill with newer ascendants Bedhead, Sixteen Deluxe, Furry Things, and Desafinado. Hüsker Dü/Sugar principal and SXSW keynote speaker Bob Mould—then living in Austin—sweetened the pot with a short acoustic set.

Later that year Coffey solidified the link between Trance and International Artists by releasing Roky Erickson's *All That May Do My Rhyme*. The album contained Erickson's first new studio recordings in years and featured guest work from local musical luminaries like guitarist Charlie Sexton, vocalist Lou Ann Barton, and Butthole Surfers guitarist Paul Leary. At the time Erickson was living with untreated schizophrenia and surviving on disability checks in the Austin-adjacent town of Del Valle. As a result, Coffey's role as label head expanded to include more traditional caregiver functions like bringing his artist groceries or taking him out to eat at Pancho's Mexican Buffet.[3]

Poster for Trance Syndicate SXSW Showcase at the Terrace, March 17, 1995, by JasonAustin.

With Trance going great guns, Stewart launched the Emperor Jones imprint in 1995. Emperor Jones counted some Texas acts, but Stewart's far-reaching tastes necessitated going beyond state lines. The label's first release was My Dad Is Dead's *For Richer, For Poorer*, a collection of deep-water indie-pop paeans to broken love from Ohio's Mark Edwards. Emperor Jones also released albums by Australian folk outcast Pip Proud and Jad Fair's long-running indie outfit Half Japanese. When not running the label, Stewart helped lead booking for SXSW, which helped ensure the music festival's vitality.

By 1996 the Butthole Surfers had pulled off the wholly improbable stunt of crossing over into mainstream musical consciousness. Three years after signing a major label deal with Capitol and enlisting Led Zeppelin bassist John Paul Jones to produce *Independent Worm Saloon*, they had a bona fide hit record. "Pepper," the lead single off *Electriclarryland*, topped *Billboard*'s Modern Rock chart for three weeks and cracked the Top 40. Its accompanying video featured a cameo from *CHiPs* star Erik Estrada, and the band performed the song on CBS's *Late Show with David Letterman*.

This broad commercial success ensured a steady stream of braver souls who would seek out the Buttholes' earlier Touch and Go albums. But when the band was unable to negotiate a more favorable royalty rate with Touch and Go, they filed suit to obtain their back catalog. Although Trance was not party to the lawsuit, Coffey was a member of the Buttholes, and this created rifts in the previously collegial relationship he had with Touch and Go founder Corey Rusk.

In the meantime, Trance and Emperor Jones maintained a steady schedule of releases. After springing to life as a four-track amalgamation of Beach Boys and My Bloody Valentine axioms, Furry Things began exploring dance and electronic avenues starting with their 1996 EP, *hedfones*. Windsor for the Derby arrived in Austin from Florida and almost immediately delineated themselves from the loud, fast set with cinematic, post-rock meditations. Fort Worth transplants the American Analog Set plied their lo-fi living room sound on Emperor Jones, as did Cavity-era garage punk stalwarts Pork, who worked with Stewart to release *Slop* after a deal with Elektra fell through.

Trance's success was inexorably linked to Touch and Go's robust distribution network. This network was all the more impressive considering that Chicago-based Touch and Go maintained a DIY-inspired ethos of operating on handshake deals that split profits fifty-fifty with artists. It was difficult to imagine the label maintaining primacy without Touch and Go.

"I personally thought the lawsuit was a really bad idea," Coffey said in 1998. "I was against it, but it seemed to me that my bandmates and Corey, who runs Touch and Go, could not reach an agreement. They were being really stubborn, and no amount of mediation on my part was going to resolve anything. Both parties were sticking to their guns. I realized all I could really do is just sit back and let those guys have their lawsuit, which for me was really depressing."[4]

Even before the lawsuit, burnout was setting in. After eight years of running a label, Coffey began to realize this was not something he had to keep doing. Then Rusk delivered an ultimatum.

"He said it's our decision if we keep putting out records, and certainly all the records will be kept in print," Coffey said. "But he said as much as he liked me as a person and knew I wasn't the instigator behind this lawsuit, he still knows that I was one of the band members named in the lawsuit, and I need to take some accountability for this. Therefore, he didn't want to be releasing any new Trance records."[5]

Coffey decided to shut down Trance in the fall of 1998, but not before making one last divot in the course of Austin music history by releasing the self-titled debut LP from . . . And You Will Know Us by the Trail of Dead. Trance's final release was Starfish's *Instrumental* EP. The Butthole Surfers' lawsuit would ultimately be decided in favor of the band by the US Seventh Circuit Court of Appeals on March 26, 1999. Stewart's Emperor Jones imprint survived the closure, continuing to release new music until 2007.

While Austin's underground music scene was poised to flourish in the 1990s regardless, it's hard to imagine as many people paying attention without Trance's formation. Even for local bands not on the label, Trance served as a calling card both in the United States and overseas. Significantly, the label evolved beyond its foundational loud-and-weird output to document the evolution of local underground music as bands moved further afield to explore new sounds not as grounded in punk's sneering aesthetic. If Trance's demise ended an era, at least its finely curated existence ensured that era was well-chronicled.

King Coffey: So many great Texas bands either broke up because nobody was putting out their records, or nobody cared. Trance's focus was to work with bands in Texas—specifically Austin.

I was attracted to art-punk stuff—people who came from a punk background but were doing different things with it. It had to be music that I liked, people that I liked, that I could see as helping the label. And also, what would make sense for Touch and Go? They were our distributor. You're asking them to sink their money and time to promote whatever record you want to work with. Almost anybody running an indie label is not in it for the money. You're only in it for the fun of it. That really was the case with Trance. We just broke even every year, so I really had to like the music and the people.

Jonathan Toubin: Austin was one of the most regional places in the world. They had this Antone's blues scene. They had the folk guys. One other thing that Austin was known for around the country was being the home of the Butthole Surfers. There was a little bit of attention being paid to the Austin underground even though there was no real underground, except for maybe the things that Trance Syndicate was starting with, from the first Crust album.

King Coffey: Crust were insane. They were part performance art. They had industrial aspects of their music, grounded in noise and punk rock. I think it was a very Texan creation too, with the singer, the Reverend Art Bank Lobby. His whole take of the televangelist was very specific to the South. I related to what they were doing as far as weird, performance, Texas freak art. Instead of playing bass guitar they were banging on metal springs. Nothing made sense, yet it all worked.

TR01 was my first attempt to make a label. I wanted to do it right, so I sent them to a real nice studio, and we spent way too much money. By the time it came time to make the covers, I ran out of money. We got it together and that was TR01.

Jonathan Toubin: Crust had a big showmanship thing. John Hawkins was like a preacher. They were far scarier than the Butthole Surfers. It blew my mind.

All over town, the cops were trying to get John Hawkins because he would always get naked and oiled up, and the TABC wouldn't allow that. I remember at the Ritz—this giant, cavernous theater—he's covered in all this oil, all lubed up, and he's got worms sewed into his pubic hair. He's setting the worms on fire. The cops come in and he had to split. The band kept playing, and he went out through a classic old stage door and starts running. He jogged all the way home to Hyde Park covered in oil and worms. The cops had nothing. He was a role model.

Marc Fort: I was playing with FuckEmos at the Austin Music Hall[6] on New Year's Eve. Crust was headlining, and their singer had sewn live earthworms into his testicles. I don't think I had eaten any hallucinogens or anything, but it sure felt like I was tripping.

Gary Chester: Every time we played with Crust, their show would eclipse the music. We're backstage putting a little paint on and then we look over at the guys from Crust and they're weaving living worms into their arms. How can we compete?

Lyman Hardy: Luke Savisky had four 16mm projectors and would change film loops, running them over each other. It looked crazy. We did that for the Austin Music Awards, but the awards had all been given out. All the mainstream bands had played, and all the masses of people were like, "Who is this guy Ed Hall? It looks weird." And they started leaving. There's this great moment in the video where we're playing this crazy music and there's films and we're in black light and the camera pans around to the back of the auditorium. There's one dude sweeping.

Gary Chester: We were trying to be like the poor man's Butthole Surfers. We had paint and black lights and art films on loop.

King Coffey: I was just a huge fan of Ed Hall. I saw some authentic vibe to what they were doing, as far as what the Buttholes were doing. A freaky, almost tribal, very Texan take of punk and art in general. I poached them from Boner.

Gary Chester: Our Boner [Records] guy—Tom Flynn—would say, "I'm going to put your record out but I'm on tour with the Melvins right now playing the bass." And we were like, "Dude you're taking too long! This guy down the street wants to put our record out *right now* and he's in the Butthole Surfers. And our dogs are friends."

Larry Strub: We recorded *Gloryhole* at Butch Vig's studio, and he was supposed to record us, but he was off recording Nirvana.

Gary Chester: They said, "We can only give you three days in the studio, and Butch is not going to be here because he is going overtime with this band, Nirvana." We were just like, "Why three days?" "Because L7 has got the place booked for six weeks and they're cutting into your turf. But the good news is, I can mix one of your songs and mail it to you."

We came up here to make an album in three days and you're going to *mail* us the mixes?

Larry Strub: And then he accidentally recorded over a vocal part I did, so I had to do it by phone long-distance.

Gary Chester: We mixed *Gloryhole* and then Kevin said, "This band Cotton Mather that I'm in is going to be huge. I have to quit." He also mentioned this band Cherubs.

King Coffey: Cherubs were great. They'd only been a band for a few months, and I said, "This is just great. Let's make a record now." They did *Icing*, the first LP.

Brent Prager: King was being distributed by Touch and Go and so his idea was to come out of the gate strong and to send us up to Smart Studios in Madison [Wisconsin] to record. But it wasn't the greatest idea in retrospect because we did it in a hurry. We didn't know who we were yet or how we wanted to sound. Then we recorded at Sweatbox for a fifth of the price and did the cool shit that I like. *Heroin Man*.

King Coffey: Many people think *Heroin Man* is the best record that Trance did. It is one of the heaviest, meanest, but also funniest. They'd play these crazy time signatures.

One time I was hanging out at their house for a practice, and they're waiting for Brent the drummer to show up. They said, "Can you just sit in here for a bit and help with this song?" The time signature was like 3, 7, 12, 8, 5, 9, and my mind was melting. I couldn't do it. I realized how dumb I am. I'm 4/4 caveman. You would never guess the mental gymnastics it takes to do what they're doing because it's so brain-melting, fantastic. It made me appreciate the whole craft to their music.

Brent Prager: The whole punk rock thing was starting to sound dull to the ears. It had been going on for twenty years. All of a sudden, it's the resurgence of the hypnotic weird time signatures. It was a lot of bands who got their influences from Scratch Acid and the Butthole Surfers and—to really go back to the roots of it—the 13th Floor Elevators.

King Coffey: Roky was a hero. Casey Monahan—the Texas Music Office director—was able to get Roky into a good studio with good backing musicians. He recorded a really solid album. Casey was looking for a way to release it, and Trance seemed like a good fit because he wanted to keep it local. It was a comeback record, and it really had to make some money as a fundraiser for him. I was told that I was the first person to really give a royalty check to Roky Erickson, which is touching, but also really sad because—out of this huge body of work that he's done through the decades—he is finally getting a royalty check for this one record.

Carrie Clark: The Trance Syndicate showcase at the Ritz [during SXSW 1991] was brilliant. It was Lithium X-Mas, Ed Hall, the Pain Teens, Crust. I just remember being in a heightened state of awareness, sitting on the edge of the balcony of the Ritz, and the pit was swirling so much. A hurricane force wind was coming up off of the crowd. Whoosh! I want to be in the middle of that!

King Coffey: That SXSW showcase was bands who played on the *Love & Napalm* seven-inch. We were just a brand-new label with a handful of releases.

Carrie Clark: My Bloody Valentine at Liberty Lunch was the game-changer. They came on stage, and they made that sound that sounds like a jet-engine taking off on your face. After that, all these other bands cropped up in Austin. It changed everything.

Frenchie Smith: February 8, 1992. My Bloody Valentine were the support band for Dinosaur Jr. I was turned on to that band by Jon Sanchez, who's the singer and guitar player in Flying Saucers. Jon is someone that we all revered. Carrie and I both auditioned for Flying Saucers.

Carrie Clark: Frenchie and I were at Emo's, and I was like, "I didn't make the Flying Saucers!" And he's like, "I didn't make the Flying Saucers!" So it's like, "Ta-da! Let's be in a band!" It was that simple.

Frenchie Smith: Just being around Carrie—she had a magic to her. The doors were open to her, and she dragged me through them with her. She was a bad motherfucker. She could sing. She went to hit a note on the guitar, it was like a high five and a karate kick.

Carrie Clark: What I hoped people would walk away with is a beautiful, visceral assault on all of your senses . . . the lights coming at you! We prided ourselves on being so loud that you would feel it.

Carrie Clark (*left*) and Frenchie Smith (*right*) of Sixteen Deluxe play a KVRX benefit. Photo by Richard Whymark.

Mark Fagan: Lyman and I recorded their first demo, and I gave that to Trance.

Carrie Clark: Then King was like, "This is great. You guys want to do a record?" It was incredible to be associated with Trance because at that point, a record label sold you. People came to see us because we were a Trance band. It was a big deal.

King Coffey: I got taken to one of their early shows, and just fell madly in love with the band and the people. They had a great guitar-laden sound. Kind of psych, but they wrote such great three-minute pop songs. Noisy, catchy, and crunchy. I was excited to work with them.

"Idea" was our hit. What a great song, and that video's great. It captures the band so well. Those guys have made such perfect pop songs.

Carrie Clark: Wally [Walton] Rowell and Heyd Fontenot were just starting to do their film work. We were following direction of some guys that were just out of film school. The innocence and invincibility of being twenty-four. The video ended up on MTV on "120 Minutes" after a Sugarcubes video. That was something that was beyond anybody's wildest dreams.

John Spath: We actually had notification that they were going to play "Idea" on MTV, and we had a watch party with about a hundred people in my living room. It felt really nice.

King Coffey: Trance bands were visual performance art, so a lot of those bands worked really well in front of a camera. But it was also a shoestring kind of thing too. For MTV, you're talking about a budget of thousands of dollars. We had a budget of tens of dollars. It was a gamble, but it paid off sometimes, so it was fun. We did one compilation—*Love & Napalm*—which had all of our videos at the time.

Marc Fort: Jon Sanchez from the Flying Saucers was like, "Man, if you are into the Flying Saucers, you're going to like Chris and Carrie's new band Sixteen Deluxe." Seeing them for the first time at Emo's was magical. You had these exquisitely beautiful pop songs drenched in feedback and distortion, combined with a very beautiful girl's voice singing pop melodies.

Carrie Clark: We had formed in the summer of '94. Marc Fort did a piece on us in the brand-new XL. We recorded *Backfeedmagnetbabe* over Christmas. That following SXSW we played the Trance showcase, and we had nine labels courting us. It was a ridiculous fast track. There was one offer that was, "We'll sign you, but we're in charge of your image." I was like, "Are you going to try and turn me into Gwen Stefani?"

King Coffey: It was the post-Nirvana '90s experience in indie record world. A lot of bands might make one or two records on an indie and then be scooped up and go major. I was concerned about us sinking a lot of time and money on a band, to promote one or two records, only to have them go immediately to a major label.

Carrie Clark: When all the people came diving in, King saw it a mile away. He was like, "Be careful. . . . Take it slow." We interpreted his advice that he wanted to get another record out of us. We just rode the wave and said, "Thanks, Trance. Bye!"

If we would've done the right thing for us, emotionally, and karmically, we would've put the brakes on it a little bit and done another record for Trance because they busted their butts for us. Then maybe Warner Bros. could've bought the Trance catalog and thanked King for his time and effort. We really did Trance wrong. King was a real mentor.

King Coffey: Carrie's being really sweet, as she is. I just know that I felt sorry for them. They barely had a chance to even be a band and all of a sudden major label types were just descending upon them and promising them the moon. It really put pressure upon them really early.

Carrie Clark: We went with Warner Bros. because Rick Gershon—who works at Warner Bros.—was our publicist and he also worked with the Flaming Lips. He was a good friend and a real fan.

Mark Fagan: Carrie was very charismatic, and Frenchie is an amazing guitar player and puts on a show. But as soon as they started getting successful, everybody's like, "Sixteen Deluxe isn't that good." And you get a backlash whenever that happens.

Chuck Trend: When that *Spin* magazine came out and had a page on Sixteen Deluxe, they felt they were under pressure to try and keep it real, which was at odds with the fact that they were getting all this media hype and attention. I think people had the somewhat unrealistic expectation that's borne out of the mid-eighties SST bands that just got in a van and toured their asses off.

Mark Fagan: Well, Sixteen Deluxe did tour a lot before they signed to a major. When you signed with a major label it was almost like you were selling out. Now everybody wants to be in commercials. But back then Neil Young was writing songs railing against this. And so they had to deal with that whole backlash of selling out. The perception at the time was that it wasn't cool to sign with Warner Bros.

Frenchie Smith: I don't think we were anti any kind of musical progress, but the idea of doing Big Business wasn't something we ever talked about.

Carrie Clark: The band took off really quickly. We are a band of strong, individual personalities and strong opinions. I am happy to say I love each and every one of those guys dearly, again, but there was a chunk of time that it was not good. Everybody had their turn to put each other through rough times. Everything moved so fast. We didn't have time to mature as a band. It was just, "Boom! Here we go!"

Frenchie Smith: We'd be at dinner with a record producer and like, "We're in L.A.! It's party time!" Carrie would ask a very profound question to the record producer, and that male record producer would answer *me*.

At the end of the dinner she was like, "You suck." I'm like, "What did I miss?" "I'm asking him questions and this guy answers *you*." I'm like, "All right, that's fucked up. This is our band. I'm totally with you."

But I could've been more aware of what the fuck was happening to her more often.

Frenchie Smith: [The album for Warner] was recorded in San Francisco at Hyde Street. At one time it was Wally Heider. They had made Santana records there. Dead Kennedys records. Green Day had made *Insomniac*. James Brown had recorded there. So it was away from Austin, but we took John Croslin from the Reivers with us to produce. It wasn't mind-blowing to him that a female could be brilliant and have ideas.

Carrie Clark: Then when we did *Emits Showers of Sparks*, rock and roll was dead. It was time for electronica. All the people that we loved and worked with, except for Rick [Gershon], had been fired.

There was a point where the label were like, "You can go on tour with Spoon now, or you can do this with Trail of Dead now." I'm like, "Can't do it. I got really good personal reasons not to do it."

That was the nail in the coffin. To make the right choices for ourselves personally, were the wrong choices businesswise. Sometimes those two aren't compatible. The label dropped us and said, "If you can't do this now, then we can't do anything for you."

Frenchie Smith: That's okay. I'm just pleased that everybody's alive and in one piece, and we can look each other in the eye. We see things in each other that no one else will see and that's really precious.

King Coffey: They found a good label, and they made a good record, and they came out winners in the end.

Carrie Clark: Then there was the post–Sixteen Deluxe, shoe-gazer thing that was happening. Furry Things.

Ken Gibson: Me and Cathy Shive started Furry Things to make really noisy melodic pop music in the vein of the bands that we were into at the time. My Bloody Valentine, Medicine, Spacemen 3. Plus, Beach Boys were a huge influence on it. The first place we played was Blue Flamingo with a bunch of crazy transvestites getting all wild. And they were playing pornos on the TV. It was pretty chaotic. Even before that happened, Cathy and I were making demos on the four-track. I sent it to *Flipside* and they reviewed us, and then Craig Koon heard it and wanted to do a seven-inch. In the meantime, we sent King Coffey demos.

King Coffey: Furry Things was so much great guitar noise crafted into some really great pop songs. They were also experimental really quick. They were really a quickly evolving band, and yet I think every record they made was just fantastic. They worked in dub and electronica towards the end.

Ken Gibson: We did a seven-inch, two EPs, and then an album. Furry Things played all over. Electric Lounge was the big one. We played there a bunch of times. Emo's. Liberty Lunch. Hole in the Wall's another one, man. Really loud. A lot of people ran out. We started most of our sets with this one track where every string was tuned to E. We definitely tried to push it as loud as possible. To this day I still got some ringing in my ears from Furry Things.

King Coffey: I think Ken is one of the few geniuses I've ever worked with. When he expressed an interest in working with samplers, I gave him my first sampler. He just went to town on it. Eight Frozen Modules was just him doing the drum and bass thing but in his own way. The guy's a genius.

Ken Gibson: Eight Frozen Modules was my first electronic project that came out on Trance. That was '97. When Furry Things ended, I concentrated on that for a long time. I didn't even think King would like it at all, but he had already released an electronic record [with a side project] called Drain.

Brian McBride: Windsor for the Derby are an Austin band that wanted to do things a little bit different. At times you could hear a little bit of Cluster or moments of Joy Division in their music. A lot of dissonance and arpeggios.

Windsor for the Derby's first two records were recorded by Adam [Wiltzie], who's in Stars of the Lid.

King Coffey: Again, geniuses. They made some beautiful records. Real experimental but not inapproachable, and they were really good live too. They were one of the most interesting acts on the label.

FACING PAGE AND ABOVE Ken Gibson and Cathy Shive of Furry Things at the Blue Flamingo. Their first show. Photo by Richard Whymark.

Jason Morales: Dude, the things that followed the whole crazy freak rock scene of Trance went on and on. Windsor for the Derby. Trail of Dead, all that stuff. It just kept on changing.

Erik Conn: I played in Wookie, which is now basically half of Little Cap'n Travis. Dave, the bass player, was like, "You got to see Starfish!" And I recognized Scotty [Marcus] right away because of Glass Eye. For me it was Ed Hall, Cherubs, and Starfish, which coincidentally were all on Trance. After the Northwest exploded with Nirvana and Soundgarden, it seemed like the next thing.

Jason Morales: This friend of mine is like, "Why are you moving to Texas, dude? You guys play power pop, and all that's down there is Trance stuff, like fucking freak rock." And then we moved down here and then the first label we get on is Trance. So I guess we transcended from power pop to freak rock on the drive down.

King Coffey: It really made sense when they got Bob Mould to record them. Bob was living in Austin at the time and had a similar take on music, as far as punk background, but with pop structures. Starfish were doing that, and Bob Mould totally locked into what they were doing.

Jason Morales: Blondie's was a major gig for Starfish. It was a skate shop on Rio Grande between Sixth and Fifth. A nice warehouse area. It was free and they usually had a keg of beer. Every fucking skater was there, and they were partying and it was awesome.

Carrie Clark: I love Starfish, so I'm not deriding Starfish in any way, but they wrote a song about us. It was a conversation at the Wookie House, and we were talking about getting signed. I said something about how I was really tired of sleeping on people's floors on tour. And that was *so un-punk* to say that. There were a couple of instances where—as the girl in the band—I had to sleep next to one of the guys for my safety. There were a couple of creepy situations. I didn't want to do that anymore, and somehow that was selling out.

Erik Conn: And then the new kids—Trail of Dead—changed the scene overnight. Instead of freak flag flying with weird colored socks and postpunk hippies, they're like, "We're all just going to wear black." Remember that? Those are my friends, and I dug that band, but all of a sudden there was a *code* again. That wasn't old-school Austin.

King Coffey: I first saw Trail of Dead at Blue Flamingo, and I was just blown away. I've never seen a band explode the way they would. That club was so small, and—it sounds like a cliché—it was a band that really blurred the line between the stage and the audience because half the audience was on stage, half the band was in the audience, all flowing back and forth. The album that we did is wonderful to me. It really captured what they were doing live at the time. They're nice guys as well.

Conrad Keely: We were extremely kind of standoffish and arrogant at the time. We knew that Craig was part of Trance Records, and when he came up and talked to us we were just like, "Yeah. Maybe we can do something with you guys." We were definitely not going to make it easy for them. We don't know why because they were so nice about it. We had this opinion that any label was going to take you over in some way or another. Even the indies.

Jason Reece: King Coffey was going to the shows quite a bit. I'd see his face there and I'd be like, "Okay what's going on? He likes us." We just started talking a bit more and finally one day he said he wanted to put out our record. We were excited.

Conrad Keely: Neil Busch from Andromeda Strain had started playing with us. He would make all these sample noises with us, and then once we decided we were going to do this recording for Trance, Neil played bass. Just the fact that we were on Trance gave us a wider thing. People have heard of Trance Records.

Jason Reece: And then we brought in Kevin Allen on guitar.

Conrad Keely: I was still working at UT. We had a lot of downtime and were allowed to use the internet for whatever we wanted because they hadn't made all these rules about productivity yet. I would make all the flyers for the shows and work on the website. We probably were one of the first bands that started having websites. It was really early HTML, but it allowed us to get out there.

We signed to Trance and suddenly we were getting interviews from places in Italy. There were fans of Trance around the world. That really helped us because there was this thing going around that there was an Austin curse—if you were from Austin, Texas, you'd never get out. We were determined not to allow that to happen to us.

King Coffey: I didn't want to fall into a local rut of putting out some records locally and that was it. We had distribution overseas and really tried to promote the label and the bands as best we could, all over the place. There was a reason why we only just broke even every year. We spent so much money on promotion. We took out lots of ads.

This was all pre-internet, by and large. There were no downloads. It was all very old-school. You just had this huge list of things to do . . . Making a CD or tape and shipping it out by mail to various writers and radio stations, making posters to send out to all the record stores, and taking out ads in all the various print publications.

And then make phone calls. It was really expensive to call outside of your home city—fifty cents a minute! Our most expensive monthly bill was our phone bill, because we were talking to people all over the place, trying to get them interested in this band, or this label, or whatever. That's the way a business was run back then. Says the old, cranky man! "You and your kids with your cell phones! Damn you!"

Jason Reece: Being a part of a label like Trance had this iconic feeling to it because you have Cherubs, Pain Teens. But when we were on it, it was Bedhead and American Analog Set and Starfish, so it was kind of a different vibe. It wasn't this noisy stuff that they had in the earlier days. Trance was a little broader sound-wise.

Conrad Keely: We wanted the old cobra head logo on our record. We asked for that.

King Coffey: I stole the logo from the Symbionese Liberation Army, which was the premier terrorist organization in the US in the '70s. They were on every news story. I found myself rooting for them in this strange way, just because they were trying to take down The Man. And they just seemed really exotic. Not that I'm promoting terrorism. That seven-headed logo always had some fascination with me. I stole it from the SLA and just slapped "Trance" on it. I was pretty sure the SLA weren't going to sue me. I took my chances there.

Marc Fort: Obviously, Spoon and Trail of Dead are two of the most import-ant bands to come out of Austin in the 1990s. I remember seeing Trail of Dead at Electric Lounge when it was just the two guys and I was like, "This is the worst band I've ever seen in my life." It was like they were tiptoeing through art rock, almost getting a little self-indulgent, falling over, not playing well. But the next show I saw of theirs, I really don't think that's the same band I saw at Electric Lounge. It was several years later. They took my head off.

King Coffey: Emperor Jones was our sister label. My focus with Trance was to keep it Texas, specifically Austin. There were a handful of bands that didn't really work on the Trance label. My husband [Craig Stewart] was running Trance with me. I said, "You should just run your own label of bands that you like. That way you can work with non-Texas bands." He worked with Mountain Goats, My Dad Is Dead, and other bands that he liked. One of those bands was American Analog Set. Fantastic band, beautiful songs. We were working with really quite minimal bands like Bedhead.

One of the last albums we did, but a personal favorite, is Monroe Mustang. It's the best album that Trance put out that few people have heard. Paul New-man were another one of the last bands we worked with. Again, very dense

Sixteen Deluxe "Idea" seven-inch on Trance Syndicate.

music. Experimental but also just engaging. It wasn't remote. They just made some fantastic records and I love the two that we did.

Jason Reece: After Trance folded, Jason Ward helped us get onto Merge. And from that relationship, we got Spoon on to Merge, because of Mike McCarthy who produced *Madonna*. And so that's how all that started happening.

Conrad Keely: Also, timing-wise, things were starting to happen for a lot of bands here. Spoon was doing well. Fastball, too. And then shortly after bands like the Sword and Explosions in the Sky started to break out of here. Sixteen Deluxe were on Warner Bros. And so we were just on the early part of that wave. Then, in a huge sense, Austin broke. Suddenly SXSW became this big deal. All eyes turned to here.

King Coffey: I'm just glad that we documented some bands that might have gone unrecorded or unknown at the time. We did our best to take bands that I thought were worth recording and putting them in the studio and getting them out there beyond Texas—really trying to give these bands a chance to be heard and fly the Texas flag. We had a good ten years. 1990 to 1999 is when Trance did our thing. It was a great bookend for me to spend the '90s promoting and working with bands I love, mostly from Austin.

ELECTRIC LOUNGE

MY CHILDHOOD HERO IS GETTING PELTED BY ROSES

THIS IS A ROCK SHOW VENUE
IT IS LOCATED ON 302 BOWIE STREET IN AUSTIN, TEXAS
THIS VENUE IS CALLED ELECTRIC LOUNGE
IT IS A VENUE TO ROCK AND HANG OUT
IT HOLDS UP TO THREE HUNDRED PEOPLE

WESLEY WILLIS

ALTHOUGH THE FORTY-TWO-STORY SPRING CONDOMINIUM TOWER NOW stands on its footprint, it would have been a stretch to call the Electric Lounge a downtown club when it opened.

In 1993 the southwestern frontier of Austin's central business district petered out around Nueces Street, giving way to a low-slung commercial/industrial area defined by car dealerships and proximity to the Union Pacific rail line. The area wasn't blighted so much as underutilized—zipping up not long after business hours concluded.

The Seaholm Power Plant and Shoal Creek effectively divided the neighborhood from downtown proper. The only creek crossing between Fifth and Cesar Chavez[1] was an abandoned railroad trestle used as an unsanctioned shortcut by intrepid pedestrians. By contrast, the Union Pacific tracks were (and remain) a major north-south freight artery. Amtrak's Texas Eagle connecting Chicago and San Antonio also shared the track, affording punchy inebriates the opportunity to moon passengers on the oft-delayed southbound run.

For architect Jay Hughey and filmmaker Mark Shuman, it was just far enough off the beaten path to make their vision viable. Hughey and Shuman were onetime Austinites who had moved to Los Angeles for work. While there, they took note of shape-shifting venues like Jabberjaw that simultaneously showcased live music and performance art in a space that had a deliberate aesthetic. Upon their return to town, Hughey and Shuman decided Austin had transcended its own aesthetic reputation for shambling thrown-togetherness enough to support a venue similar to the ones they'd known in Southern California.

In the pre-skyscraper era, the neighborhood's most prominent structure was the Seaholm Power Plant. Constructed over several years during the 1950s, the hulking art deco complex was Austin's sole source of power until 1959. Ultimately renamed to honor Walter E. Seaholm, the superintendent credited with stopping the municipally owned power system from being privatized in 1927, the plant generated power until 1989. When Hughey and Shuman signed a lease on the industrial building in the shadow of the Seaholm at the corner of Bowie and West Third, they christened it the Electric Lounge.

The Lounge opened on April 9, 1993, with a performance from the Horsies. Formed by veterans of Happy Family, the Pocket FishRmen, and Poison 13 who wanted to start a band audiences could dance to, the erudite sextet's cross of skittering Afro-pop rhythms and lyrical paeans to Noam Chomsky epitomized the new club's eclectic booking policy. A 1994 compilation disc, *Overload: Live at the Electric Lounge*, bears witness to this anything-goes approach by pitting jazz-fused prog-punk troupe Hominybob against romantic pop-punk purists Miss Universe and postdoctoral power trio El Flaco.

By the fall of 1993 the Electric Lounge was the "it" new place in town to see shows. Part of the club's appeal was a wall—later a Plexiglas shield—separating the bar area from the showroom. This enabled a semblance of lounge-like conviviality over the squall. Video cameras allowed people outside the showroom—in what was called the Elbow Room—to keep up with the action on TV monitors. Those who desired more privacy could take up residence in a side room with couches.

The club's most distinctive physical delineator was a red neon sign above the stage, spelling out "Electric" in a Reddy Kilowatt–inspired font. Toward the end of a Muffs show in 1995, bassist Ronnie Barnett smashed the

"Electric" sign with the neck of his instrument in a fit of pique. Following substantial repairs, the emblematic sign was returned to its rightful perch.

Smashed neon pales in significance to the club's greatest trial—an electrical fire that broke out in the wee hours of February 19, 1994. The building's interior was gutted, but Hughey and Shuman persevered.

The club managed to take part in SXSW less than a month after the fire by holding shows in a tent set up in the parking lot. Veruca Salt, a biting pop fourpiece from Chicago, showcased at the Lounge, got signed to Geffen, and wound up with a gold record for their debut, *American Thighs*. With assistance from their landlord and even competing local club owners, the Electric Lounge reopened in earnest by early May.

As it became better established, the Lounge cultivated both early and late crowds. Syracuse, New York–bred transplant Ed Hamell was the de facto artist-in-residence. Delivering pizza to make ends meet, Hamell captivated early-evening clubbers with his acerbic antifolk and ultimately signed with Mercury Records for a brief spell.

Wednesday nights belonged to the Asylum Street Spankers, a shapeshifting hokum jazz collective featuring a motley bunch of notable-in-their-own-right scene veterans, including onetime Cannibal Club DJ Billy Dave Wammo on vocals and washboard, blues belter/guitarist Guy Forsyth, and vocalist/ukulele player Christina Marrs. Aside from reintroducing songs and styles from the '20s and '30s, anyone in the audience celebrating a birthday might find themselves getting spanked.

Hughey and Shuman made longtime booker Mike Henry general manager in 1997. The club continued to successfully mine a fruitful niche of touring acts that weren't yet shoo-ins to pack Liberty Lunch, including subgenre definers like Spiritualized and Sleater-Kinney. Working in tandem with promotion collective Hip-Hop Mecca, Henry brought in emergent national hip-hop artists like DJ Spooky, Hieroglyphics, and Mix Master Mike.

Sometimes Henry's astute booking secured a major act just before they crested, which was how Cornershop played a sold-out Lounge on February 2, 1998, right after their indie/Indian music-hybridizing debut *When I Was Born for the 7th Time* topped many 1997 best-of lists. Overwrought Floridian grunt-rockers Creed played the Lounge on October 30, 1997, two years before their multiplatinum chart-topper *Human Clay* was released.

Henry was also a principal figure in Austin's poetry slam community, which helped make the club an epicenter for spoken-word performance. When the National Poetry Slam came to Austin in 1998, Henry served as event codirector, and the Lounge was a primary venue.

There were also occasional stunt bookings of acts on their heels. Original

Kiss drummer Peter Criss showed up for a 1994 solo set only to have his arena rock posturing mocked. Revived Tex-Mex (by way of Michigan) garage rock heroes Question Mark and the Mysterians fared much better when they played the Lounge in 1997.

While the club's stature was solid as the decade wound down, its business fundamentals were anything but. Developers began eyeing the no-man's-land around the Lounge to build close-in residential buildings aligned with the city's smart growth initiative. Land value began creeping up along with rent. How incoming residents would respond to having a loud rock club in their midst was another concern.

As the first of many lots began to be cleared for new construction, the Lounge had more prosaic business problems to face. In 1998 the alcohol tax deposit the club had to pay the state to maintain its liquor license increased by more than $10,000.[2] In January 1999 Henry noted that the club's expenses had nearly tripled over the past year.[3] The conditions that had once allowed the Lounge to survive and even thrive a little were no more.

Following a series of farewell shows, the Electric Lounge breathed its last in the wee hours of Monday, April 12, 1999. Still between labels after getting dropped by Elektra after just one poorly promoted album, Spoon headlined the final night of music on April 10. Then fellow major label reject Ed Hamell took the stage to play a Hendrix-style "Star Spangled Banner." The next night at a "private" party, clubgoers mournfully liquidated the venue's remaining alcohol stock.

Jay Hughey: There was nothing going on in this town. Mark and I said, "We need to open a cool place of the type that we went to in L.A. . . ." These multicultural art venues that embraced visual arts, music, performance art, and crazy, spontaneous happenings. That was the impetus.

Mark Shuman: We decided right away that we didn't want to be on Sixth Street. We wanted to be removed from it.

Jay Hughey: The industrial zones that were left in downtown Austin were ripe for a catalyst and cheap for rent. There were landlords saying, "Hmm, maybe. How much money do you have to fix up my building for me?"

Mark Shuman: Ultimately, we found a space. Jay—being an architect—says, "Oh, this is perfect! This will be a club." We got into it, and we hammered away for four or five months to get open.

The first night we thought we were loaded. It sold out! It was amazing! We thought everybody was going to show up the second night. Well, that doesn't happen. We were sitting there about a week into it, and all these cars would come into the parking lot, look in the empty window, and drive off. We called a bunch of our friends and said, "Come down here! We got free drinks!" They would sit in the windows and it would be like a primer. It probably wasn't a month and a half and we had people stopping by the club bringing us tapes. That's how we met Mike.

Mike Henry: I was booking what we called college rock bands—Wannabes, Cotton Mather, Black Irish, Spoon. In the *Chronicle* there was a story about a new club opening. I got my stack of cassette tapes and headshots and walked in.

Jay Hughey: We were all over the map for the first several months. Bands like Rockbusters and Skatenigs that would draw a big crowd and fill a big room. The Horsies were the epitome of what we wanted to aspire to—that crazy eclectic nature of Austin music. There was no pretense of, "If we follow this formula we'll be noticed."

Brant Bingamon: The Horsies never played Emo's. It didn't fit in the punk philosophy in any way. The Electric Lounge was its own thing. Consciously they were purveying their own type of music for a different part of the scene. Almost creating a new scene. And the Horsies played their inaugural night. They played when the place burned down, and they played it when it came back. So yeah, the Horsies were really identified with that club.

Cris Burns: The Horsies had elements of western swing, maybe country flavors. There's elements of jazz, as well as dance music and Afro-beat kind of stuff. A lot of different elements in the Horsies soup.

Jay Hughey: Swine King was maybe a little crazier version of the eclecticism of the Horsies. Our dearly departed Randy "Biscuit" Turner was, to me, a really great bellwether of just how crazy people in Austin can be.

Dotty Farrell: We would do themes and take turns making props to throw out into the audience. At Electric Lounge we did a luau. Biscuit decorated it like a Hawaii theme and made a big thing of cream of wheat, put some honey in it and walked around saying, "Eat the poi!"

Jay Hughey: Every time Biscuit was coming in, there were hours of production before. Here was a guy who made art with tiny dolls and things like that. His shows were crazy.

Dotty Farrell: We worked at Planet K and would be on the clock cutting out stuff for Swine King. For the Hyde Park Baptist Church show, I'd be making Bible pamphlets that said, "Get Stoned and Fuck!" and throw them out into the audience.

Jay Hughey: We just knew what we liked and what was good, so we started booking an amazingly eclectic array. It was organic and had no pretense.

Ed Hamell: I played the Electric Lounge one night. Six people came. A table of four girls are talking, and so I'm like, "Can you stop talking?" And they kept on talking. Finally, I screamed, "*Shut the fuck up or get out!*" And they got up and they left. So now I play the remainder of the set to my wife. We walk out to the car and all of a sudden Mark Shuman runs up. He goes, "That'll never happen again."

He booked me in front of Spoon and other high-profile bands. He totally got it. He had the vision to see that some screwball telling jokes and doing these long narrative dialogue songs could turn the thing around. There was real support for idiosyncratic stuff in that place and that scene really responded to me. And then the fans from the postgrunge bands dug me. It really worked for me when I got signed to a major.

Kelly Linn: At the Electric Lounge, we [Moist Fist] did the Chain Show and got this chain-link fence to separate us from the audience. If it's any form of art, it has to do something for me, right? It has to give me that sort of reaction. And that's what I wanted to create—something that is not normal.

Ed Hamell: It was a literary venue. They were having film and poetry readings at the beginning of the night. People said it was hipster, but it really wasn't. It was very embracing of the arts.

Mark Shuman: Margaret Moser walked in and she dropped a tape recorder on the desk. She goes, "Hi, I'm Margaret Moser from the *Chronicle*. I'd like to interview you. What does it feel like to be a pioneer of the West End's Art District?" I had no idea what she was talking about.

Jay Hughey: Whether it brought money in or not, we wanted to provide a venue for people who didn't have a home, for people who were making a film, or who had a performance art piece.

Mike Henry: It was ballsy. It was performance art and all kinds of music all crammed together. We like Swine King, and we like Hominybob, and we like the Wannabes, and we're going to just put them all together.

Mark Shuman: It wasn't about dollars. That's how we got Morphine in. They sent us their first two CDs and we were like, "This is amazing!"

Jay Hughey: It was sold as a package—Morphine and Babe the Blue Ox. We wanted Sincola to open the show. We thought that would be the perfect fit with the zeitgeist of the moment and so forth. Rebecca [Cannon] had listened to both the CDs and said, "Well, this Morphine thing, they're okay. Babe the Blue Ox—they should be the headliner."

Mark Shuman: Morphine had been on a tour where they weren't selling out, but they got to Austin and sold out. It really was just posters and word-of-mouth. No internet. It wasn't our advertising budget because we had none. We advertised in the *Austin Chronicle*, but that's all we could ever afford.

Mike Henry: Shortly after the Morphine show, I started doing the booking. We had a telephone[4] with an answering machine with a tape. I have no idea how a show ever got booked. There's drunk bartenders writing down messages. That was it. I think this is the greatest booking letter ever written in the history of all booking letters. It's handwritten . . .

It says, "Dear Mike, This demo doesn't do us a damn bit of justice. We are loud and fast and we all breathe fire on stage. We got a stripper/dancer/crazy woman also. And someone who breaks appliances—especially cash registers—with a flaming sledgehammer. We can mellow out if the place is too small, but if it's okay we will freak the fuck out. Call me. We will be touring through Austin the second week of September. Love, Joe from Empire of Shit."

I opened that up and I called those guys and gave them a gig. They brought people, and they brought sledgehammers. And they broke shit on stage.

Jay Hughey: There was this explosion of new bands. We saw this amazing pool of talent in Austin that was mixing and interspersing itself and generating an amazing quantity of quality new stuff.

Mark Shuman: The club became Daniel Johnston's home away from home. He did a lot of solo shows. I made a deal with his family. I said, "He won't smoke. He won't eat candy. We'll just pick him up."

I sent Mike Mariconda to pick him up in Waller, Texas. They pull up to the club. Here comes Daniel with a cigarette and a big box of chocolates. I'm like, "Mike, what happened?" He goes, "I don't know. He's a grown man. What are you going to do?"

We had great shows though, man. He was amazing!

Mike Henry: Also, Elliott Smith played the club a few times. He would show up by himself early in the day. No tour bus. No handlers. Just him. A guy and a guitar. He'd say, "Hey, do you mind if I just hang out?" He would sit at the bar, practice, play songs. It was the coolest thing.

Ryan McDaniel: The Electric Lounge was more upscale and adult. One thing that was really cool about Gomez is we were one of those bands that we kind of fit in everywhere with every band. They let us open up for a lot of different kinds of bands from Material Issue to Agent Orange to Mr. T Experience. And it was awesome to play with bands like the Wannabes and Spoon.

Britt Daniel: We played a lot of shows there. Saw a lot of great shows there. I think it probably held maybe 350 people or something. You'd see a lot of shows for bands that were just starting out, but you had heard of. Sleater-Kinney on their first tour. That kind of thing. Jonathan Richman would play there a couple times a year.

Travis Higdon: Britt used to like to play pranks a lot. There was a band that had an obnoxious reputation around town. They were playing a show at the Electric Lounge. The power breaker was on the outside of the club. Britt shut it down in the middle of their set, put a padlock on it, and drove off. I don't even know what happened to the rest of their show but basically, they were screwed because there was a padlock on the power breaker.

Ed Hamell: There was another band called Hominybob. Very similar to Cake. They ultimately morphed into Drums & Tuba that got signed to Righteous

Babe. Brian Wolff has now played with Buckethead and Tom Waits and Drums & Tuba.

Mike Henry: Drums & Tuba, there's a great band. They were like, "We have this new band that we'd like to get a gig. It's drums and it's a tuba." I was like, "Awesome. What's it called?" He said, "I think we're going to call it Drums & Tuba."

Chepo Peña: I played there the night it burned down. They had my money and it burned.

Mike Henry: The night of the fire I was managing the club. Pocket FishRmen played and had twenty smoke machines on stage. Snoopy was naked, of course. It *seemed* like there was a fire in the place. It was a great show and we got out of there as usual at four a.m.

Jay Hughey: I was mortified. I got phone calls from the security company because all the wires had melted, and so they're getting an alarm as though we'd been broken into. The calls kept coming and I was saying, "Nah, it's a mistake. I just left there. It's a mistake."

Mike Henry: The phone rings at eight a.m. It's Jay saying, "What are you doing? Get up! The club's on fire!" As I got there, the firemen were walking out. There's still smoke hanging in the air.

Jay Hughey: Then I became immediately mortified because the last thing I remember was cavalierly casting my cigarette over the bar. All I could think was that it landed in the bottle cap box, which was the origin of the fire. It happened right there. We found out later that it was a compressor in a cooler, so I could at least be absolved of the overwhelming guilt.

Mark Shuman: We thought our club was gone. We worked our butts off to rebuild the club again. It's amazing that we made it for another five years.

Jay Hughey: Let's be clear, the only reason we reopened was this wonderful eighty-year-old man named Eldon Hill, who rented us our place. He said, "Hey, you boys don't have insurance?"

We laughed. He pondered that for a couple of minutes and said, "Well, I know how hard you boys worked on this place. Boy, I tell you, against all of my better judgment I'm going to tell you that I have insurance. I can't help you with all the equipment and the other stuff that goes into there, but I'm going to call the insurance company and we're going to get you rebuilt."

Mark Shuman: The funny thing is, once he found out how much insurance money he was getting, Eldon would ask us over and over, "Now, are you boys *sure* you want to open this club again?" We're like, "Yeah!"

He could've just made it a warehouse and rented it and taken a big pay-check, but he stuck by us, and he was an amazing guy. This town rallied around us, and one of the first people to come to us was Danny Crooks from Steamboat who said, "Hey, listen guys. I know I don't do your kind of music, but I heard about your situation. I want to throw a benefit for you guys."

Mike Henry: It was his best line-up. Sister 7. Bob Schneider. Danny handed us $700 cash, and this is in 1993 dollars. He provided us an impetus to go forward. We went in and spent hours wiping the smoke off of chairs. We rebuilt it out of nothing.

Jay Hughey: Our closed-circuit video camera that piped the image of the stage into the Elbow Room was this puddle of black about fifteen feet below. You get the sense that everything in our world is transitory.

Mark Shuman: That year we won the *Austin Chronicle*'s Best Rising from the Ashes Critics Award. I think it's the same year we won Best Club. Then during South By Southwest—right before we opened—Brent Grulke called us and said, "Hey, I know you're out of business, but we're going to try to help you guys do a venue." They helped us finance a tent and we used the parking lot and that became our venue.

Chepo Peña: Sincola got discovered at that tent. The label guy canceled his flight and stayed to see our show. And then that's how we met Caroline [Records].

Kris Patterson: I think Craig Koon had said something to somebody at Caroline. Brian Long was our dude at the label.

They flew us to New York to sign. Jason Cohen interviewed us up in New York for *Texas Monthly*. We were on top of the world. Caroline gave us $10,000 to buy a van. It just seemed like every show we played we were just having a really good time and stuff couldn't go wrong. With *What the Nothinghead Said*, we had the big release party at Scholz Beer Garden. We were playing with Ben Folds Five and it was packed. Amy Ray from the Indigo Girls was there, and I was just super-fan-girl.

Rebecca Cannon: We got on a major label. We got a crowd really quickly. Things just went really well. We toured, we made videos, and we traveled to Europe.

Kris Patterson: We went on tour to England with Ben Folds Five. I remember getting so angry at Greg. He wouldn't go get his passport. I could just see him not doing it so he could go to the Showdown and smoke cigarettes and drink and say, "I'm supposed to be in London right now but, you know."

I remember calling his sister, Amy. "You better get your brother to go get his fucking passport!" When we picked him up, he's just got his ripped jeans, a dirty white undershirt, and his few little clothes in a paper sack. "We could go on tour for two months and that's all you brought?"

"Yeah. I got my cigarettes and my little sack of clothes."

Rebecca Cannon: After about five years, things had been going really well. So fast, so good. We had a tour with Joan Jett.

Kris Patterson: Our last show of that Joan Jett tour was at Electric Lounge. It was really surreal. We hung out with her in that little side room.

We play our shows and it's really great, and she's like, "Let's go get a drink somewhere." So we all go to Emo's and King Cheese[5] are playing. Joan got some fruity rum drink, and we start playing air hockey and I'm beating her because I'm just high on adrenaline. And then all of a sudden you hear King Cheese start playing, "I Love Rock n' Roll." It was just the most surreal thing ever.

Rebecca Cannon: We had done two records with Caroline Records. And then Brian Long, our A&R guy, was let go. Then all of the bands that he signed were dropped. We didn't get to do our third album.

Kris Patterson: We're back in Austin and Caroline is not returning our calls. The new Caroline president was like, "Do you do dance music?" And we were like, "No, we do not."

Rebecca Cannon: And at that same time there were a lot of power struggles in the band.

Michael Letton: Toward the end, I could tell Chepo wasn't happy with Sincola. The last show I saw him playing in Houston, he was basically facing the wall. Chepo has no problem expressing his feelings in no uncertain terms.

Rebecca Cannon: Me and Greg just quit one day. We met at Taco Bell. It's kind of ridiculous, but I remember saying, "Should we do it?" At the time, it was a really big deal, and the girls didn't talk to us for like seven years, but we're all friends now.

Kris Patterson: It was hard. I think Chepo was the first one to say he was leaving. This was in a matter of days, and we were just falling apart. Rebecca was like, "I'm not doing this anymore," and I said, "Okay, well then it's all done." Everyone had a very important role to play, and I don't think they were replaceable.

Rebecca Cannon: It all happened at once for all these bands beginning with the letter "S." It was kind of weird. Starfish, Sixteen Deluxe, Spoon. . . . Spoon stayed together, so there is a part of probably all of us that thinks, "What if we stayed together and stuck it out? Would we be as big as Spoon?"

Jay Hughey: That tent during SXSW opened our eyes to this whole realm of possibility. As a result, we hosted a couple of festivals. The Fringe Festival was one of the most memorable of just how weird things could get. This whole crew of guys were outside welding this sculpture together and telling people, "Don't look directly at the welding arc!"

What are we going to do with this sculpture? We could let it live in perpetuity outside, but it's taking up two parking spaces. We didn't have to worry, because part of their program was to beat the fucking thing back down to the earth.

Then they were like, "I just can't stop the beat!" There was a train parked and they were climbing up all over this train, doing this unbelievable, staccato percussion. People were showing up going, "I heard this thing from way down Lamar and I just came over." Who knew that they were playing a train?

Mark Shuman: That was the crazy thing too. We were next to the train tracks. It had the sharpest curve between Laredo and Austin, so a lot of guys jumped off the train coming from Mexico.

Hunter Darby: Every year Ringling Brothers would come to town, and they would do their show. That was the greatest night to be at the Electric Lounge

Sincola, 1993 (*left to right*): guitarist Greg Wilson, vocalist Rebecca Cannon, bassist Chepo Peña, guitarist Kris Patterson. Photo by Greggae Giles.

because the circus people would come in and drink and they would watch the show. To talk to a guy about elephant training was really surreal.

Mark Shuman: We ended up having this relationship with the guys that worked with the railroad. They'd come into the club and go, "Hey, we can't switch tracks! There's a car on the track! You got to move it."

Hunter Darby: My wife worked at South By when the Frogs were playing and someone drove a car onto the railroad tracks, got stuck, and just left. And the train was coming. Everyone went outside and realized we can't get the car off the track, so we just watched it hit.

Jennings Crawford: Yeah, alcohol mixed with railroad tracks . . . What could possibly go wrong?

Hunter Darby: The guy that got his arm cut off, that was a gruesome night. That was bad.

Mike Henry: He lost an *arm*.

Jay Hughey: He didn't "lose" an arm because Tom Beach went out and put the arm on ice. He was later reprimanded by the EMS guys who said, "Do not put a raw arm on ice! Do you not know? You've got to wrap the thing in cloth!"

Mark Shuman: The hospital called us the next day, and they said, "Hey, listen. We got your ice chest. They brought an arm in it last night."

Mike Henry: "We don't need that chest back."

Mark Shuman: After the fire, we had the Peter Criss show. Those guys brought the whole *rock show* and packed it in there. We kept blowing power. The Aussie manager comes up to me and goes, "Listen, mate. If the power blows here again this show is over."

I just looked at him and go, "Pal, if the power blows again, you guys are all out of here!" He didn't say anything else.

Mike Henry: The greatest thing about the show was Gomez opening. Criss wouldn't move any of their setup, so Gomez is playing on two and a half square feet of the stage.

Ryan McDaniel: I was on the road with Jesus Christ Superfly as their roadie. I called Chepo, who was like, "Dude, you got to come off the tour early. We're going to play with Peter Criss at the Electric Lounge!" So of course I hop on a bus.

Before the show we go out and get a bunch of flowers because during "Beth," Peter Criss likes to throw out flowers. We were like, "Let's give our own salute to our favorite drummer of Kiss!" So we played the show and this crowd does not want us one bit. They wanted the cheesy heavy metal Peter Criss. So we're like, "Screw it." We played maybe four originals and we're like, "Okay, you want to hear some Kiss?" We did "Deuce" and "Strutter."

Chepo Peña: We did "Heaven's on Fire." We did "I Love It Loud." We tried to do all of them.

Gomez (the Austin version) opening for Peter Criss at Electric Lounge, 1994. Photo by Greggae Giles.

Ryan McDaniel: During "Lick It Up," we decided to dedicate it to Eric Carr—Peter Criss's replacement—and throw out flowers at the same time, which didn't go over well with a whole lot of people.

Mike Henry: The really serious Kiss fans are there early. They're all in acid-washed denim and drinking a Bud Light with their girl. Gomez is up there just obliterating every Kiss song that they know or don't know. It was perfect because everyone in there was totally confused, and also they like it but they're not sure if they're supposed to.

Ryan McDaniel: Peter Criss gets on stage and the singer of his band is the most ridiculous '90s trying-to-be-cool guy with a little stubby mohawk and they lunge into the most ridiculous heavy metal that anyone has ever heard. And it's not packed. There's maybe a hundred people there.

Mike Henry: On the rider, Criss had half a dozen roses because the encore was "Beth" and "Hard Luck Woman," and it was all acoustic. It was like the *Kiss Unplugged* thing. During "Beth," he throws the roses out. And then people start throwing the roses back and it was the saddest moment ever. My childhood hero is getting pelted by roses . . .

Ryan McDaniel: After the show, Peter Criss was doing an autograph signing session. Kind of. It was ridiculous. To get a Peter Criss autograph, you had to give your item to the guy standing at the door of the bus. My friend Aesop [Dekker]—the drummer from Hickey—gets his signed drumhead back, looks at the autograph, and he's like, "Man, I've been looking at *KISS Alive 1* since 1975. I know what those guys' signatures look like. That's *not* Peter Criss's signature."

I put Aesop on my shoulders, he looks into the bus window, and it's Peter Criss and three other guys sitting at this table all signing "Peter Criss" autographs. So now we're throwing rocks at the bus going, "Hey, Catman! Come on out, you pussycat! You can't sign your own autographs?"

Mike Henry: We were making some money. We were doing okay. But then, right as our lease came to be renewed, all the smart growth stuff started to happen downtown. They were trying to revitalize downtown and make a dense urban core. We were over there by ourselves with nothing around us.

Kerthy Fix: Because of SXSW and probably *Slacker* and the sort of broadcasting of this little world, there was a commodification of the Austin lifestyle, and it was kind of unstoppable.

Mike Henry: I think that what the Lounge was about would translate to today. It was about this creative spirit, bringing together a bunch of different kinds of art forms, different kinds of genres, but always being about an amazing show. There are venues that strive to do that today. I think that we were representative of a time that happened. And time marches on.

LIBERTY LUNCH

BY THE '90S, WE WERE ROCKING

REGARDLESS OF SENTIMENT, THE ASSERTION THAT LIBERTY Lunch was at the heart of Austin is geographic fact.

Long before Anglo settler Jacob Harrell pitched a tent in 1833 near where Shoal Creek empties into the Colorado River, nomadic Native Americans utilized the nearby low-water crossing to ford the river. If not for that crossing now under the waters of Lady Bird Lake [called Town Lake until 2007], the hamlet of Waterloo—soon to be renamed after revolutionary empresario Stephen F. Austin and envisioned by president to-be Mirabeau B. Lamar as the frontier seat of an empire stretching all the way to the Pacific—would not have come into being where it did.

The land that would one day become Liberty Lunch first took commercial form as a wagon yard for the adjacent J. P. Schneider general store in the years immediately following the Civil War. The Houston & Texas Central Railroad arrived in Austin in 1871 with a depot at the corner of Fourth and Congress.

Though officially known as the First Ward, the neighborhood between the train station and the wagon yard would come to be known as Guy Town, a red-light district with a thriving prostitution trade. Biennial legislative sessions and the opening of the University of Texas in 1883 ensured a steady supply of johns until the city shut it down in 1913. When the area was excavated for redevelopment in 2001, archeologists found hundreds of beer bottles along with dice and birth control devices.[1]

By the 1920s the Liberty Lunch site was surrounded by the Calcasieu Lumber Company, which would ultimately grow to a teeming, six-block complex of lumberyards, mills, offices, and warehouses. In the post–World War II years, the building that would eventually house the club's offices and a small game area was a restaurant called Liberty Lunch.

As downtown land became more valuable, Calcasieu started moving their operations out of the central business district, leaving behind industrial spaces unsuitable for offices or shops but ripe for repurposing in more imaginative ways. In 1975 Shannon Sedwick and Michael Shelton rented the dilapidated property at 405 West Second Street. The future founders of venerable comedy cabaret Esther's Follies envisioned a freewheeling performance art space that also served Cajun food.

The plan was to call the place Progressive Grocery, but then Shelton and Sedwick scraped paint off the front of the building and found a ghost sign for Liberty Lunch. With the nation's bicentennial months away, that became the name. The "new" Liberty Lunch opened for business on December 6, 1975.[2] A month later, the city took over the property, setting in motion a unique blessing/curse relationship that would continue for the entirety of Liberty Lunch's existence.

While chef Emil Vogley's gumbo was the first big draw, weekday residencies by dance-friendly bands like Beto y Los Fairlanes and the Lotions made live music and cheap beer the stock-in-trade. Revelers would stomp on the gravel floor until clouds of dust coated the instruments. The bands made good money for late-seventies Austin unless the open-air venue got rained out.

Charles Tesar took over the Liberty Lunch lease in 1979. Across the river, the Armadillo World Headquarters closed down in 1980. The Armadillo's demise set the stage for Liberty Lunch to become the go-to venue for touring acts too small for arenas but too big for smaller nightclubs. A spiritual torch of sorts was passed in 1981 when beams and trusses from the demolished Armadillo were trucked over to Liberty Lunch to construct an erstwhile roof.

Mark Pratz started working the door at Liberty Lunch in 1978, eventually working up to owner-manager. Pratz and future SXSW cofounder Louis Meyers started Lunch Money Productions in 1982, booking an eclectic array of local and national acts into Liberty Lunch, the Continental Club, and three other venues. A long list of notable reggae acts played Liberty Lunch during this era, including Burning Spear, the Gladiators, and Steel Pulse. New Orleans R&B royalty the Neville Brothers made multiple visits, culminating with a three-night stand in January 1989.

Katrina and the Waves played on June 14, 1985, just as "Walking on Sunshine" became the pop hit of the summer. Five nights later, emergent hip-hop icons Run-D.M.C. performed a Juneteenth set so energetic that DJ Jam Master Jay struggled to keep his records from skipping. On July 13, 1985, a quavering Daniel Johnston sang "I Live My Broken Dreams" and Zeitgeist performed "Things Don't Change" for an episode of MTV's *The Cutting Edge* that would air the following month.

During that episode, host Peter Zaremba notes that Liberty Lunch is slated for closure over footage of downtown Austin shot from a construction crane. Months later, the commercial real estate lending bubble began its years-long collapse, snuffing out Austin's boom but allowing Liberty Lunch to live another day. The ongoing recession also put the kibosh on plans for a new city hall building on the site.

The upside of the club's tenuous relationship with the city was that rent stayed cheap. Pratz was paying $500 a month to rent Liberty Lunch and three times that to rent the Continental Club, so he pulled out of the latter in 1987. The decade's latter half saw the club's focus shift toward college radio favorites like the Replacements, Fishbone, and the Meat Puppets.

By the '90s Liberty Lunch was firmly established as the go-to Austin stop for touring bands on the verge of breaking big. Green Day, Smashing Pumpkins, Beck, and Alanis Morrissette all played there within months of going platinum. Booking agent Frank Riley funneled many of these shows to the club.

Nirvana sidled into Liberty Lunch on October 21, 1991, with support from former Austinite and ex-Dicks vocalist Gary Floyd fronting his new band, Sister Double Happiness. *Nevermind* was less than a month old, but the album had already begun its insurrectionary campaign to dethrone Michael Jackson's *Dangerous* from the top of the charts. Key to the coup was Samuel Bayer's anti-pep-rally music video for "Smells Like Teen Spirit." One of the moshing extras in the video was former KTSB DJ Marc Schlossberg, who is briefly seen wearing a Bouffant Jellyfish T-shirt.

Liberty Lunch was also the pinnacle of a local ecosystem of venues built on a forever-changing foundation of plywood and cinder block stages in backyards, house parties, college co-ops, and smaller clubs. A packed show at Liberty Lunch was as far as a local band could go without expanding its horizons beyond the city.

Local bands could also expand their fanbase by opening for touring acts. Before packaged openers started crowding out this arrangement toward the end of the '90s, local bands like Gomez and Miss Universe would find themselves opening for Green Day and Pavement, respectively.

Pratz and his co-owner/manager/spouse J'Net Ward took over the lease from Tesar in 1992. They carried out renovations to shore up the roof and shore up the front wall, both of which had proved vulnerable to gate crashers during the aforementioned Nirvana show, but the club's shambling character remained intact.

As the '90s rolled on, Rage Against the Machine, Weezer, and No Doubt alternated with big local draws like Ed Hall, Sincola, and Sixteen Deluxe. Because Liberty Lunch was all-ages, a parallel scene of younger bands like ska-laden punks the Impossibles could pack the house with underage kids while going all but unnoticed by the over-twenty-ones.

Fans and bands didn't keep coming back to Liberty Lunch because of the edifice itself. It could be oppressively hot in the summer and teeth-chatteringly cold in the winter. There was no backstage restroom, so bands had to use the same Pittsburgh basement–style toilets with no privacy stalls as their fans. In 1996 the road-hardened male members of North Carolina indie rock institution Superchunk positioned Liberty Lunch's facilities in a three-way tie for first place in their list of the worst rock club restrooms in the United States.[3]

What Liberty Lunch did have was Pratz, J'Net Ward, and longtime staff like Betsy Nissen, Mileah Jordan, and Scott Anderson, who ran the club with an endearing mix of pragmatism and soul. During the time he ran the club with Ward, Pratz simultaneously built a successful career in elementary education, a skillset that undoubtedly came in handy when dealing with drunk patrons, overzealous slam-dancers, and sensitive artists.

Relative to everyone else in this book, Pratz and Ward strike an equanimous tone about the club's demise. Perhaps that's because the club was never not living on borrowed time. After more than a decade of the Lunch site being slated for a new city hall, Austin's city council approved a plan to raze Liberty Lunch and replace it with an office building housing software developer Computer Sciences Corporation on December 10, 1998.

Then in the wee hours of December 12, Afghan Whigs vocalist Greg Dulli got into an altercation with Liberty Lunch bouncer Teitur "Taiter" Gentry following the Whigs' show there. Dulli claimed Gentry blindsided him, knocking him to the concrete floor, then kicking him while he was down. The club maintained Dulli only got hit after coming at Gentry with a two-by-four. Dulli wound up at Brackenridge Hospital with a fractured skull, missing several tour dates. Though police never filed any charges, Dulli filed a lawsuit,[4] and the incident made national news.

Even as MTV News coined Dulli's account of the incident "shocking," most music fans in Austin were more concerned that Liberty Lunch really was shutting down this time. A few even remembered that Dulli found similar trouble during the Whigs' first Austin appearance at the Cannibal Club back in 1990, when he threw a beer pitcher into the crowd and hit an unfortunate bystander in the head.

Throughout the first half of 1999, calls to designate Liberty Lunch as a historical institution worthy of preservation grew in both number and intensity. *Austin Chronicle* music editor Raoul Hernandez accused the mayor and city council of paying nothing more than lip service to Austin live music, even calling out a former colleague-turned-council member. "Daryl Slusher, you've got a lot of gall divorcing yourself completely from the left-wing agenda you ranted and raved about here at the *Chronicle* as politics editor," Hernandez wrote.[5]

The shouting continued right up through July, but the deal was done. The Lunch's final month of shows was a memorable one. Sonic Youth played a farewell two-night stand on July 7 and 8. Then came the Gloria-thon on July 23 and 24, where a constantly rotating cast of local musicians played Them's "Gloria" for twenty-four hours straight. They were briefly joined by Van Morrison, composer of the 1964 garage rock gem, who called in from overseas to sing a few lines.

Oddly enough, the final bill at Liberty Lunch on July 31, 1999, wasn't locally grown. Instead, platinum-plated Fort Worth alt-rock combo Toadies shared the stage with Denton's Baboon as the gathered assemblage burned Mayor Kirk Watson's visage in effigy.

Despite his fervor for smart growth, Watson also attended shows at Liberty Lunch, and he knew it was bad politics to displace a beloved long-running local business. As a consolation, the city arranged a low-interest loan for Pratz and Ward to reopen Liberty Lunch on Red River next to Stubb's, but the project fell through during planning. The sweetheart lease on city-owned land was gone, the economics of presenting midlevel touring bands was more daunting, and Liberty Lunch wasn't coming back.

Now newer Austinites who'd long grown tired of old-timers carping about the end of the Armadillo World Headquarters had their own ghost club to carp about. Like the Armadillo, Liberty Lunch was replaced by an office building—one housing a *tech company*, no less—in a poetic example of commerce displacing art.

In the well-worn narrative of moving to Austin, falling in love with the city, and then becoming disenchanted, the end of Liberty Lunch was a milemarker in a story that stretches both backwards and forwards. But if you were a local music fan who hit your stride in the '90s, Liberty Lunch was the heartshot that stung the most.

Liberty Lunch. Photo by Richard Whymark.

Mark Pratz: Second Street was one of the main streets when the Colorado River was a low-water crossing. People could come across the river in their wagons. In the 1800s it was the old red-light district in town. It was a very trafficked part of town.

The site is a historical building. If you've seen the plaque, it was called the Schneider Store. In the digging and rebuilding downtown there, they discovered a tunnel all the way underneath the street that came up in the Schneider store. It's really interesting history down there. They dug up a lot of bones and animals. Both domestic and—they think—prehistoric. And Indian sites. It is a site that has just incredible energy.

During World War II, some guy went into the little office building and did a restaurant called Liberty Lunch. Named after—we believe—liberty bonds and the whole liberty theme of World War II. Then it shut down and disappeared for years. But that's why we called it Liberty Lunch and Wagon Yard.

Marc Fort: Clubs come and go all the time, but Liberty Lunch was different. It had this literal physical connection to Austin music history.

Mark Pratz: Liberty Lunch was the grace of the city. They gave it to us for $500 a month. The city always thought they were going to tear it down the next day. The place had fallen into really bad disrepair. In the '90s we took over the lease with the agreement we would remodel it. Then the city rented us that property behind what is now Lambert's, so we got that big beer garden area where you could go out and smoke and hang out.

J'Net Ward: Most of the city council back then were all music people, and they would love to come down. They believed in us and what we were doing.

Marc Fort: Going to Liberty Lunch as an impressionable eighteen-year-old was really cool. They created this energy inside where it felt like that was the best place you could be anywhere in the world. Cheap Shiner Bock in the original formula before Corona bought 'em. Weed from Mexico that was really cheap. It was an eighteen-year-old's nirvana.

Ryan McDaniel: Mark and J'Net were cool. They were like your cool punk rock aunt and uncle.

Tim Kerr: They're totally coming from the right place to begin with. They are more community-minded than they are a business. And it was just a really great place to play.

Marc Fort: Maybe it was special because their first bookings were reggae. Reggae has that positive vibe of "anybody can come and be a part of it." That trailed over into the energy and vibe of the rest of the place and bookings.

Mark Pratz: We started booking a lot more national and international reggae. Burning Spear. The Meditations. Culture. Inner Circle. Lucky Dube. That had a big audience, and then word gets around in the agencies. "Hey! Someone's got a thousand-person room down there!"

Marc Fort: Something really special started happening with the bookings there when Mark and J'Net took over the club. Both with local bands and with roadshows. That was when Generation X took over.

Frenchie Smith: In the summer of 1990, I got a job at Whole Foods Brodie Oaks. That immediately put me in a subculture that was very Austin-tastic. Cindy Toth—bass player from the Reivers—was my coworker. I would work with Brian Beattie from Glass Eye. I soon figured out that he had produced the Dead Milkmen.

Graham Williams: At the time it was such a big club and such a small scene. The first show I saw there was Dead Milkmen. And then I saw Fugazi a few months later. So you would see bigger stuff, and you'd see a local opening band for those artists.

Mark Pratz: The smaller clubs, like Brad First's clubs, really did a lot to build and become feeders. Our hope was the local bands would then start having a draw.

Frenchie Smith: I would see Ed Hall be masters of curating bills at Liberty Lunch. Seeing and hearing them play, I had some kind of an epiphany that "Okay, there's international music. There's national music. And then locally we have bands that are also making records and doing tours. This band is one of them." It was shockingly good. The band would be barely clothed and paint themselves with weird stick figure cave drawings. There would be black lights. Maybe a bag of flour would go up in the air. All of a sudden they would start looking like some kind of indigenous being that escaped "Danger Island" from *The Banana Splits*.

Luke Savisky was doing film work for them. Luke had a relationship with Butthole Surfers, so he brought 35mm film projectors and made loops of film. He would scratch some pattern into the film that would be dancing. So you have a crazy sound, sweaty heat, low end that altered your bodily organs, and cymbals on the drum kit going like a jet engine.

Kelly Linn: We would open for Ed Hall a lot, but our biggest show was when we opened for Glass Eye's last show at Liberty Lunch, and there were seven hundred people. That was awesome. That was the Orange Show. We made these crazy freaky orange-and-white striped dresses with wire on the bottom so they stuck out. And we had orange slices on our chests. It was this complete scene and there was so much support. It was the same thing with the Big Boys, you know?

Jane Sanders: Talk about Austin music royalty—that was Biscuit, starting back with the Big Boys. For a Swine King Halloween show, Biscuit came in

Dotty Farrell (*left*) and Randy "Biscuit" Turner (*right*) of Swine King at Liberty Lunch. Photo by Richard Whymark.

and he hung baby dolls from the ceiling that he had painted green and put wings on and stuff. He was an incredibly kind man, and so talented.

Chepo Peña: The amount of people that a local band got to play to was amazing. It made you feel special.

Ryan McDaniel: For bands like us, if you got a slot playing at Liberty Lunch, it was like Madison Square Garden. If you could headline Liberty Lunch, no one could touch you.

Tim Stegall: As far as Austin venues went, it was the best possible stage you could play. It was this really nice, huge, well-maintained stage. The first time we played there, I thought I was in the Clash all of the sudden. I winded myself running back and forth across that stage!

Susie Martinez: Mileah Jordan, who used to book Liberty Lunch, would get us [Handful] a gig whenever she could. It is a *big* stage. Terri [Lord] was really nice and gave us an opening slot when she could.

Frenchie Smith: You had one hour a week to get a hold of the booking person. So by the time you got your foot in the door, you better be doing mischief to let people know about your band playing or you're never coming back. Orange Mothers had that raw white sheet hanging from the railroad bridge on Lamar and it just said, "Liberty Lunch, Orange Mothers." It hung up there for days.

Chepo Peña: They were supportive of all types of bands. When I started going there, local bands like Agony Column or Retarted Elf or Bouffant Jellyfish would pack that place. But when Sincola would play there, maybe the floor would be full, but you could walk around the outside.

Edith Casimir: We played at Liberty Lunch when we were brand new and horrible. People would go, "Oh my gosh! You played at Liberty Lunch?" "Well yeah, but there were only six people there."

Graham Williams: Bands like Mineral or Trail of Dead did great when they toured, but no one really cared here. Like they would play to a couple hundred people maybe, but then they toured and played to tons of people because they were bigger in other cities. But Impossibles were big everywhere. They got on a lot of big tours right away. I put out their first record when I was in

Ned's Atomic Dustbin at Liberty Lunch, SXSW 1994. Photo by Richard Whymark.

high school, and then a label re-put it out because we didn't know what we were doing.

Chepo Peña: The thing that was great was they let local bands open for touring bands. They would call the shots—not the touring bands. We opened for Material Issue and Juliana Hatfield and all these other people. You don't see that anymore. You don't see a local band opening a touring show at Stubb's. They always get a package deal.

Mark Pratz: I don't know how much is in control of local promoters anymore. I have this feeling that it's pretty tightly dictated when you start doing big-name acts. I think Charles Attal has perfected that now in terms of owning everything and booking everywhere. What I loved to do was get a headliner, and then get two or three other local acts all in one night.

Michelle Rule: It's really weird how shows get booked nowadays. It's completely different from how it was before. We opened for Pavement at Liberty Lunch after we had opened for them in Iowa City. I called Bob [Nastanovich] the percussionist, and I asked him to call the owners of Liberty Lunch. He called them and got us the opening slot. It was fun to play that huge stage.

J'Net Ward: A lot of the Waterloo Records people really helped a lot, saying, "This would be a good band to play. We're selling a lot of their music right now." A lot of times the local bands would say, "We'll do the posters and stuff to help promote the show." All before the internet.

Frenchie Smith: Mark and J'Net were booking the coolest bands in the world. My Bloody Valentine, Nirvana, Smashing Pumpkins.

J'Net Ward: By the '90s, we were rocking. We had the cutting-edge stuff. If they were going to play *Saturday Night Live* or the *Tonight Show* in the '90s, they'd be at Liberty Lunch. But I'm at a Xerox machine making advanced tickets. I'm getting the same card stock that anyone else could get. The person next to me could buy one of our tickets and then copy it. And then I thought I was being cute by putting a stamp on the back of it. A *colored* stamp.

Mark Pratz: The road manager for Michelle Shocked took me to the cleaners about these little funky tickets. "You got two girls at the door taking money!" And he was convinced we were stealing from him.

I just went, "Dude, I'm sorry that it's crude and primitive, but you walk around the room and you count every head in this hall and you see what I pay you tonight." He was half upset because there were only four hundred people there instead of the nine hundred they thought would be there.

Janet Hammer: We all braved ten-degree weather to go out and to see Dinosaur Jr. right when *Bug* came out. They never played anywhere. So everybody's wrapped in blankets. They played three songs. J Mascis marched offstage and refused to play any more music.

Mark Pratz: Hootie & the Blowfish. They were big shit in North Carolina, apparently. Their record was just breaking, and we made the mistake of booking them on OU weekend. We paid them a pretty decent sum of money, and nobody showed up. A hundred people. Darius [Rucker]—very nice guy— went, "Man, this is not what we do. This is terrible, and we'll be back."

Well, they went on to skyrocket sales for that album. Their agent called back six months later and said, "I can't believe I'm asking you this. But will you have Hootie & the Blowfish come back? Darius is insisting."

I said, "Are you kidding me?" Because at that time it's the number-one

Poster for Dinosaur Jr., My Bloody Valentine, Babes in Toyland, February 18, 1992, at Liberty Lunch. Photo by JasonAustin.

album. It's gone nuts. But to Darius's credit and the band's credit, they came back and played two killer freaking nights.

J'Net Ward: The musicians loved coming to Austin and hanging out. It was such a musician-friendly place. If there were only ten people there but we said we were going to pay you five grand, you got your five grand. We didn't whine or cry. Musicians liked the way we treated them as family when they came.

Jane Sanders: One of my favorite memories of Liberty Lunch was the twenty-four hours of "Gloria." Our sound guy, Mike Odell, managed to somehow patch in Van Morrison. And then Van Morrison himself sang the song!

Tim Stegall: I can remember Ron [Williams] and I getting our hearing blown out by Sugar the night they played there. Sugar were so loud, they had inadvertently damaged the Liberty Lunch PA system. Bob [Mould] just very calmly reached in his pocket and paid them for the damage.

Mark Pratz: My Bloody Valentine is the loudest band in the world.

Tim Stegall: I can remember seeing My Bloody Valentine play a D7 chord at five million watts for fifteen minutes.

Jane Sanders: We had everything from local bands that might have five people at the show to all of the big popular bands. Anywhere from Fishbone, Alanis Morissette, Bush, Joan Jett, Sean Lennon. NOFX were the greatest. They came to play, and we were sold out. There were well over a hundred people that wanted to get in but couldn't, and they were threatening to bum-rush the door. They were all crowded in the street on Second Street right in front of Liberty Lunch. Mark Pratz went out to talk to the crowd. Pretty soon he starts banging on the front door. We creak it open to let him in. He's disheveled with a ripped shirt but with a grin ear to ear. It was wonderful.

Robert Zimmer: October 1991. It was literally three weeks after *Nevermind* had been released. Our [KTSB] music director was like, "They're going to be the next big thing! They've just gone from Sub Pop to Geffen Records." You just had a sense that you were witnessing something incredibly magical and special. Nirvana was about to change the entire landscape of the music scene.

Mark Pratz: Nirvana had just played [in Dallas] at Trees the night before. Kurt had gone crazy and smashed their monitor board with his guitar. He had completely wrecked their stage gear.

J'Net Ward: All of our workers were like, "Are we going to let them play?" I'm like, "Yeah we're going to let them play!"

Jonathan Toubin: On every level, the grunge revolution got people into punk and underground music. It's like, "Wow! The cheerleaders from high school are here?" All these people got involved in the culture. Some of them were just tourists. Some of them stayed, but a lot of the bands started getting signed and that changed it. There was a higher level of record sales for indie stuff.

Tim Stegall: This was a band that was readily accessible, and suddenly they were selling lots of records. It seemed like suddenly every little independent rock band thought they could become rock stars.

Robert Zimmer: You just had a sense that history was changing. I remember the crowd just going bonkers when they played "Smells Like Teen Spirit."

Mark Pratz: It was 1,400 people. Tickets sold out in twenty-three minutes. We had these little advance tickets that we used. Someone had found out how to duplicate them. They were selling them out front, and they were dead on, so we ended up with way too many people in there.

J'Net Ward: They just overran the club.

Mark Pratz: People made a run for the door. We were trying to pull the door shut while all these fingers were pulling from top to bottom. It was like a horror show! We shut it and put a bar in.

J'Net Ward: We locked people in.

Mark Pratz: No one could get in or out. People were coming down through the big holes in the roof and sliding down the pole. We had to go up on the roof and put the caps on, so it turned into a freaking oven in there. Thank goodness there was no fire.

Ryan McDaniel: People were going nuts. It was back when they didn't have the barricades. As security, you basically had to kneel on the front of the stage the whole time. What I remember the most is getting knocked in the back of the head by Krist Novoselic's bass. He was just knocking us all in the back of the head, and I couldn't tell whether he was doing it on purpose or if he was just rocking out. Either way, it hurt. Then after the show I played Kiss pinball with him and that was pretty fun.

J'Net Ward: Our security was the Friendly Skinheads.

Jane Sanders: They might have been skinheads, but they were nonracist. We had Teitur, his brother Oscar, and Pork Chop. Our door guy was Jason Saenz. As a woman working the door, they looked out for me better than I looked out for myself, you know? If they saw that there was going to be trouble, they were right there.

Mark Pratz: We would've been beat up many times if they hadn't been around.

Jane Sanders: The Afghan Whigs showed up for sound check. Bands would usually come in the back door. For whatever reason, Greg Dulli starts banging on the front door, and of course the doors were locked. One of our guys, Teitur Gentry, took a little bit of time to get those doors unlocked. There were several keys, chains, and all that. Greg Dulli comes in and he's mad. Teitur had a goatee, so Greg starts calling him Billy Goat Boy. Like I say, Greg Dulli was an asshole. Teitur just ignored him.

After the show, all the customers were gone. I was sitting on the stage. Greg Dulli went into the women's bathroom. He pried a 2×4 off the wall. Teitur was standing at the front door area. Greg Dulli reached up to clock Teitur over the head with the 2×4, and Teitur punched him. Teitur was a pretty tough guy. Greg Dulli fell and smashed his head on the concrete, and that darn near killed him. We called 911. I had just got the door open when the EMTs showed up. I've seen stuff in the press that says, "Liberty Lunch wouldn't open the doors." That is false. I was the one that got the doors open. That's what happened. And it obviously became a big, horrible thing. There was a court case. I'm glad Greg Dulli lived, but it was serious.

Mark Pratz: All those big shows were just kind of crazy. Most of the time it was not bad. It was just people having fun. So much fun and so much energy. We were in the golden era of Austin's live music scene. I guess everybody thinks they are.

And as much as Liberty Lunch could not survive, it was a huge mistake closing it. Something should've happened to try to preserve it. When you look down there now and look at that town that's been built on top of it, it's fabulous. But it was also the death knell on just a kind of way of doing things.

Kathy McCarty: From working at the Cannibal Club, I knew that every single rock music venue in America is hanging on by the skin of its teeth. Owning a rock club is just not a lucrative way to make a living. It's almost as bad as being in a band.

Mark Pratz: We were big on keeping prices down. If you want to play Liberty Lunch, then you're not going to charge twenty-five bucks at the door. We'll charge fifteen. The reason we could do that is that cheap rent we had. And slowly but surely, that stopped.

Kathy McCarty: Everybody knew the city would eventually sell that land. It's right downtown on the river. It's worth millions of dollars. They're not going to let it be this little rock club forever. And it's bad that we live in a kind of society where people don't look at something like Liberty Lunch and consider it to be like the Vienna Opera House. This is a cultural gem that we want to preserve.

J'Net Ward: The city had a vision for Second Street. People were coming in with money because the only thing down there was City Hall. The city really tried to help us move to a different location, but we were going to have to spend so much money, and we already spent all of our money in the '90s. There's nothing bad I can say about the city at this point. They did what they could, and we just couldn't make it. We couldn't find the magic.

Marc Fort: In a perfect world, Liberty Lunch would still be open. There'd be the tall high-rise condos built all around. They'd have a City of Austin historic landmark right on the front.

Jett Garrison: I remember being at Liberty Lunch on the last night, and hugging Mark and J'Net and crying about it, because the reason it was shutting down was because we had had the tech boom and everybody started to realize, "Oh, let's build up downtown! These little venues—that's great real estate! They just need to get the hell out of there!"

Marc Fort: I totally get that. You don't want downtown having empty, dilapidated buildings. Believe it or not, that's the way Second Street, Third Street, Fourth Street in downtown Austin was at the time. You want to do your urban renewal, but you don't want that at the sake of the town's culture.

Rick Carney: Liberty Lunch was the greatest venue in all of the United States. I've never seen a place that had such diversity in booking. Such a great staff. Such a good vibe. And to be lost really for no good reason but a bad real estate deal was really a tragedy. But it was totally legal. It's not what I wanted to see happen, but is it wrong? It's the way business goes.

Marc Fort: The irony is the city owned the property Liberty Lunch was on. And they have their council meetings every week, starting off the whole meeting talking about [how] Austin's the Live Music Capital of the World.

Tim Kerr: Then you get off the plane and it says, "We Support Austin Music!"

Marc Fort: That damn building sat empty for years. And Liberty Lunch could've been there making money as Austin turned into this boomtown. Everybody from MTV to Swedish television to people from Japan wanted to move here, let alone all of California. So everyone and their brother and sister wants to move here in the 2000s and there's a venue with great historical/

cultural significance that should be still there. Senator Watson, wherever you are . . . love you, bro, but you goofed on that one.

(On December 13, 2022, more than two decades after his last mayoral term ended, Kirk Watson narrowly defeated state representative Celia Israel in a runoff election to win another term as Austin's mayor.)

THE END

IT DOESN'T GO ON FOREVER

IF YOU COULD GO BACK IN A TIME MACHINE WITH DOCTOR WHO, YOU
COULD BE RICHER THAN DELL.

GARY CHESTER

THE CHRONOLOGICAL END OF DECADES AND THE cultural era we associate those decades with don't always coincide, but sometimes the seismicity
of events aligns with the calendar in a manner that puts an exclamation point
on the passage of time. The Rolling Stones didn't set out to end the sixties
when they decided to play a free concert at Altamont Speedway on December
6, 1969, but the chaos and violence of that day couldn't help but take on a
poetic resonance as the calendar ran out.

On December 31, 1999, the headline for the *Austin Chronicle*'s year-end
music wrap-up declared 1999 "The Year It All Went Wrong." If one went
looking for a decade-ending Altamont moment for the Austin music scene
in 1999, the drumbeat of venerable club closures followed by the unexpected
death of Doug Sahm in November made for a convincing argument. In his
final years it was common for the author of "Groover's Paradise" to warn local
music fans that they were in danger of losing a good thing.

"Remember, Austin, Texas, we've got a heritage here," Sahm said from the stage of the 1997 Austin Music Awards. "Don't ever lose it, man."

That same week, the Wannabes unveiled their new T-shirt for the far-flung throngs assembled for SXSW. It was a laughably simple design, with yellow block letters on a black shirt. The front read, "Wannabes, Austin, Texas." The back read, "DON'T MOVE HERE."

Things were changing. The sleepy, midsized college town of 1990 was now an emerging metropolis. Austin's population had grown to 629,769 by 1999 and the metro area had surpassed one million residents. Developers were busy consolidating tracts of land at the corner of Fourth and Congress for the Frost Bank Tower, which would briefly reign as Austin's tallest building upon completion in 2003.

In May the city closed the convenient-but-obsolete Robert Mueller Municipal Airport and opened a new airport with room to grow at the former site of Bergstrom Air Force Base. Austin, as an ongoing series of news stories about growth and development on KXAN-TV liked to remind us, was "On the Move."

The city's cultural fabric was evolving, too. By 1999 the Red River space once occupied by the Cavity was a high-end dance club called Spiro's. And unlike the Blue Flamingo, Spiro's really did have valet parking.

When the 1990s started, the closest most Austinites came to quaffing local beer from a small brewery was Shiner Bock. Then Belgian emigre Pierre Celis opened a small craft brewery on the east side of town in 1992. The following year, the Texas legislature passed House Bill 1425, which amended the state's alcoholic beverage code to allow brewpubs to operate. Later that year, brewpubs began popping up around downtown Austin.

Billy Forrester's Waterloo Brewing Company at the corner of Fourth and Guadalupe was the first brewpub in modern Texas history. Waterloo's brewmaster was Steve Anderson,[1] an eighties-era punk veteran who was Scratch Acid's vocalist for their first two shows. While both Waterloo and Celis Brewing were gone by 2001, the two businesses helped set the course for a craft brewing renaissance that would ultimately transform an anonymous light industrial section of North Austin into a "Brewing District."

At the same time, the holy trinity of barbecue, Tex-Mex, and Southern comfort cuisine was losing its dominance over Austin's restaurant scene. Upscale eateries like Mezzaluna and Sullivan's Steakhouse in the city's Warehouse District exemplified this shift. The latter's cigar-and-martini vibe was savaged in Boomland's swart anthem, "Go Back to California," from 1998's *South Austin Kicks Ass* compilation.

Despite such protests, Austin's national reputation—once confined to sentinel hosannas like the June 1990 cover story in *National Geographic*—was sealed. The success of *Slacker* and years of positive SXSW dispatches fueled by friendly vibes, free grub, and fair weather certainly helped, but word-of-mouth from previous Austin transplants—many swelling with civic pride for the first time in their lives—ensured more would follow.

As the city grew, the local music scene couldn't help but become less inwardly focused. Of all the nineties-era Lollapalooza tours, only the 1995 edition came through Austin. For years Austinites had gotten used to driving to Houston, Dallas, or San Antonio for big shows, but that became less necessary as the decade wore on. More roadshows effectively increased competition for local music and the clubs presenting it. While the costs of sustaining local live music climbed upward, the sheer number of bands combined with a live audience weaned on free shows and cheap beer kept payouts flat.

Simultaneously, the primacy of live music as Austin's best-known cultural export began to recede amid technology's growing reach. In 1994 Hugh Forrest launched the SXSW Multimedia Conference alongside the music conference with game developer and future astronaut Richard Garriott as keynote speaker. Initially nested with the film festival, multimedia became its own event in 1995 and rebranded as SXSW Interactive in 1996.

That year the emergence of interactive technology was largely still viewed through a prism of promise. The 1993 release of Mosaic had introduced a whole new audience to surfing the web. As soon as bandwidth was no longer a constraint, many musicians assumed the internet would allow them to bypass the mediators and transact directly with fans all over the world. Only a handful really understood just how much things were about to change.

Even before SXSW Interactive, there were less formalized confluences of music and technology. In 1993 the first issue of *FringeWare Review* was published by Jon Lebkowsky and Paco Xander Nathan. Ostensibly a zine dedicated to covering the emerging cyberculture with a punk-inspired DIY ethos, *FringeWare* also became a brick-and-mortar underground bookstore and pioneering online retail website. Sometimes the confluence was more quotidian in nature. When Spoon drummer Jim Eno first started performing with Britt Daniel in the short-lived Alien Beats, the onetime electrical engineering student spent his days designing microchips for Motorola.

The dot-com boom ushered in another wave of prosperity in the latter half of the '90s. Capital gains taxes were lowered, and flush investors sought to get in on the ground floor of e-commerce. Unlike old-guard local tech stalwarts like IBM, startups often had a cachet of coolness. Dress was casual, tattoos didn't have to be covered, and you might find beer stocked in the office fridge. The multimedia design firm Human Code actually took out an ad in the *Chronicle* in 1999 to promote the bands of its employees.

Of course, many of those bands ended 1999 with fewer venues to play a show. While the end of Liberty Lunch was the *coup de grâce*, the bloodletting started in January when the Bates Motel lost its lease. In 1995 owner Joe Bates[2] turned over booking of the room at 317 East Sixth to manager/harp blower Randall Stockton, who steered toward punk as a countermeasure to the blues bands next door at Bates's Joe's Generic Bar. The club's most noteworthy furnishings were the neon "BATES MOTEL/NO VACANCY" sign in the front window and a men's room completely covered in seventies-era centerfolds from *Playboy* and *Penthouse*.

While Angela Tharp's Flamingo Cantina at 515 East Sixth mixed in punk shows during the 1990s, it was primarily a reggae and world music club. Emo's was still going strong, but its hulking calendar, chock-full of road-shows, couldn't accommodate everyone. With the Blue Flamingo's closure in 1997, Bates Motel became the primary incubator for everything from street punks the Lower Class Brats and pyrotechnic goof-pop quintet the Kiss Offs to prolific genre-switching collective Brown Whörnet and young scruffs Dynamite Hack, who would soon generate marginal alt-radio heat with their droll cover of N.W.A's "Boyz-N-The Hood."

That all came to an end when the building was sold to a new owner with designs on housing a frat-oriented bar called the Blind Pig Pub there. The Kiss Offs were the last band to play the last show at Bates Motel on January 30, 1999. Mourners in attendance decided to help the new owners out by starting demolition early.

One bright spot in the decade-ending spate of club closures was the opening of the Red Eyed Fly in the summer of 1999. Located at 715 Red River, the Fly upped the aesthetic ante in a manner far removed from the Cavity's squalor. Unlike Liberty Lunch, the toilets were demarcated with stalls. Unlike Bates Motel, the men's room walls were not decorated with an erstwhile collage of '70s pornography. Mixed drinks were served in plastic cups with the club's logo. While the Fly's roost as an underground rock venue would only last until 2001, the club served a pivotal go-to function in the wake of losing the Bates Motel and Electric Lounge. Situated between Stubb's and Emo's, it was also a connective building block for the music venue cluster now known as the Red River Cultural District.

Some of Bob Ray's 1999 film *Rock Opera* was shot at the Bates Motel. This low-budget romp semifictitiously chronicles the vile underbelly of Austin '90s underground music in autumn. Stars included Pigpoke vocalist Jerry

Poster for Flaming Lips, Sonic Boom Experimental Audio Research, Robyn Hitchcock, Sebadoh, August 7, 1999, at Stubb's. Photo by JasonAustin.

Don Clark, FuckEmos vocalist Russell Porter, and larger-than-life raconteur Chad Holt.[3] Even Dave Prewitt from *CapZeyeZ* made a cameo. The soundtrack featured an almost all-local array of bands, including Squat Thrust, Ed Hall, Honky, and the Crack Pipes.

Though loosely tied together by a drug-score-gone-bad plot, this narrative thread is primarily a vehicle to showcase the seeds-and-stems lifestyles of ne'er-do-well Austin underground musicians eking it out in broken-down rent houses soon to be razed to make way for what city leaders called "smart growth." With the benefit of rear-view-mirror vision, *Rock Opera* can be viewed as a logical endpoint to the Austin portrayed in *Slacker* at the start of the decade.

Rock Opera premiered at the original Alamo Drafthouse Cinema. Before growing into a respected national chain of movie theaters, the first location opened by Tim and Karrie League at 409 Colorado in 1997 furthered the city's music-film convergence with a series of shows featuring local bands performing original soundtracks to classic silent films. In 1998 Dong Huong–era space-rock stalwarts ST 37 wrote and performed a new score for Fritz Lang's *Metropolis*. That Halloween, Brown Whörnet did the same for F. W. Murnau's *Nosferatu*, followed by the Golden Arm Trio's live score of Sergei Eisenstein's *Potemkin* in December.

With composer Graham Reynolds as its sole constant, the Golden Arm Trio presented an avant spin on highbrow forms like classical and jazz to lowbrow underground rock audiences at clubs like Emo's. An erudite shape-shifter, Reynolds's approach avoided the potential constraints of patronage art while broadening the horizons of what was logistically possible in a DIY setting. On June 22, 1999, the Tosca String Quartet performed a series of string compositions written by Reynolds and Brown Whörnet pianist/composer Peter Stopschinski at a sold-out Hyde Park Theater. It was a hot summer night, and the air conditioners were turned off so the performance could be recorded, but the rapt audience didn't mind. That show was a prelude to the premiere of two full-fledged symphonies composed by Reynolds and Stopschinski and performed by a forty-one-piece pick-up orchestra at the Scottish Rite Temple on February 12, 2000. It was a long way from the Cavity.

Peggy Ellithorpe: In '91, the economy was really, really awful. Finding a job fresh out of college was really tough. Then, around about '94, there was this whole high-tech surge. All of the craziness that is well documented in Ondi Timoner's film *We Live in Public*—a lot of that same stuff was going on in Austin. Very sky's-the-limit signing bonuses that were completely insane.

Tim Stegall: When I initially lived in Austin, I could name one sushi restaurant. When I came back, I suddenly discovered six. A rather slummy area of South Congress was suddenly being called SoCo and had boutiques where young hipsters could buy skinny jeans for ridiculous prices.

Peggy Ellithorpe: The climate became different. A lot of people started looking at that and saying, "Austin is going to be the next tech capital." People started moving in. There were articles in the *Austin American-Statesman* about the Californication of Austin. And we got to see a lot of people purchasing a home that was far and above what any Austinite could afford. And calling it cheap.

Tim Stegall: Austin was starting to get expensive. It was starting to get traffic problems. It was starting to get where there weren't a lot of marginal jobs that would support you. Although, by that point, at least the economy was strong.

Mike Henry: For Austin's economic health, it makes all the sense in the world why all this happened. There were some of us that got erased. Some of the culture got knocked off in that time.

Mark Shuman: I didn't realize how much smart growth was going to do that. I'm on record talking about how "smart" that growth was because they didn't make any accommodations for small businesses that were around.

Sean McGowan: It's a changing world. You can't fight city hall. But it doesn't mean you got to take it all willingly and happily.

Jonathan Toubin: Rents kept going up. All of our favorite businesses were closing. It's funny that we were saying this in '98 because I'm sure someone said this two years ago, too. In 1998, Austin pay-scale was still roughly the same as when it cost nothing to live here.

Tim Storm: Probably the defining moment for that scene—the crushing moment—was the Motards breaking up. I believe they did in 1999, which was fitting. End of the decade. And I remember at the time that this was so big, when I heard the Motards broke up. I went into the next Reclusives rehearsal and said, "The Motards just broke up. We need to break up. This scene is done."

King Coffey: In 1990 there were very few clubs and not as many bands. By the end of the '90s you had more clubs, more bands, more options, more opportunity. Austin was just growing bigger in general. You had more fractured scenes, more diverse things going on. The whole scene just grew because the city of Austin grew itself.

Carrie Clark: When Sixteen Deluxe started, Austin was a big town. Austin's a city now, and the dynamic's different.

Mike Henry: One of the biggest differences between now and then? People could afford to be in bands. It was a lot cheaper to live downtown. Music wasn't as driven by the bottom line. Sure, everyone wanted to succeed. Everyone needed to draw crowds and stuff like that, but you could take chances on people.

King Coffey: It's harder to be in a band now. You can't just be a slacker and play in your band and work half-assed. You really have to work all the time and hope you have time to promote your band. It's just a grind.

Jay Hughey: The densification and urbanization of our downtown has been great. It's absolutely the right kind of thing for a longer-term trajectory for the future of Austin. That is what you want. You want people living downtown. By the same token, those kinds of plans have to incorporate incentives and support smaller businesses as well.

Craig Koon: The reason Austin was the "Music Capital of the World" is gone no matter what they want to tell you. The whole slacker thing. The only reason those people were there to inspire *Slacker* is because they had no rent to speak of. So all this creative stuff began bubbling out of Austin.

I don't think the punk and garage stuff from the late eighties and early to mid-nineties encouraged people to move here so much, but it made noise. And as we know, punk rock broke. That whole geyser shot forth and Austin was dragged along with the cultural explosion.

Sean McGowan: You have to get out of the way and let the kids have their fun. Sean Powell's like, "We're like those dudes who were wearing tie-dye shirts when we were fifteen." They were hanging on to the Grateful Dead, and we were like, "You heshers man, get with it!" And I'm aware of that.

It doesn't discount what we've done at all, but it does make me feel like the level of energy and output and emotion that was once present isn't going to be there again. One of the last songs we wrote was called "The Mild One." In a nutshell it's just like, "Oh how the wild ones become the mild ones." And that's what it is. It was just a phrase that Frankie [Nowhere, Chumps guitarist] uttered.

The guy that you were twenty years ago—he wouldn't want to talk to you now. You're nothing he would want to identify with. And you didn't see that coming, but that's the nature of living and experiencing stuff. You sometimes wind up learning lessons you didn't see coming. Or being a person you didn't imagine being.

Lisa Rickenberg: Inner Sanctum [record store] was like the epicenter of the '70s scene. And when I got here it was this old guy complaining about how the punks had chased all the hippies out of Austin! And I remember just rolling my eyes thinking, "What a pain in the ass!"

Michael Toland: I'm sure there are twenty-year-olds who are going, "I wish they would shut the fuck up about the Electric Lounge."

Dave Prewitt: Are we going to talk about the clubs that used to be cool? Or are we going to take what we have that's amazing and recognize it and embrace it? Go out and make a club for *you*.

Graham Williams: All the '90s people that I got to watch, they set the tone for the next generation, and those people will help build something for the next generation. Without it, Austin definitely wouldn't be what it is now. Everyone is part of these interesting building blocks.

Laura Williams: When I first came, Armadillo World Headquarters was there. And as those venues shut down, other things took their place. And the music did the same thing, but that thread doesn't leave.

Kerthy Fix: Those of us involved in that scene were all drawn here for a reason. We didn't create it. We got dropped into the incubator and stayed. The incubator existed because Texas has a really crazy history. Sam Houston was wearing a jaguar vest in the 1830s. Ma Ferguson was governor. Pappy O'Daniel got elected with the Light Crust Doughboys electioneering for him on the radio. You always had an intersection of politics and culture and the common person. It's this thread.

Ken Dannelley: I had this idea that somebody was going to make it. And I thought, well, maybe it's Sincola. No, Sincola's gone. Maybe it's Pork. Well, no. Suddenly everyone's gone.

Brant Bingamon: But that's the thing about Austin music, it's not as saleable as you might think or you might assume.

Cris Burns: I think outside of Austin they just don't get the joke.

Jonathan Toubin: New, more cosmopolitan bands were moving to Austin that sounded like every kind of scene around the world. All these people saw *Slacker* and came. Instead of Austin being this inbred, weird thing, it was more diverse. You're meeting more people every day from all over the world, and you're like, "Oh, you moved here to Austin? Right on."

Graham Williams: Outside of a handful of people, no one's from here. But everyone's mad that people are moving here. This is the hipster equivalent of "Go back to Mexico!" Who are you to say someone does or doesn't belong anywhere because you got here first? If you're in a progressive cool city. It's not going to slow down.

Jonathan Toubin: We were not like people are today with people moving here. We were like those friendly natives welcoming the Spaniards at first. And we got slaughtered. We were like, "Come have some Shiner Bock! Have some barbeque! This is a breakfast taco from Tamale House. It's 65 cents." We were very happy to have our guests back then. Then, by the late '90s, all our guests ended up owning our house.

Tim Kerr: I've had people ask me, "Does it make you mad that Austin's changed?" It's never really affected me that much. It's just going to happen. We all change.

Kerthy Fix: Sadly, the leadership of this town have not protected artists and musicians. They have not protected inexpensive housing. They have not protected the rock clubs. They've overcharged. In 1999 a lot died. Once those places died, an energy vacuum is created. And, sadly, what's filled the space is a kind of commercialization of a fiction of Austin to be sold. Once you start selling a culture—like the creators of Austin City Limits Music Festival did—it's over.

Tim Kerr: I think the part that bothers me more is to have a city that really uses "We Support Austin Music" and all this kind of stuff as something to rally around. And in reality these places are folding up left and right because the city isn't supporting them like they say they are.

Rebecca Cannon: I don't miss the '90s at all, but I don't know what I would've done without Sincola as an escape from all these terrible things that happened to me personally. Music, for me, was a cathartic thing. Most of my family died in the '90s. My aunt, my uncle, my mother. And all this was happening within three years. So I would get on stage and I would write about this and I would perform it. I wasn't wrapped up in the scene. I was wrapped up in these personal things that were happening to me that were out of my control. And I was going to take these terrible, painful things and put them into my music.

Carl Normal: I think it was a great scene, and I think it was a totally happening scene. I think most people who look back on Austin in the '90s don't have any idea of what the underground was then. They're more likely to mention Joe Rockhead or Twang Twang Shock-A-Boom than they are Gomez or Stretford or Miss Universe or the Inhalants. A sense of community. Like-minded people doing what they love to do. It may not pay off further than a lot of good memories, but I don't think I'd have done it any differently. With about five exceptions.

Conrad Keely: In other places there was always a strong emphasis in having to "make it." But it wasn't like that here. I think a lot of people were just doing music for music's sake. And it was a very DIY aesthetic.

Kerthy Fix: One of the things I think was not possible to address when we were active musically was the racial divide. That's something that continues to bother me about Austin, and it's more clear to me how white our little scene was. That's a disappointment. We weren't political racially, but we were political in terms of queerness and feminism. But it wasn't in the same way that Riot Grrrl was very strongly feminist and very angry and aggressive.

Graham Williams: I don't feel like anything is gone. It's just changed and morphed and grown. If anything, there's just more of these DIY scenes. There's this guy who has a warehouse that they do skating in, bands practice there, and they have shows every weekend. There's this whole community of people.

John Spath: A lot of people see the music scene as a through line from punk to today, and it's not. It's broken up. You can break them up into three-year periods when music scenes really hit their stride and then they demise. And if you go from year one to year three in any scene, they're completely different scenes.

Lisa Rickenberg: There's a pretty healthy house party scene that has kind of the same feeling as the Blue Flamingo. It's easy to park, and people just hang out. So I think it's more not being in touch with what's actually going on that makes people think that Austin has kind of been wrecked.

John Spath: There is still a house party scene—it's one of those things that keeps me going out because I'm curious about what's next. Who are these new people?

Graham Williams: We were lucky to be part of it. So many people didn't have that. Man, you could have been wherever-the-fuck working at Dairy Queen for ten years, taking a bus to go see a band once a year, and that was the thing you talked about all year—that time you saw Metallica at the stadium in Dallas. *That* could have been your life.

Britt Daniel: That was a long time ago, and things were so different then. Not only in terms of the way that the band operated and the way that commerce operates but also, musically we were a lot different back then. I look back on the '90s in general as like the first time that I was ever in a bit of a scene. Then, the reality of our band putting out records and it being hard for a long time happened. But it needed to happen that way. We kept going because I felt like I could make it work. But also, we had some pretty key people that really believed in us.

Dotty Farrell: My mom was a scholar, and she really, really wanted me to stay in school. She didn't like those punk people I hung out with. One time we were at Whole Foods and there were three people in this aisle that were Swine King fans. They dropped to their knees and just started genuflecting. They were like, "You're in Swine King! You're a goddess and you fucking rock and you're the best and we love you, Dotty!" My mom was standing there, and if I'd won the Nobel Peace Prize, she couldn't be fucking happier, you know what I mean? It kind of made it okay.

Russell Porter: I'm still in a band. I'm still in my fucking band. Jesus.

Kerthy Fix: It was a very sweet time to grow up, and I hope that young people making art and music now can have that safe space. And I would like to think that Austin can do a better job of preserving that safe space because our humanity is at stake. When we kill Barton Springs or we kill a rock club, we're killing a part of ourselves.

In the '90s in Austin, it was a safe place to do adventurous performance work with sexual themes. You weren't going to get attacked. You might draw some weird attention, but it wasn't a rape culture environment. For the women in bands here, you were accepted on your own terms. It's not that you were sexually neutral, but there was an even-handedness and a friendliness.

I got to do all this music, all this art, the zines, short stories, poetry, writing music, performance art, theater. Because of all those things all functioning together in this temporary autonomous zone, that's what makes me a mature creative person now. I performed with Annie Sprinkle. I performed a group orgasm with thirty women for an audience. And I don't have any regrets.

Andy Maguire: I just hope that it's better for women in the future. There are prejudices we all hold, and sometimes they direct your actions without you even being aware of it. Hopefully the world will get to a place where that doesn't happen, and we can just judge people on their work and not what color they are, what gender they are, or anything else. In the meantime, we're going to get through and do our DIY.

Kelly Linn: Somehow there was this connection there. A place to connect. A place to come together and connect and either express or to get it out listening. A Curious Mix of People, right? That's what it was.

Tim Kerr: I always have a problem with these kinds of things because so many times people want to put a start and an ending to something like this. DIY started way before any of us could even imagine, and it's going to be going on way after we're gone. So you can't say, "This is the best," because it's constantly going . . .

ACKNOWLEDGMENTS

THERE WOULD BE NO *CURIOUS MIX* WITHOUT Chepo Peña, who started this project as a documentary in 2010. A key figure familiar to just about everyone in the story, Chepo's vision and the interviews he conducted led us to realize: first, we had the makings of a book; and second, the story had to be told by the people who were there.

Casey Kittrell, our editor at UT Press, provided astute direction that opened new avenues of inquiry and made our narrative richer as a result. We were lucky to have two fine writers and subject-matter experts like Chris Riemenschneider and Alan Schaefer read our draft manuscript and provide insightful comments and suggestions that improved our work. UT Press manuscript editor Lynne Ferguson, copyeditor Leslie Tingle, and proofreader Luke Torn used their superb editorial acumen to wring clarity out of every last character. We also thank editorial assistant Christina Vargas for helping us wrangle all the details and Eric Redpath for his last-minute scanning assistance. We could not ask for a better marketing team than Danni Bens, Cameron Ludwick, and Bailey Morrison. Finally, a special thank you to Krissy Teegerstrom for putting us in touch with UT Press.

Richard Whymark: Thanks to Jack and Rachel for all their love and support, to everyone who has supported this project with photos, videos, zines, flyers, posters, records, and stories, and to KVRX for getting me into the DIY mentality in the first place.

Greg Beets: I'm forever grateful to my wife Kate Harrington and our son Alex for giving up hours of family time while I wrote. Thanks to the *Austin Chronicle* and especially music editor emeritus Raoul Hernandez for letting me cover local music for twenty-seven years. Lastly, thanks to all the bands, artists, writers, DJs, sound engineers, bartenders, friends, volunteers, and fellow travelers who made this place home.

CAST OF CHARACTERS

Gerry Atric
Vocalist, the Bulemics.

Greg Beets
Vocalist, Cheezus, Noodle, the Peenbeets; DJ @ KTSB; music writer, *Austin Chronicle*; copublisher, *Hey! Hey! Buffet!*

Brant Bingamon
Vocalist/guitarist, Pocket FishRmen, the Horsies, the Meat Purveyors.

Jimmy Bradshaw
Guitarist/vocalist, Squat Thrust, Unicorn Magic, and Voltage; cofounder, the Cavity.

Melissa Bryan
Guitarist/vocalist, the Shindigs; later served on board of directors for Girls Rock Camp.

Cris Burns
Guitar antihero, Pocket FishRmen.

Rebecca Cannon
Sincola vocalist, Stretford trumpeter, and DJ @ KTSB.

Rick Carney
Vocalist/guitarist for EMG and Jesus Christ Superfly; booked the Cavity in 1992.

Edith Casimir
Drummer, Pork.

Gary Chester
Guitarist/vocalist, Ed Hall; guitarist/bassist, Moist Fist.

Jason Christian
Vocalist for early incarnation of Squat Thrust; later performed with Victims Family.

Carrie Clark
Guitarist/vocalist, Sixteen Deluxe.

King Coffey
Drummer, Butthole Surfers (1983–present); founder/owner, Trance Syndicate Records.

Erik Conn
Drummer, Wookie, Tia Carrera.

Buckner Cooke
Live programming director, Austin Music Network.

Jennings Crawford
Guitarist/vocalist, the Wannabes; trumpeter, Stretford.

Michael Crawford
Photographer, *Austin Chronicle*, *Thora-Zine*.

Laura Creedle
Guitarist, Happy Family, Power Snatch.

Britt Daniel
Guitarist/vocalist/bandleader, Spoon; previously played in Skellington, the Alien Beats, and solo under the pseudonym Drake Tungsten; DJ @ KTSB.

Ken Dannelley
Drummer, Stretford, the Hamicks, Airport Noises.

Hunter Darby
Bassist/vocalist, the Wannabes, Neil Diamond tribute band the Diamond Smugglers, and scatalogically minded Fab Four cover band the Dung Beetles.

Bones DeLarge
Vocalist, Lower Class Brats, 1995–present.

Jim Ellinger
Founder, KOOP-FM; longtime community radio activist.

Peggy Ellithorpe
SXSW volunteer coordinator, 1994–2004.

Mark Fagan
Bassist, Bayou Pigs and Noodle; guitarist, the Paranoids; longtime Sound Exchange employee; copublisher of *Apathy Trend*.

Dotty Farrell
Founding member/bassist for Biscuit-led band Swine King and the Punkaroos; actress with Big State Productions.

Kerthy Fix
DJ @ KTSB; Austin Music Network host; vocalist for Olive and Gallus Mag; filmmaker, performance artist, and all-around Renaissance woman.

Marc Fort
Bassist, Bo Bud Greene, Schatzi, and the FuckEmos; music writer and photographer for the *Austin American-Statesman*; DJ @ KVRX and KOOP.

Scott Gardner
Host of *Stronger Than Dirt*, Saturday nights on KOOP-FM.

Jett Garrison
Formerly known as Jenn Garrison. DJ @ KVRX; station manager, KROX (101X); DJ @ KGSR; and Austin Music Network host.

Ken Gibson
Guitarist/vocalist/producer for Furry Things.

Tim Hamblin
Music video producer and host/producer at Austin Music Network.

Ed Hamell
Syracuse, New York–bred singer/songwriter/storyteller performing as Hamell on Trial; held popular residency at the Electric Lounge.

Janet Hammer
Music writer; contributor to *Destroy All Movies!!! The Complete Guide to Punks on Film* (Fantagraphics Books, 2010).

Lyman Hardy
Drummer for Houston bands Sugar Shack and Bayou Pigs before moving to Austin in 1991; played with Cheezus (1991–1992) and then replaced Kevin Whitley in Ed Hall.

Eric "Emo" Hartman
Founder/owner (and namesake) of Emo's Houston and Emo's Austin, 1989–2001.

Tim Hayes
Guitarist/vocalist, the Cryin' Out Louds; Sound Exchange employee.

Jennifer LaSuprema Hecker
Copublisher of zines *Hope You Die* and *Geek Weekly* with Susan Shepard; founded Austin Fanzine Project in 2012.

Mike Henry
Booking agent turned co-owner for the Electric Lounge; documentary filmmaker and founder of Austin Poetry Slam.

Dave Hermann
Owner/operator/resident, the Cavity, 1991–1993; later moved to Mexico's Pacific coast to run a bed and breakfast; died in October 2015 at age 53.

Travis Higdon
Publisher of *Peek-A-Boo* zine; founder/CEO of Peek-A-Boo Records; guitarist/vocalist for the 1-4-5s; guitarist for the Kiss Offs; DJ @ KVRX.

Tom Hudson
Drummer for Silver Scooter.

Jay Hughey
Cofounder/co-owner of the Electric Lounge at 302 Bowie Street,
1993–1999.

Ray Ject
Guitarist, the Bulemics.

Bill Jeffery
Trumpeter/court jester for Stretford.

Conrad Keely
Vocalist/multi-instrumentalist, . . . And You Will Know Us by the Trail of
Dead.

Tim Kerr
Guitarist for cornerstone Austin punk band the Big Boys (1979–1984);
also played in Poison 13 and Bad Mutha Goose. During the 1990s Kerr
played with Jack O'Fire, Lord High Fixers, and the Monkeywrench and was
one of the most active producers working out of Sweatbox Studios. Also a
celebrated painter, illustrator, and muralist.

Craig Koon
Manager, Sound Exchange; cofounder, Rise Records; publisher, *Yet Another
Fanzine*; owner, Prole Art Threat record pressing facility.

Nanette Labastida
Music superfan since childhood; was married to Fastball bassist Tony
Scalzo when "The Way" became a hit; now a successful real estate agent.

Andy Langer
Music writer, *Austin Chronicle*; DJ @ KROX-FM (101X); host, *Live & Interactive*, Austin Music Network.

Michael Letton
Friend of Chepo Peña.

Fawn Li
Vocalist, 10" Maria.

Kelly Linn
Vocalist, Moist Fist.

Andy Maguire
Bassist in early incarnation of Spoon, Ursa Major.

Jeff Martin
Guitarist, Buzzcrusher.

Susie Martinez
Drummer, Handful, Ursa Major, Tallboy, the Hormones.

Brian McBride
KVRX DJ behind *The Dick Fudge Show*; member of ambient band Stars of
the Lid.

Kathy McCarty
Vocalist/guitarist for Glass Eye (1983–1993); 1994 solo album of Daniel
Johnston songs, *Dead Dog's Eyeball*, helped introduce Johnston's songs to
a wider audience; played the Anarchist's Daughter in *Slacker*.

Ryan McDaniel
Guitarist/vocalist for Austin pop-punk combo Gomez and ska band the
Bowler Boys.

Sean McGowan
Sneering vocalist for the Chumps (1995–2000), prolific photographer of
the '90s Austin punk scene, ardent defender of the little guy.

Richard McIntosh
Vocalist, Gut.

Miss Laura
Founder/hostess of the Blue Flamingo and coiner of the phrase "A Curious
Mix of People."

Jason Morales
Guitarist, vocalist for Starfish, Tia Carerra; drummer for Migas, Gorch
Fock.

Roger Morgan
Owner/operator of Unclean Records and Sound Exchange employee.

John Motard
Fearless frontman for full-contact punk quintet the Motards (1993–1997).

Nick Nack
Cofounder, Hip-Hop Mecca; DJ for KVRX's *B-Side Mixshow*.

Bryan Nelson
Recording engineer, Sweatbox Studios, 1995–2012; bassist, Peglegasus; drummer, School Trauma Flashback; cofounder, Australian Cattle God Records.

Carl Normal
Publisher, *No Reply*; bassist/vocalist turned guitarist/vocalist, Stretford.

Alice Nutter
Vocalist/percussionist, Chumbawamba.

Nevie Owens
Director, *Breakin' In*, Austin Music Network.

Kris Patterson
Guitarist/cofounder, Sincola.

Rob Patterson
Early '90s music editor, *Austin Chronicle*.

Ty Pearson
DJ @ KVRX; vocalist, the Yuppie Pricks.

Chepo Peña
Bassist, Sincola; cobandleader, Gomez (not the UK band); copublisher, *The Mouth* fanzine; also played with Figbash, Pop Unknown, and the Peenbeets.

Gretchen Phillips
Vocalist/multi-instrumentalist, Two Nice Girls (1985–1992); performed in the Gretchen Phillips Experience and Lord Douglas Walston Phillips during the 1990s.

Russell Porter
Vocalist/trombonist, Warthog 2001, FuckEmos.

Brent Prager
Drummer for Cherubs, FuckEmos, and Sugar Shack.

Mark Pratz
Co-owner/manager of Liberty Lunch along with spouse J'Net Ward during the 1990s. Pratz also booked the Continental Club during the 1980s and ran Lunch Money Productions with future SXSW cofounder Louis Jay Meyers (1956–2016).

Dave Prewitt
Producer/host of long-running Austin cable access shows *CapZeyeZ* and *rAw TiMe*.

Trina Quinn
DJ @ K-NACK (KNNC-FM) and KROX-FM (101X).

Jason Reece
Guitarist, vocalist, drummer, . . . And You Will Know Us by the Trail of Dead.

Lisa Rickenberg
Bassist/vocalist, the Inhalants.

Lauren Robertson
DJ @ KVRX; Sound Exchange employee; drummer, the Search Party.

Debbie Rombach
Hole in the Wall waitress turned booker turned owner, 1974–2002.

Michelle Rule (née Molnar)
Vocalist, Miss Universe (became Miss Galaxy after cease-and-desist notice from the Miss Universe Pageant).

Jason Sabala
Bartender turned bouncer turned co-owner of Emo's; currently owns Buzz Mill Coffee and Plow Burger.

Jane Sanders
Worked the door at Liberty Lunch, 1992–1999.

Susan Shepard
Copublisher of zines *Hope You Die* and *Geek Weekly*; engaged music scene while still in high school; landed interview with a former bandmate of drummer-turned-mass-shooter George Hennard.

Mark Shuman
Cofounder/co-owner, Electric Lounge.

Bob Simmons
KTSB/KVRX broadcast adviser, 1988–1989, 1993–1999; worked at seminal San Francisco underground FM station KSAN in the 1960s.

Susannah Simone
Vocalist, Moist Fist; cast member, *Slacker*.

Officer Charles Smith
Responding Austin Police Department officer to GG Allin show/melee at the Cavity, February 18, 1992.

Chris "Frenchie" Smith
Guitarist, Sixteen Deluxe; owner/operator, The Bubble recording studio.

Dana Smith
Guitarist, Pork.

John Spath
Music video director/producer, the Administration.

Jimmy St. Germaine
Bassist, Down Syndrome Army.

Karla Steffen
One of several people who sometimes slept at the Cavity between 1991 and 1993.

Tim Stegall
Guitarist/vocalist/bandleader, the Hormones; music writer for the *Austin Chronicle*, *Alternative Press*, and *Flipside*.

Tim Storm
Vocalist, the Reclusives.

Paul Streckfus
Vocalist, Glorium; owner/operator, Golden Hour Records.

Larry Strub
Bassist, Ed Hall (1985–1996).

Michael Toland
Reviews editor, *Pop Culture Press*; music writer for *High Bias*, *Blurt*, and *Austin Chronicle*.

Jonathan Toubin
Guitarist, Cheezus, Noodle, the Hamicks; DJ @ KTSB; Sound Exchange and Kinko's employee.

Chuck Trend
Copublisher of *Apathy Trend*; music writer, *Austin Chronicle*.

Mike Vasquez
Owner and recording engineer, Sweatbox Studios, 1992–2012.

Charlie Void
Drummer, Down Syndrome Army.

Marty Volume
Guitarist, Lower Class Brats.

Staryn Wagner
Owner/operator/resident, the Cavity, 1991–1993.

J'Net Ward
Co-owner/manager of Liberty Lunch along with spouse Mark Pratz during the 1990s.

Richard Whymark
Photographer and DJ @ KVRX; producer and director, Austin Music Network

Cindy Widner
Vocalist, Happy Family and Power Snatch; longtime managing editor, *Austin Chronicle*.

Graham Williams
Talent buyer/manager, Emo's (late '90s/early '00s); founder, Fun Fun Fun Fest (2006–2015), Transmission Entertainment, and Margin Walker Presents; owner, Resound Presents.

Laura Williams
Booking manager, Chances; Graham Williams's aunt.

Luann Williams
Publisher/editor, *Pop Culture Press*.

Robert Zimmer
Station manager and DJ @ KTSB. In a plot twist right out of *Welcome Back, Kotter*, returned to UT Austin to serve as KVRX's broadcast adviser from 2015–2019.

CHRONOLOGY

1990

- Ed Hall, Bouffant Jellyfish @ Texas Tavern, January 20.
- The Jesus Lizard, Skatenigs, Happy Family @ Cannibal Club, February 10.
- Austin Music Awards @ Palmer Auditorium, March 14. Daniel Johnston shares bill with Townes Van Zandt, Nanci Griffith, and Poi Dog Pondering. Stevie Ray Vaughan makes one of his last public appearances in Austin, receiving award for Artist of the Decade.
- Ultramagnetic MCs featuring Kool Keith play SXSW @ Raven's (future Emo's location), one of the first (if not the first) national hip-hop acts to do so, March 15.
- Folklorist John Henry Faulk dies of cancer in Austin at age 76, April 9.
- Trance Syndicate releases Crust's *Sacred Heart of Crust* on Good Friday, April 13.
- Happy Family release *Lucky* on 50 Skadillion Watts.
- Butthole Surfers, Ed Hall, Pocket FishRmen @ Austin Opry House, May 4.
- *Slacker* premieres @ Dobie Theater, July 27.
- Mudhoney @ Cannibal Club, July 27.
- Stretford plays first show @ Texas Tavern with Happy Family and the Friendly Truckers.
- Stevie Ray Vaughan killed in helicopter crash after playing show at Alpine Valley Music Theatre in East Troy, Wisconsin, August 27.
- Pocket FishRmen release third single, "Dead Dog/Sodom and Gomorrah" on 50 Skadillion Watts; played by BBC Radio DJ John Peel on November 4.
- Butthole Surfers release *The Hurdy Gurdy Man* EP on Rough Trade (first post–Touch and Go release).

1991

- BBC Radio DJ John Peel plays Happy Family's "Big Ass on Fire," January 12.
- Hand of Glory record release @ Cannibal Club, February 16.

Poster for Sonic Youth at Liberty Lunch, October 27, 1990, by JasonAustin.

- Butthole Surfers release *pioughd* on soon-to-be-bankrupt Rough Trade label, February 20.
- Trance Syndicate Records hosts its first SXSW showcase @ Ritz with Ed Hall, Crust, Pain Teens, Sugar Shack, Lithium X-Mas, and ST 37, March 22.
- *Billboard* begins using SoundScan data to compile album sales charts, March 25.
- Carl Normal and *No Reply* present first Sid Vicious Birthday Bash with Pocket FishRmen, Wannabes, Stretford, Jesus Christ Superfly, Rockbusters, Happy Family, Friendly Truckers, Hollywood Indians, and the Danned (Damned cover band featuring future Stretford guitarist Dan Carney) @ Ritz Theater, May 20.
- Helmet, Jawbox @ Cannibal Club, August 7.
- First Lollapalooza skips Austin for Dallas. Butthole Surfers share bill with Jane's Addiction, Siouxsie and the Banshees, Living Colour, Fishbone, Ice-T (with Body Count), and the Rollins Band @ Starplex Amphitheater, August 22–23.
- Austin City Council approves resolution sponsored by council member Max Nofziger and Mayor Bruce Todd declaring the City of Austin "Live Music Capital of the World," August 29.
- Cavity grand opening with Meat Lover's Pizza, Stumpwater, Warthog, September 20.
- Nirvana's *Nevermind* released September 24.
- Nirvana and Sister Double Happiness @ Liberty Lunch, October 24.
- KNNC-FM (aka K-NACK), Austin's first commercial alternative station, goes on the air, October 31.
- The Jesus Lizard @ Cannibal Club, November 29–30.
- Ed Hall releases *Gloryhole*, third LP overall and first on Trance.
- Four teenage girls are murdered at a North Austin yogurt shop, December 6.
- Cannibal Club closes, December.

1992
- Cannibal Club reopens as Jelly Club, January.
- Nirvana's *Nevermind* replaces Michael Jackson's *Dangerous* as the nation's top-selling album, January 11.
- Dinosaur Jr., My Bloody Valentine, Babes in Toyland @ Liberty Lunch, February 8.
- GG Allin @ the Cavity, February 18.
- Drummer Lyman Hardy debuts with Ed Hall along with Crust and Drain @ Liberty Lunch, February 28.

- Craig Koon releases Pork's "Wanna Ride" seven-inch on SubPar/Worthless.
- Cavity turns down SXSW to host official showcases, instead booking three nights of local underground bands like Pork, Cherubs, and Crust, March 12–14.
- Grand opening weekend of Austin Emo's with Trouser Trout/Jesus Christ Superfly (April 24), and Agony Column/Chaindrive (April 25).
- Sid's Birthday Bash II with Pocket FishRmen, Cheezus, Jesus Christ Superfly, Wannabes, IV Violent People, Inhalants, Blister Fetish @ the Cavity, May 16.
- Killdozer, Poor Dumb Bastards, Cherubs @ Emo's, May 29.
- KNNC hosts K-NACK Fest with the Soup Dragons, Peter Murphy, Flaming Lips, Cracker, and more @ Lake Walter E. Long Metropolitan Park, June 26.
- Craig Koon and Frank Kozik launch Rise Records with Jesus Christ Superfly's "Big Shit" seven-inch.
- Roger Morgan relaunches Unclean Records with the Flying Saucers' "White Out/Rise And Fall" seven-inch.
- Glorium releases "Dive Bomb/Chemical Angel" seven-inch on Ryan Richardson's Existential Vacuum label.
- Bikini Kill @ the Cavity, September 28.
- "Hell-O-Ween" rooftop show @ the Cavity with Pocket FishRmen, Myra Maines, Smell of Blood, October 31.
- Thinking Fellers Union Local 282, Sun City Girls @ Emo's, November 17.
- The Jesus Lizard, Jon Spencer Blues Explosion @ Emo's, November 20.
- Short-lived teen club Bookers opens downtown.
- Ween @ Emo's, November 26.
- Trance Syndicate release party for "Love and Napalm" video with Ed Hall, Pain Teens, and Cherubs @ the Back Room, December 12.
- Blue Flamingo opens as a low-rent gay/trans bar.
- The Bad Livers @ Emo's, December 31.

1993

In 1993, you could have been in a craptastic hair-metal band called, oh, Hellavator, and if you cut your hair, threw on a flannel shirt, and stuck a Tad sticker to your guitar case, you could have gotten a fucking record deal. This is not an exaggeration.

Tim Sommer, former Atlantic A&R rep

- Sound Exchange employee Mark Fagan launches Bunkhouse Records with *Penis Cowboy* seven-inch compilation (Noodle, Andromeda Strain, Tabitha, Sourball).

- Sincola first show @ Texas Tavern, January 27.
- Cavity loses lease and shuts down with final show featuring Pork, February 20.
- Butthole Surfers release John Paul Jones–produced major label debut, *Independent Worm Saloon*, March 23.
- Turkey Baster Records releases *Comping an Attitude* ten-inch punk compilation (Gomez, Figbash, Minority, Kid's Meal, Stretford, El Santo).
- Electric Lounge opens at the corner of Third and Bowie with the Horsies, April 8.
- Glass Eye plays final show @ Liberty Lunch, April 9.
- Superchunk, Rocket from the Crypt @ Emo's, April 17.
- Kilamanjaro begins hosting punk shows at the corner of Seventh and Red River in the former Cave Club/Planetarium/Sanitarium location.
- West Campus pizza parlor Zeppoli's hosts all-ages shows during the summer featuring bands like Glorium, Rig (Crown Roast), and the Unliked. The venue is well liked but short-lived.
- Ed Hall's *Motherscratcher* released October 18.
- Smashing Pumpkins @ Liberty Lunch, November 2.
- City of Austin amends land development code to effectively ban posting flyers on utility poles.
- KVRX releases *Fallout: A Radioactive Compilation*, recorded live at Acropolis (future site of Austin Music Hall), featuring Spoon, Stretford, Sincola, and others.
- The Makers, Mono Men, Jack O'Fire, Sugar Shack @ Emo's, December 31.

1994

If Seattle has already been "harvested," as one Washington recording executive put it, it's time to seek out another place where bands that started out playing for one another are coming up with music everyone will want to hear.

Jon Pareles, *New York Times*, July 17

- Sincola *S/T* EP released on Rise. "Bitch" goes into heavy rotation on K-NACK.
- Poster artist Frank Kozik leaves Austin for San Francisco.
- Electric Lounge catches fire on February 19, closing club for three months. *Overload: Live from the Electric Lounge* CD compilation released in the interim.
- The Offspring @ Emo's, February 25.
- Green Day, Gomez @ Liberty Lunch, March 5.

- Sincola wins Austin Music Awards for Best EP and the newly launched Best Alternative/Punk category, March 16.
- Johnny Cash plays Emo's during SXSW, March 17.
- Blue Flamingo hosts series of non-SXSW shows, including March 17 Spoon gig attended by Matador Records head Gerard Cosloy.
- Austin Music Network signs on, April 1.
- Kurt Cobain found dead of self-inflicted gunshot wound, April 8.
- Punk Prom with Power Snatch, Stretford, Hormones, Sons of Hercules, and emcee Gretchen Phillips @ Chances, April 16.
- Sincola signs with Caroline Records.
- Sincola plays New York's New Music Seminar, July.
- Online book retailer Amazon is founded, July 5.
- Chances closes in the summer.
- KVRX begins FM broadcasting, November 15.
- Jeff Buckley @ Electric Lounge, November 29.
- KOOP begins broadcasting, December 17.

1995
- Oasis @ Liberty Lunch, February 12.
- Sixteen Deluxe's debut single, "Idea," released in February on Trance.
- Sincola's LP debut, *What the Nothinghead Said*, released February 21.
- Trance Syndicate's SXSW showcase at the Terrace (former Austin Opry House) with Bedhead, Ed Hall, Crust, Sixteen Deluxe, Furry Things, Desafinado, and a short acoustic set from Hüsker Dü's Bob Mould, March 17.
- L'Austin Space Collective--a group loosely patterning themselves on the Diggers--holds benefit show at Cedar Park VFW Post 10427 on March 22 to raise funds for alcohol-free all-ages venue. Performing bands include the American Psycho Band, Andromeda Strain, Brownie Points, Carbomb, Furry Things, Gomez, Inhalants, Lord High Fixers, and the Motards. The collective is unable to locate an affordable location for the proposed venue, so proceeds are donated to charity.
- Ed Hall releases last LP, *La La Land* and Sixteen Deluxe releases first LP, *Backfeed Magnetbabe*, on May 23.
- Travis Higdon launches Peek-A-Boo Records, an offshoot of the fanzine of the same name, by releasing a seven-inch by his band, the 1-4-5s.
- KROX-FM (101X) signs on, June 5.
- New York's New Music Seminar folds, making SXSW the biggest new music festival in the United States.
- Courtney Love has her purse stolen at Emo's during an L7 show, August 7.

- Muffs bassist Ronnie Barnett smashes neon "Electric" sign at the end of their show @ Electric Lounge, August 8.
- Lollapalooza comes to Austin's Southpark Meadows on August 9, with Sonic Youth, Hole, Elastica, Beck, Pavement, Cypress Hill, and the Jesus Lizard.
- Emo's and other clubs are fined by the City of Austin for illegally posted flyers promoting shows at the clubs, September.
- Blondie's Skate Shop begins hosting free all-ages shows on Saturday afternoons featuring acts like Starfish, Wookie, Fourth Grade Nothing, and Buzzcrusher.
- Trance Syndicate Records celebrates five years in business with the *Cinco Anos!* compilation and a September 9, Liberty Lunch show featuring Sixteen Deluxe, Starfish, Bedhead, and Emperor Jones imprint signee My Dad Is Dead from Cleveland.
- Foo Fighters play first Austin show @ Liberty Lunch, September 11.
- Roger Morgan and Unclean Records moves from Austin to San Antonio, December.
- Butthole Surfers demand that their fifty-fifty split orally agreed upon with Corey Rusk of Touch and Go Records be changed to an eighty-twenty split, which ultimately culminates in a years-long lawsuit, December 4.
- Ed Hall, Sixteen Deluxe, Squat Thrust @ Liberty Lunch, December 30.

1996
- Stubb's opens on Red River with SXSW showcase by the Fugees, March 16.
- Steel Pole Bath Tub, Sugar Shack, Polio, Drums & Tuba @ Emo's, June 7.
- Butthole Surfers score a Top 40 hit with "Pepper" from *Electric Larryland.* Video features a cameo from *CHiPs* star Erik Estrada.
- Brainiac, Shiner @ Emo's, July 6.
- Ed Hall plays last show at Emo's, August 3.
- Fronted by a young Ted Leo, Notre Dame–bred punk trio Chisel plays at the short-lived Another Cup Coffee House in West Campus, August 6.
- Butthole Surfers perform "Pepper" on CBS's *Late Show with David Letterman*, August 6.
- Makers, Motards, Chumps, Tallboy @ Emo's, September 13.
- Sixteen Deluxe signs to Warner Bros., October.
- Stereolab and DJ Spooky @ Liberty Lunch, October 31.
- The former Chances space reopens as Club de Ville in the fall.
- The Wannabes' *Popsucker* wins Indie Award for Best Alternative Rock album from the National Association of Independent Record Distributors and Manufacturers.

- Six Finger Satellite, Trans Am @ Emo's, November 4.
- Man . . . Or Astroman, the Hamicks, Phantom Creeps @ Emo's, December 31.

1997

In an economy of ideas, GSD&M takes ideas seriously. So seriously that Roy Spence Jr., 49, cofounder and president of the twenty-six-year-old Austin, Texas–based advertising agency, has launched a one-man campaign to replace Austin's current slogan "The Live Music Capital of the World" with a new tagline, "The City of Ideas."

Gina Imperato, "Greetings from Idea City," *Fast Company*, 1997

- Jo Walston, coowner of Manor Road Coffeehouse and vocalist for the Meat Purveyors, Joan of Arkansas, and Wet, is profiled in a *Chicago Tribune* story about the coffeehouse/intimate music venue's yoga classes for smokers, March 16.
- Dicks guitarist Glen Taylor, more recently of Pretty Mouth, dies of kidney and liver failure, May.
- Crust, the first band on Trance, breaks up.
- The Texas Instruments, together since 1983 and now known as the Instruments thanks to a cease-and-desist from a certain technology concern, break up.
- Sincola breaks up, April.
- California transplants Tim and Karrie League open the Alamo Drafthouse Theater with a double feature of *This Is Spinal Tap* and *Raising Arizona*, May 25.
- Sleater-Kinney @ Electric Lounge, May 25.
- Mudhoney, Lord High Fixers, Zulu as Kono play Emo's fifth anniversary party, June 21.
- Link Wray @ Electric Lounge, June 27.
- Turbonegro squeezes into Blue Flamingo, July 26.
- Members of Knife in the Water host the Flaxfield Unheard Music Festival in Lytton Springs, near Lockhart. The Hamicks, Yellow Fledgling, Wannabes, Sisterunaked, Stretford, and Trail of Dead perform, July 26.
- Locally produced sitcom *Austin Stories* premieres on MTV, September 19.
- Spoon leaves Matador to sign with Elektra, October.
- The Texas Union Film Program hosts its last screening, a double feature of Fritz Lang's *M* and the Irish drama *Some Mother's Son*, December.
- New Bomb Turks, Sons of Hercules, Econoline @ Emo's, December 31.

1998

- Knife in the Water, Experimental Aircraft @ Bates Motel, January 13.
- Unsane, Today Is the Day @ Emo's, February 13.
- Fastball's second album, *All the Pain Money Can Buy*, released March 3. Lead single "The Way" hits Top 10 and the album goes platinum.
- Limp Bizkit, Clutch, Sevendust @ Liberty Lunch, March 26.
- Bedhead, Windsor for the Derby @ Liberty Lunch, April 10.
- Spoon's *A Series of Sneaks* released May 5, on Elektra. Label drops the band four months later.
- Electric Lounge hosts Melodica Festival, May 14–17, with 7% Solution, Monroe Mustang, OMD 20/20, Paul Newman, ST 37, Lift to Experience, Sixteen Deluxe, Trail of Dead, Kitty, Mazinga Phaser, Sub Oslo, Drums & Tuba, Ohm, the Prima Donnas, the Pilot Ships, and Light Bright Highway.
- Tortoise, Oval @ Emo's, May 18.
- Gas Huffer, Lord High Fixers @ Emo's June 19.
- Austin hosts the National Poetry Slam, August 19–22. Electric Lounge coowner Mike Henry serves as codirector for the event.
- Google founded, September 4.
- Kid Rock @ Emo's, November 10.
- Austin City Council approves Mayor Kirk Watson's plan to bring software developer Computer Sciences Corp. (CSC) downtown with a new building on the city-owned land where Liberty Lunch resides, December 10.
- Afghan Whigs singer Greg Dulli gets in altercation with bouncer Teitur Gentry following the band's show @ Liberty Lunch, December 12.
- Trance Syndicate shuts down. Final release is Starfish's *Instrumental* EP.

1999

- Bates Motel closes. Following the Kiss Offs pyrotechnic-infused show, fans destroy the interior of the club, January 31.
- Director Bob Ray releases *Rock Opera*, March.
- Guided By Voices headlines free SXSW outdoor show @ Waterloo Park with Spoon, the Gourds, and Damnations TX, March 20.
- Tom Waits plays a high-demand SXSW show at the Paramount Theatre, March 20.
- Bouncers beat up Austin native and onetime Vulcan Gas Company coowner Don Hyde, a friend of Tom Waits, when he tries to go backstage at Alejandro Escovedo's SXSW closing night show at La Zona Rosa, March 21.
- Butthole Surfers/Touch and Go lawsuit decided in favor of the band, March 26.

- Electric Lounge closes, April 12.
- Purgatory Lounge, successor to the Blue Flamingo and Blue Flame, closes.
- Red Eyed Fly opens @ 715 Red River, June.
- Online file-sharing service Napster founded, June 1.
- Sonic Youth final appearance @ Liberty Lunch, July 7–8.
- "Gloria-thon" @ Liberty Lunch, July 23. Various local musicians play Them's "Gloria" for twenty-four straight hours.
- Bob Mould @ Liberty Lunch, July 30.
- Toadies, Baboon play final show @ Liberty Lunch, July 31.
- Atari Teenage Riot, Nerve Center @ Emo's, August 15.
- Melvins, Hovercraft, Honky @ Emo's, August 19.
- Launch of Club Cast Live, short-lived website that broadcasts MP3-quality live music performances from twelve Austin venues, August 27.
- . . . And You Will Know Us by the Trail of Dead release second album, *Madonna*, on new label Merge Records, October 19.
- Spoon questions the motives of their former Elektra A&R man Ron Laffitte with the single "The Agony of Laffitte"/"Laffitte Don't Fail Me Now," November 1.
- Austin closes most of downtown to traffic and approximately 250,000 people attend free A2K New Year's concert headlined by Lyle Lovett, while Honky, Pocket FishRmen, and Play Doh Squad play Red Eyed Fly, December 31.

NO.	YEAR	BAND	TITLE	FORMAT	LABEL
1	1990	Crust	*The Sacred Heart of Crust*	EP	Trance Syndicate
2	1990	Happy Family	*Lucky*	LP/CD	50 Skadillion Watts
3	1990	Two Nice Girls	*Like A Version*	EP	Rough Trade
4	1990	Wannabes	*Lucky Pierre*	Cassette	Point One Five
5	1991	Bad Livers	"Lust for Life"	Seven-inch	Fist Puppet
6	1991	Ed Hall	*Gloryhole*	LP	Trance Syndicate
7	1991	Daniel Johnston	*Artistic Vice*	LP	Shimmy Disc
8	1991	The Texas Instruments	*Crammed Into Infinity*	LP	Rockville
9	1992	Bad Livers	*Delusions of Banjer*	LP	Quarterstick
10	1992	Chaindrive	*Tear Into the Feces*	Seven-inch EP	Scratched
11	1992	Meg Hentges	*Tattoo Urge*	EP	Tim/Kerr
12	1992	Jack O'Fire	*Bring Me the Head of Jon Spencer*	Seven-inch EP	Undone
13	1992	Jesus Christ Superfly	"Big Shit"	Seven-inch	Rise
14	1992	Pork	"Wanna Ride"	Seven-inch	SubPar/Worthless
15	1992	ST 37	*The Invisible College*	LP	Over and Out
16	1992	Shoulders	*Trashman Shoes*	LP/CD	Musidisc (France)/ Dejadisc (USA)
17	1992	Skatenigs	*Stupid People Shouldn't Breed*	LP	Megaforce
18	1993	American Psycho Band	*Soul On Ice/1,500 Miles*	Seven-inch	Drive 4
19	1993	Ed Hall	*Motherscratcher*	LP	Trance Syndicate

20	1993	The Flying Saucers	*Startime*	CD EP	Unclean
21	1993	Gut	*Platypus*	Seven-inch	Powernap
22	1993	Hamicks	*Erase! And Start from Scratch*	Seven-inch	Unclean
23	1993	The Horsies	*Trouble Down South*		Austin Throw-down/Sector 2
24	1993	Inhalants	*Misanthrope*	Seven-inch EP	Unclean
25	1993	johnboy	*Pistolswing*	LP	Trance Syndicate
26	1993	Pocket FishRmen	*Future Gods of Rock*	LP	Austin Throw-down/Sector 2
27	1993	Rig	*Warthole*	Seven-inch	Unclean
28	1993	Stretford	"Zerox Love"	Seven-inch	Rise
29	1994	Cherubs	*Heroin Man*	LP	Trance Syndicate
30	1994	El Flaco	*Thub*	LP	Sector 2
31	1994*	FuckEmos	*FuckEmos Can Kill You*	LP	Rise (*tape released in 1993)
32	1994	Glorium	*Cinema Peligrosa*	LP	Undone
33	1994	Gomez	*Gomez*	LP	Little Deputy
34	1994	The Hormones	"Sell Out Young"	Seven-inch	Unclean
35	1994	Kathy McCarty	*Dead Dog's Eyeball: Songs of Daniel Johnston*	CD	Bar/None
36	1994	The Motards	"I'm A Criminal"	Seven-inch	Self-released
37	1994	The Nipple 5	"Willie of the Valley"	Seven-inch	Self-released
38	1994	The Satans	*The Satans*	Seven-inch EP	Existential Vacuum
39	1994	Sincola	*Sincola*	EP	Rise
40	1994	Swine King	"All Broke Down"	Single	Outpunk
41	1994	Teen Titans	*More Songs, Less Music*	Seven-inch EP	My Papa's Leg
42	1994	Various artists	*Live at Emo's*	CD	Rise
43	1995	The Chumps	*Invent Rock 'N' Roll*	CD	Mortville
44	1995	Roky Erickson	*All That May Do My Rhyme*	LP/CD	Trance Syndicate

45	1995	FuckEmos	*Lifestyles of the Drugged and Homeless*	CD	No Lie
46	1995	Furry Things	*The Big Saturday Illusion*	LP/CD	Trance Syndicate
47	1995	Gals Panic	*I Think We Need Helicopters*	CD	Goopy Pyramid
48	1995	Miss Universe	*DUH!*	LP	Rise
49	1995	The Motards	*Rock Kids*	LP/CD	Empty
50	1995	New Girl Art Trend Band	*A Certain Sacrifice*	Cassette	Golden Hour
51	1995	The Rudy Schwartz Project	*Günther Packs a Stiffy*	LP	Seeland
52	1995	Sixteen Deluxe	*Backfeed Magnetbabe*	CD	Trance Syndicate
53	1995	Starfish	*Stellar Sonic Solutions*	CD	Trance Syndicate
54	1995	Stretford	*Crossing the Line*	LP/CD	Unclean
55	1995	Various artists	*Peek-A-Boo Bicycle Rodeo*	LP	Peek-A-Boo
56	1995	Wannabes	*Popsucker*	LP/CD	DejaDisc
57	1996	Carbomb	*Young Heart Attack*	EP	Buddy System/ Carmelita
58	1996*	Ed Hall	*permission to rock . . . Denied*	LP	Forbidden Place (*released 2020)
59	1996	Monroe Mustang	"I Was 18, It Was Hate"	Seven-inch EP	Framed!
60	1996	Olive (Gallus Mag)	*Voluptuous Lies*	Cassette	Self-released
61	1996	Peglegasus	*So Much for King Tut*	LP	Sector 2
62	1996	Various artists	*Cooking By Strobe Light: KVRX Local Live Volume One*	CD	KVRX
63	1996	Sincola	*Crash Landing in Teen Heaven*	LP/CD	Caroline
64	1996	Spoon	*Telephono*	LP/CD	Matador
65	1996	Windsor for the Derby	*Metropolitan Then Poland*	EP	Trance Syndicate
66	1996	Shindigs	*Boyfriend/Spaceboy/ Gaz*	Seven-inch	RockHaus
67	1996	Drake Tungsten	"Sixpence for the Sauces"	Seven-inch EP	Peek-A-Boo

68	1997	The Adults	*Soothing Sounds for Baby*	CD	Fume
69	1997	The American Analog Set	*From Our Living Room to Yours*	CD	Emperor Jones/ Trance Syndicate
70	1997	Ant Man Bee	*Cut Bait and Run*	CD	Charcoal
71	1997	Drums & Tuba	*Box Fetish*	LP	T.E.C./My Pal God—reissue
72	1997	Gretchen Phillips	*Do You Ever Wish for More?*	Cassette	Self-released
73	1997	Mineral	*The Power of Failing*	CD	Crank!
74	1997	Paul Newman	*"... Please Wait During the Silence"/"Clear Baby"*	Seven-inch	Twistworthy
75	1997	Silver Scooter	*The Other Palm Springs*	LP	Peek-A-Boo
76	1997	Prima Donnas	*Live on KVRX*	Cassette	Golden Hour
77	1997	Stars of the Lid	*The Ballasted Orchestra*	LP	Kranky
78	1997	Glorium	*Eclipse*	CD	Golden Hour
79	1998	Enduro	*Half Rack of Sugar*	LP	The Self Starter Foundation
80	1998	The Golden Arm Trio	*The Golden Arm Trio*	LP	Shamrock
81	1998	Knife in the Water	*Plays One Sound and Others*	CD	Self-released
82	1998	The Meat Purveyors	*Sweet in the Pants*	CD	Bloodshot
83	1998	Morningwood	*Rock Hard*	Single	Self-released
84	1998	Pocket FishRmen	*Simian Dreams*	CD	Enhanced
85	1998	Spoon	*A Series of Sneaks*	LP	Elektra
86	1998	Wannabes	*"On the Business of Being Young"*	Single	CD included with *Pop Culture Press* Issue 44
87	1998	Various artists	*South Austin Kicks Ass*	CD	High On the Hog
88	1999	... And You Will Know Us by the Trail of Dead	*Madonna*	LP/CD	Merge

89	1999	Brown Whörnet	*Brown Whörnet*	LP	Austin Music Mafia/Bent Over Cowboy
90	1999	The Bulemics	*Old Enough to Know Better . . . Too Young to Care*	LP	Junk
91	1999	Cyrus Rego	*Cyrus Rego*	CD	Emperor Jones
92	1999	The Kiss Offs	*Goodbye, Private Life*	LP	Peek-A-Boo
93	1999	Handful	*Handful*	CD	Self-released
94	1999	Lord High Fixers	*Is Your Club a Secret Weapon?*	CD	Estrus
95	1999*	Orange Mothers	*Big Blue House*	CD	Jim Thunder (*released 2000)
96	1999	The Reclusives	*The Reclusives*	LP	Mortville
97	1999	Society of Friends aka The Quakers	*Society of Friends aka The Quakers*	Seven-inch EP	Mortville
98	1999	Teen Cool	*Teen Cool Skips Skool*	Seven-inch EP	Mortville
99	1999	Various artists	*Bands That Begin with S + Peglegasus*	CD	Sweatbox
100	1999	Various artists	*Rock Opera Soundtrack*	LP/CD	Monkey Boy

A CURIOUS MIX OF THE DEPARTED

IN MEMORIAM

Kent Benjamin
Program director, Austin Music Network; associate editor, *Pop Culture Press*

Roger Brown
Bassist, Intent

Lee Roy Chapman
Emo's bartender, artist, historian, go-go dancer

Tom Churchill
Bassist, Glitterpuss, Blort

Tim Cole
Trumpeter/vocalist, Euripides Pants

Tom Cuddy
Guitarist/vocalist, Do It Now Foundation

Russ Curry
Drummer, EMG, Jesus Christ Superfly, Gravy Boat, Boomland

Lisa Davis
Photographer

Grant Dorian
Drummer, Rockbusters, Squat Thrust, Assnipple

Bruce Dye
Photographer, illustrator

Brent Grulke
SXSW creative director; music editor, *Austin Chronicle*

Lawrence Heads
Bartender/doorman, Hole in the Wall

Dave Hermann
Co-owner, the Cavity

Chad Holt
Vocalist, Frunt Butt, Total Badass

Mileah Jordan
Office manager, Liberty Lunch

Paul Kaupilla
Music director, KTSB; DJ, KOOP; Drummer, Million Sellers; punk rock librarian

Wade Longenberger
Bassist, Squat Thrust

Frank Kozik
Graphic artist; cofounder, Rise Records; founder, Man's Ruin Records

Doe Montoya
Vocalist/guitarist, Doe Nuts, Go Juice

Alvaro Moreno
Bartender/doorman, Hole in the Wall

Sean Morrison
Bassist, Myra Manes

Travis Nelsen
Drummer, Okkervil River, Coolhand Band

Damon O'Banion
Vocalist, Drunken Thunder

Will Samuels
DJ, KTSB

Tom Smith
Vocalist/ringmaster, Dogshit Rangers.

Spot [Glen Lockett]
American record producer and multi-instrumentalist.

Handsome Joel Svatek
Lover of the Ladies

Danny Ray Texas
Vocalist, Nipple 5

Randy "Biscuit" Turner
Artist/vocalist, the Big Boys, Cargo Cult, Swine King

Ryan Walker
Bassist, Rockbusters, Bad Mutha Goose

Monte Williams
Guitarist/vocalist, Schatzi, Blunderwheel

NOTES

Introduction

1. "Savings Association Seeks Office on Astronauts' Own Turf," *New York Times*, November 24, 1984, section 1, 8.

2. In April 2023, the Salvation Army's Austin Area Command closed its downtown shelter.

3. Much of Moffett's development ultimately got built years later, albeit with more stringent watershed protections than would have otherwise been in place.

4. In another example of Austin's incestuous nature at the time, Ward (1948–2021) surreptitiously wrote food columns for the *Chronicle* while still employed by the *Statesman* under his pseudonym "Petaluma Pete."

5. Cary Baker, "The Long Road from Year 1 to Year 25," in *SXSW Scrapbook: People and Things That Went Before*, eds. Peter Blackstock, Jason Cohen, and Andy Smith (Essex Press, 2011).

6. Barry Shank, *Dissonant Identities: The Rock 'n' Roll Scene in Austin, Texas* (Middletown, CT: Wesleyan University Press, 1994) 208–209.

7. MDC had not broken up, but they had moved to San Francisco.

8. Vietnamese restaurant/punk club Dong Huong was located at 111 North Loop Blvd., next to the Austin State Hospital pauper cemetery.

9. The most recent Pocket FishRmen Fish Fry as of this writing took place in 2019.

10. Dongfest and Noisefest were a series of festival-type gigs mostly featuring bands that performed regularly at Dong Huong.

11. "AmRep" is an abbreviation of Amphetamine Reptile, a Minneapolis-based record label.

12. In Austin music, a "hoot night" is a show in which multiple bands perform songs by a single artist or with a similar theme.

13. "Dancing About Architecture" was the weekly music column in the *Austin Chronicle*, written by Ken Lieck, from September 1989 to January 2003.

The Cavity

1. The Crossing at 613 Red River and Marilyn's (soon to become the Blue Flamingo) at 617 Red River.

2. "Men suspected in slayings in custody in Mexico City," *Austin American-Statesman*, October 23, 1992, A1, A12.

3. Michael Hall, "Under the Gun," *Texas Monthly*, January 2001.

4. Warthog 2001 was alternately known as Warthog 2000 and Warthog prior to becoming the FuckEmos.

5. Formed in 1974 and led by poster artist/comedian Kerry Awn, the Uranium Savages strafed the overly serious with crude double entendres and outrageous stage shows featuring smoke bombs and penis props. One of their best-remembered nuggets was 1980's "Idi Amin Is My Yardman." As of this writing, the Savages continue to perform in Austin.

6. Peel was a highly influential BBC Radio 1 disc jockey from 1967 until his death in 2004.

7. "The Leader Is Burning" was actually one of 143 favorite singles Peel kept in a wooden box apart from his vast main collection. The box was the subject of the 2005 documentary *John Peel's Record Box*.

8. Snoopy Melvin, Pocket FishRmen drummer, 1991–1994.

9. Richard Kane—a veteran of the late seventies–early eighties New York noise scene. Briefly served as a substitute drummer for Sonic Youth after their first album.

10. "EV Records" is an abbreviation for Existential Vacuum Records.

11. The Ramones, Debbie Harry, Jerry Harrison, and Tom Tom Club played the Austin Aqua Festival on July 28, 1990, as part of the "Escape from New York" tour.

12. Letton was Peña's classmate at Westlake High School.

13. GG Allin's backing band.

14. On December 3, 1979, eleven people died as a result of injuries sustained in a crush to enter Riverfront Coliseum in Cincinnati, Ohio, for a concert by the Who.

15. All quotations from Officer Charles Smith are taken from Austin Police Department Incident Report No. 92-0500073-00, filed February 19, 1992.

16. From Richard Whymark's interview with Alice Nutter for KVRX 91.7 FM.

17. As a younger man, Steve Chaney played in a nascent Austin band called Cold Sweat, who opened for punk provocateurs the Huns at Raul's on the night of the infamous "Huns Riot" on September 19, 1978.

Emo's

1. Planet K is an Austin-based chain of head shops.

Radio

1. Ken Lieck, "Star Power," *Austin Chronicle*, December 14, 1990, 38.

2. Avrel Seale, "Sharing the Air," *Texas Alcalde*, May-June 1993, 11.

3. As of this writing, UT Austin holds the licenses to three radio stations—KUT, KVRX, and KUTX.

4. The Armadillo World Headquarters, located at 525½ Barton Springs Road, opened in 1970. The armory turned beerhall became the epicenter for the progressive country sound, hosting Willie Nelson, Jerry Jeff Walker, and Michael Murphey, among others. The storied venue also hosted the Clash, the Ramones, Frank Zappa, and AC/DC's first American show in 1977, before closing in 1980.

5. In this usage, "Tower" refers directly to UT's Main Building and the UT System's administration more generally.

6. Despite this assertion, Cunningham did record a station identification for KTSB.

7. Jenny Wong was KOOP station manager in 1994. Wong previously worked at KTSB. In 1990 she was passed over for the KTSB station manager job by the Texas Student Publications board.

Hole in the Wall

1. Michael Perchick, "The Way: How a Salado Couple's Tragic Story Spawned a Chart-Topping Song," KVUE-TV, July 27, 2017.

2. Michael Hall fronted the Wild Seeds, one of Austin's most popular mid-eighties bands, and released several acclaimed solo albums in the '90s. He also became a staff writer at *Texas Monthly*.

3. HAAM stands for Health Alliance for Austin Musicians, a nonprofit that helps local musicians access affordable healthcare.

4. Founded in 1995, the SIMS Foundation provides mental health care services to musicians. The nonprofit was started in memory of Sims Ellison, bassist for Austin hard rock

band Pariah, who suffered from depression and took his own life on June 8, 1995, at age twenty-eight.

5. Spot (Glen Lockett) is best known as the house producer for SST Records between 1979 and 1985, producing records by Black Flag, Hüsker Dü, Minutemen, Meat Puppets, and Descendents. He moved to Austin after leaving SST and was a regular presence in the local underground and Irish folk scenes. He left Austin for Sheboygan, Wisconsin, in 2008 and passed away there on March 4, 2023, at age seventy-one.

6. The Austin Rehearsal Complex, located at 1109-B South Congress from 1989 until 1999.

7. Rob Seidenberg was an A&R executive at Hollywood Records.

8. Andy Langer covered music for *Texas Monthly*, DJed for multiple local radio stations, and was the music reporter for Time Warner Cable's local news channel.

9. Multi-instrumentalist, carpenter, sculptor, and painter Thor Harris has played percussion for numerous local and national acts, including Swans, Stick People, Gretchen Phillips, and Shearwater.

Blue Flamingo

1. Author's note (GB): How bad? Koon recorded a few songs by my band the Peenbeets for the album, and it took me about thirty seconds to recognize the squall as my own the first time I heard it playing at Sound Exchange.

2. Leslie Cochran (1951–2012) was a well-known homeless cross-dresser and sometime politician who was frequently seen walking around downtown Austin in a thong bikini bottom. Despite Miss Laura's use of "she," Cochran identified as a man.

3. Named after a Fall song, Prole Art Threat was the name of Koon's short-lived vinyl pressing operation.

4. 1996's *Texas: A Collection of Texas Garage Punkers*.

Chances

1. As of 2022 the cliff wall stage remains at Cheer Up Charlie's, the current tenant at 900 Red River.

2. Spike Gillespie, "Chances Are," *Austin Chronicle*, December 25, 1998.

3. Zeitgeist changed their name to the Reivers in 1987.

4. The 1980 Punk Prom was the Dicks' first show. Although they'd only been a band for two weeks, their snarling performance of "Saturday Night at the Bookstore" from this show stands shoulder to shoulder with Frank Zappa and Captain Beefheart's *Bongo Fury* (1975) as one of the best live recordings made there. The Next, the Big Boys, the Reactors, and Sharon Tate's Baby also played.

5. Though its key provisions were rendered unenforceable by the Supreme Court's *Obergefell v. Hodges* decision in 2015, the Defense of Marriage Act was not repealed until President Joe Biden signed the Respect for Marriage Act into law on December 13, 2022.

6. Gillespie, "Chances Are."

7. In 2018 the festival became the All Genders, Lifestyles and Identities Film Festival.

8. Gillespie, "Chances Are."

9. McCarty played in Buffalo Gals between 1981 and 1983 before starting Glass Eye with bassist/vocalist Brian Beattie, keyboardist Stella Weir, and drummer Scott Marcus in 1983.

10. Veteran Austin drummer Terri Lord played in Sincola, Power Snatch, Lord Douglas Phillips, Bad Mutha Goose, and Sexy Finger Champs during the 1990s.

11. Bassist Darcee Douglas played in Power Snatch, Swine King, Girls in the Nose, and Lord Douglas Phillips during the 1990s.

12. An urban legend attributes "Mama" Cass Elliot's 1974 death to choking on a ham sandwich. Her actual cause of death was heart failure.

13. Guitarist/vocalist/composer Hentges performed in Two Nice Girls from 1989–1992 before embarking on a solo career. Her 1999 album, *Brompton's Cocktail*, was produced by Fountains of Wayne's Adam Schlesinger.

14. Teresa Taylor, a.k.a. Teresa Nervosa, played drums in the Butthole Surfers alongside King Coffey from 1983 through 1989. She may be best known for her role as "Madonna Pap Smear Lady" in *Slacker*.

15. Vocalist Wing (1994–2017) formed Sharon Tate's Baby in 1979. They changed their name to Jerryskids in 1981.

16. David Stain, a.k.a. Dave Dictor, formed nascent Austin punk band the Stains in 1979. After releasing the classic single, "John Wayne Was a Nazi" in 1981, they changed their name to Millions of Dead Cops and moved to San Francisco. MDC remains active as of this writing.

Sweatbox Studios

1. Harry Whittington died on February 4, 2023, at the age of ninety-five.

2. Christopher Gray, "TCB: Sweatbox Sweats One Out," *Austin Chronicle*, January 13, 2006.

3. Drew Knight, "Westin to Pay for Club's Soundproofing System after Filing Lawsuit," KVUE.com, July 11, 2017.

4. Kevin Curtin, "Playback: Cheer Up Charlie's Sounds Off," *Austin Chronicle*, August 31, 2012.

5. Greg Beets, "Cherubs Flourish in the Afterlife at SOS Fest," *Austin Chronicle*, November 4, 2016.

6. Mike Carroll previously played with Kerr in Poison 13. The mid-eighties Austin garage-blues combo counted pivotal Seattle bands like the U-Men and Mudhoney as fans. Carroll died of complications from bacterial meningitis in 2018.

TV and Video

1. Cynthia True, "Off with the Show," *Texas Monthly*, August 1998.

2. Austin Community Television Collection, ACTV Press Conference, February 8, 1989, https://youtu.be/6GbdFBzs29s.

3. Austin Community Television Collection, ACTV Press Conference, February 8, 1989.

4. Michael Bertin, "Sleeping with the Television On: Teething Problems at Austin Music Network, Austin Chronicle, February 21, 1997.

5. Vocalist/multi-instrumentalist John Hawkins, aka the Rev. Art Bank Lobby.

6. Darcie is the daughter of singer/songwriter and onetime Texas poet laureate Steven Fromholz (1945–2014).

7. Former Austin Chronicle politics editor Slusher served on the Austin City Council from 1996 to 2005.

Zines, Flyers, and the Press

1. Jesse Jarnow, "Call Them Hippies, But the Grateful Dead Were Tech Pioneers," wired.com, July 3, 2015.

2. International Telecommunications Union/World Telecommunication/ICT Indicators Database, 1998–2020.

3. Mark McKinnon quote from "Chapter 1: Before the Beginning," *Austin Chronicle*, September 7, 2001, 24.

4. Ramsey Wiggins quote from "Chapter 1: Before the Beginning," 34.

5. Texas Penal Code, Sec. 43.23, "Obscenity," makes it illegal to promote or possess more than six "obscene devices," including dildos, artificial vaginas, and any other device "designed or marketed as useful primarily for the stimulation of human genital organs."

6. Louis Black, "Page Two," *Austin Chronicle*, September 13, 1996.

7. Kate Eichhorn, *Adjusted Margin: Xerography, Art, and Activism in the Late Twentieth Century* (Boston: MIT Press, 2016).

8. Sign Ordinance 25-10-103 remains on the books as of 2022.

9. Andy Langer, "Postage Decrease?," *Austin Chronicle*, October 27, 1995.

10. Marc Savlov, "Violators Will Be Punished," *Austin Chronicle*, September 12, 1997.

Sound Exchange

1. US Sales Database, Recording Industry Association of America, retrieved January 19, 2021. Revenue figures not adjusted for inflation.

2. David Basham, "Backstreet Boys, Britney Spears, Ricky Martin Dominate Year-End Sales," mtv.com, January 6, 2000. Revenue figures not adjusted for inflation.

3. Jupiter Media Matrix press release, "Global Napster Usage Plummets, But New File Sharing Alternatives Gaining Ground, Reports Jupiter Media Matrix," July 20, 2001.

4. US Sales Database, Recording Industry Association of America, retrieved January 19, 2021.

5. Sound Exchange owner Mark Alman sold the Houston location to Kurt Brennan and Kevin Bakos in 1998. After thirty-eight years in three Montrose area locations, Brennan and Bakos moved the store to 101 North Milby St. on Houston's East End in 2018.

6. Thirty Three Degrees opened in 1996 just north of UT at 2821 San Jacinto and later moved into an old pharmacy across the street from Austin State Hospital at 4017 Guadalupe. The store featured a richly curated mix of punk, experimental, and avant garde music and regularly hosted live performances by local and touring acts. After Thirty Three Degrees closed in 2004, co-owner Plunkett opened End of an Ear Records in 2005.

7. "Dragworm" is a pejorative term to describe panhandlers on the Drag.

8. Located at 1908 Guadalupe through the mid-nineties, G&M Steakhouse was known for their cheeseburger platters and employees who verbally accosted diners.

9. The space at 2402 Guadalupe is a CVS that is now closed at the time of this writing.

10. Renowned blues club Antone's was located at 2915 Guadalupe from 1981 to 1997.

11. By the time of its closure, the roof of Sound Exchange was festooned with a large wooden-masked wrestler painted in garish colors.

Record Labels

1. Rob Patterson, "Unclean Thoughts," *Dallas Observer*, January 11, 1996.

2. In addition to his label, Twistworthy cofounded the Texas Punk Treasure Chest blog, an indispensable resource for checking out rare recordings from Texas punk bands.

3. Raoul Hernandez, "7 and 7 Is," *Austin Chronicle*, May 31, 1998.

4. Greg Beets, "Empire of the Mind," *Austin Chronicle*, September 4, 1998.

5. This quote is the last line in chapter five of Oates's 1990 novel, *Because It Is Bitter, And Because It Is My Heart*.

6. Kozik went on to recycle this cover for the Melvins' album *Electroretard*.

7. Prior to the Sons of Hercules, Frank Pugliese fronted the Vamps, who opened the Sex Pistols' San Antonio show at Randy's Rodeo on January 8, 1978.

8. Before starting Little Deputy, Edwards sang for the Unliked and was cohost of KTSB's hardcore show.

Trance Syndicate

1. Over twenty years after their demise, the Cherubs reunited and released the widely acclaimed *2 Ynfynyty* in 2015. They continue to perform together as of this writing.

2. The Terrace was initially constructed as part of a motor hotel and convention center just off South Congress Ave. in the 1950s. From 1977 to 1988, the property was owned by

Willie Nelson and operated as the Austin Opera House. As of this writing, there are plans for an 800–1,200 capacity music venue to be included in a new mixed-use development on the property—plans that are opposed by nearby neighbors concerned about the noise and traffic such a venue would bring.

3. Scott Schinder et al., *Rolling Stone's Alt-Rock-A-Rama: An Outrageous Compendium of Facts, Fiction, Trivia and Critiques of Alternative Rock* (New York: Delta, 1996), 85–87.

4. Greg Beets, "Weird Bands from Texas," *Austin Chronicle*, November 20, 1998, 64.

5. Beets, "Weird Bands from Texas."

6. At the time of this December 31, 1993, show, the building at 208 Nueces that would become the Austin Music Hall was a club called Acropolis.

Electric Lounge

1. Downtown's southernmost east-west thoroughfare (north of Lady Bird Lake) was first platted as Water Street and later First Street. It was posthumously renamed for farm labor activist Chávez in 1993.

2. Michael Bertin, "The Year It All Went Wrong," *Austin Chronicle*, December 31, 1999.

3. Ken Lieck, "Dancing About Architecture—Throw the Beat in the Garbage Can," *Austin Chronicle*, January 15, 1999.

4. The Electric Lounge's phone number was 476-FUSE.

5. King Cheese was a duo that performed raucous versions of '70s and '80s hits.

Liberty Lunch

1. Rachel Feit, "Guy Town," texasbeyondhistory.net, October 1, 2001.

2. Chris Riemenschneider and Michael Corcoran, "Liberty Lunch: An Oral History," *Austin American-Statesman*, July 15, 1999.

3. Schinder et al., *Rolling Stone's Alt-Rock-A-Rama*, 328.

4. *Dulli vs. Liberty Lunch*, Case No. D-1-GN-98-014038, Travis County 200th District Court, was dismissed for want of prosecution on August 25, 2002.

5. Raoul Hernandez, "You Do Not Tear Down Landmarks," *Austin Chronicle*, February 5, 1999.

The End

1. Following Waterloo Brewing Company's closure, Anderson became brewmaster for Live Oak Brewing Company in Austin and Big Bend Brewing Company in Alpine before his death from cancer in 2015.

2. Bates was murdered in his home in October 2004, not long after closing Joe's Generic Bar. The crime remains unsolved as of this writing.

3. Holt—whose exploits could easily fill another book—was the subject of *Total Badass*, a 2010 documentary also directed by Ray. Holt died of rectal cancer in 2019.

Photos and illustrations are indicated by italicized page numbers.

Sound Exchange wall, 203; on women in music, 139
Buckethead, 261
Buferd, Marilyn, 179
Buffalo Gals, 134, 332n9
Bulemics, the, 111, 154–155
Bunkhouse Records, 217
Burning Spear, 275
Burns, Cris, 24, 58, 146, 257, 295; on the Cavity, 21
Burrell, Eloise, 134
Busch, Neil, 51
Bush (band), 282
Bush, George W., 179
Butcher, Joe, 153
Butthole Surfers, 8, 161, 193, 209, 232, 238, 276; on 101X, 65; Austin attention and, 237; commercial success of, 235; lawsuit, 235–236; shock value, popularity of, 7; time signatures and, 239. *See also* Coffey, King

C3 Presents, 42–43, 61, 62
Cake, 260
Calamity Jane, 142
Cannibal Club, 1, 13–15, 74, 183, 217; Afghan Whigs trouble at, 273; Hole in the Wall and, 82
Cannon, Rebecca, 97–101, *100*, 139, 142, 168; on the Cavity, 25, *26*, 31; on DIY, 75; on inclusivity, 13; roast interview of, 171; on Sincola, 263, 296; on working at Kinko's, 184; on zines, 186
CapZeyeZ, 45, 159, 161–163, *162*, 167–169
Carbomb, 49, 117, 118
Carney, Rick, 37, 60–61, 86, 108, 122, 225; on Emo's, 45; on Liberty Lunch, 285; on move to Austin, 9, 10; on Rise Records, 219
Caroline Records, 263
Carr, Eric, 267
Carroll, Mike, 154, 332n6
Cash, Johnny, 43, 48–49
Casimir, Edith, 91–92, 93, *93*, 94; on the Cavity, 34–35; on

Koon, 218; on Liberty Lunch, 278
cassette tapes, 199–201, 213
Cavity Club, The, 15, *26*, 27, 82; atmosphere, 30; bands nurtured by, 19; close of, 103, 108; context for opening of, 17–18; decade end aesthetics compared to, 290; fake blood and, 24; filth and violence, 31–34; first band at, 21–22; freak shows, 23; FuckEmos at, 58; Hartman on Emo's and, 46; keg parties, 28; last six months of, 38; living space in, 22; location of, 18, 19, 330n1; as nonalcoholic venue, 25; nudity, 24; owner of, 18; personal reflections on, 20–38; Sweatbox and, 151; underage shows, 29
CBS, 206
CDs. *See* compact discs
Cervenka, Exene, 5, 90
Chaindrive (band), 130–131
Chaindrive (club), 130–131
Chances, 208; benefits hosted by, 127; Cher impersonator show, 127; cliff wall stage of, 125, 332n1; closing of, 128; Frampton visiting, 132; lesbian/gay community and, 125–128, 133, 136; marriage ceremony at, 131; personal reflections on, 128–143; Punk Prom at, 127, 139–140, 327n4; "Running Through the Woods" show, 132; Swine King first show (ham sandwiches), 136; SXSW and, 125–126, 130, 132, 133
Chaney, Steve, 35, 326n17
Chapman, Lee Roy, 55, 322
Cheezus, 18, 23
Cheney, Dick, 150, 156–157
Cher, 127
Cherubs, the, 39, 147, 151, 154; albums, 213; reunion, 329n1; time signatures of, 239; Trance Syndicate and, 233, 239, 250
Chester, Gary, 9, 132, 137, 220;

on Crust, 195, 238
chickenhawks, 109
Childish, Billy, 152
Chomsky, Noam, 254
Christian, Jason, 12
Chumbawamba, 19, 31, 34
Chumps, the, 94, 105, 111, 117, 119, 120, 294
Clark, Carrie, 134, 184, 194, 241–243, 293; on record producer ignoring, 244–245; on "selling out" perception, 248; on SXSW 1991, 240; on Trance Syndicate, 240; on Warner Bros. decision, 245–246
Clark, Jerry Don, 290–291
Clinton, Bill, 79
Close, Glenn, 137
CMT. *See* Country Music Television
Cobain, Kurt, 50, 55, 206
Cochran, Leslie, 108, 327n2
Coffey, King, 193, 214, 248, 252, 333n14; on Cherubs weird time signatures, 239; on club scene growth, 293; on Crust, 237; on Ed Hall, 238; on Furry Things, 246, 247; on Gibson, 247; on husband (Stewart), 250; on joining bands in current climate, 293; on promotion spending, 249; record label started by, 7–8; Rusk and, 235–236; on Sixteen Deluxe hit, 241, 246; on SXSW 1991, 240; on template bands, 8; Touch and Go partnership, 236; on Trail of Dead logo source, 250; on Trance budget *vs.* MTV, 242; Trance shut down by, 236; on Trance Syndicate focus, 236–237, 250; on Windsor for the Derby, 247
Cohen, Jason, 262
Coleman, Bob, 72, 214
college radio, UT and, 63, 65–67, 216, 271; Koon show on KTSB, 199; personal perspectives on, 68–78; UT opposition to students, 71, 331n6